DISABILITY-AFFIRMATIVE THERAPY

ACADEMY OF REHABILITATION PSYCHOLOGY SERIES

Series Editors
Bruce Caplan, *Editor-in-Chief*
Timothy Elliott
Janet Farmer
Robert Frank
Barry Nierenberg
George Prigatano
Daniel Rohe
Stephen Wegener
Lester Butt

Volumes in the Series

Ethics Field Guide: Applications in Rehabilitation Psychology
Thomas R. Kerkhoff and Stephanie L. Hanson

The Social Psychology of Disability
Dana S. Dunn

Disability-Affirmative Therapy: A Case Formulation Template for Clients with Disabilities
Rhoda Olkin

Forthcoming in the Series

Suicide Prevention after Neurodisability
Lisa Brenner and Grahame Simpson

Disability Law, Discrimination, and the Handicapped
Rochelle Balter

Women Living with Physical Disabilities: A Framework for Practice in Rehabilitation Psychology
Margaret A. Nosek

Embracing Disability as Diversity: Developing Cultural Competence
Erin E. Andrews

Validity Assessment in Rehabilitation Psychology and Settings
Dominic A. Carone and Shane S. Bush

Disability in the Global Context: A Practical Primer and Integrative Approach to Multi-Systemic Challenges
Jacob Bentley

Disability-Affirmative Therapy
A CASE FORMULATION TEMPLATE
FOR CLIENTS WITH DISABILITIES

Rhoda Olkin

OXFORD
UNIVERSITY PRESS

OXFORD
UNIVERSITY PRESS

Oxford University Press is a department of the University of Oxford. It furthers
the University's objective of excellence in research, scholarship, and education
by publishing worldwide. Oxford is a registered trade mark of Oxford University
Press in the UK and certain other countries.

Published in the United States of America by Oxford University Press
198 Madison Avenue, New York, NY 10016, United States of America.

© Oxford University Press 2017

All rights reserved. No part of this publication may be reproduced, stored in
a retrieval system, or transmitted, in any form or by any means, without the
prior permission in writing of Oxford University Press, or as expressly permitted
by law, by license, or under terms agreed with the appropriate reproduction
rights organization. Inquiries concerning reproduction outside the scope of the
above should be sent to the Rights Department, Oxford University Press, at the
address above.

You must not circulate this work in any other form
and you must impose this same condition on any acquirer.

Library of Congress Cataloging-in-Publication Data
Names: Olkin, Rhoda, author.
Title: Disability-affirmative therapy : a case formulation template for clients with disabilities / Rhoda Olkin.
Description: Oxford ; New York : Oxford University Press, [2017] |
Series: Academy of rehabilitation psychology series |
Includes bibliographical references and index.
Identifiers: LCCN 2017006175 (print) | LCCN 2017011867 (ebook) | ISBN 9780199337330 (updf) |
ISBN 9780199337347 (epub) | ISBN 9780199337323 (acid-free paper)
Subjects: LCSH: Disability evaluation. | People with disabilities—Psychology. |
People with disabilities—Rehabilitation.
Classification: LCC RA1055.5 (ebook) | LCC RA1055.5 .O45 2017 (print) | DDC 616.07/5—dc23
LC record available at https://lccn.loc.gov/2017006175

9 8 7 6 5 4 3 2 1
Printed by WebCom, Inc., Canada

Contents

1. *Rationale for Disability-Affirmative Therapy and Definitions* 1

2. *What Do We Know about Outpatient Psychotherapy with Persons with Disabilities?* 12

3. *A Case Example: "Sam"* 34

4. *D-AT I: Current Disability Status—Disability Sequelae and Their Management* 46

5. *D-AT II: Developmental History—Disability, Medical, Educational, and Advocacy* 71

6. *D-AT III: Models of Disability* 79

7. *D-AT IV: Context and Intersectionality—Interplay of Disability and Other Demographic Variables* 97

8. *D-AT V: Disability Culture and Community* 115

9. *D-AT VI: Microaggressions—Experiences and Effects* 132

10. *D-AT VII: Friendships and Social Interactions* 145

11. *D-AT VIII: Affective Prescriptions and Prohibitions Imposed on People with Disabilities* 156

12. *D-AT IX: Families and Intimate Relationships* 165

13. *Disability-Affirmative Therapy Applied to the Case of "Sam"* 188

APPENDIX: OTHER WORKS BY R. OLKIN 199
REFERENCES 201
ABOUT THE AUTHOR 237
INDEX 239

DISABILITY-AFFIRMATIVE THERAPY

1 Rationale for Disability-Affirmative Therapy and Definitions

Rationale

Why does there need to be a special book on psychotherapy with clients with disabilities? There are multiple reasons:

- Virtually all clinicians are likely to see clients with disabilities. Persons with disabilities comprise approximately 19% of the U.S. population (http://census.gov). While rates are higher in some geographic areas (across the south), in some ethnic groups (American Indians, African Americans) and some economic strata (lower income), disability is ubiquitous. About 50% of all families are directly affected by disability of a family member (Olkin, Abrams, Preston, & Kirshbaum, 2006).
- Most clinicians are not trained in treating people with disabilities (Olkin & Pledger, 2003) and may not know much about this population (Strike, Skovholt, & Hummel, 2004). Typically they have had a diversity class in which one class period was spent on disability, heard a few lectures devoted to assessment of intellectual disabilities or dementia, and studied advanced psychopathology, including the classification of mental disorders. But the intrapsychic, psychosocial, familial, economic, political, and legal aspects of disability typically are not included in graduate clinical programs. Furthermore, psychologists may hold the common belief that

it is non-psychologists who hold less favorable attitudes toward disability (Castaneto & Willemsen, 2006) and thus fail to address the prejudices within the field.
- Attitudes toward persons with disability are, on the whole, more negative than those toward persons without disabilities (c.f., Dunn, 2015; Wright, 1988). Therapists are not immune to those attitudes, and, in fact, training in psychology, with its emphasis on pathology, may further contribute to the view of disability as deviance. Obviously such attitudes will affect treatment. Thus, self-examination is a prequel to effective implementation of disability-affirmative therapy (D-AT).
- Specialized knowledge is required for conducting psychotherapy with persons with disability. Although one person is unlikely to know the details about most disability types, some general knowledge about all disabilities is important. Further, clinicians should be prepared to do some homework in order to gain knowledge more specific to the individual client or family. However, a basic understanding of commonalities across disabilities will be helpful.
- Certain skill sets are particularly important in practicing D-AT. Some may be skills the clinician already possesses. What is critical is the understanding of how behaviors that mean one thing to able-bodied persons may take on a different meaning to people with disabilities. Simple acts, such as holding a door open, asking about sexuality, filling out a depression inventory, all will carry some disability baggage—that is, a personal history of interactions related to the disability. That baggage will look different for each person, but there will be a disability twist to it.
- There is a disability culture and community that the clinician needs to be aware of (Olkin, 1999). If the therapist is able-bodied, then therapy is cross-cultural therapy (Gill, 1994), which carries higher risk of misdiagnosis and incorrect case formulation and, hence, treatment. Understanding of disability culture can help bridge the gap.

Focus of this Book

There are myriad causes of disability, a plethora of possible impairments, and pronounced differences across categories of disabilities. I do not claim expertise in all of these factors, and I do not imply that D-AT will be the most appropriate fit for every client with a disability. My familiarity is mostly with physical and systemic disabilities (both visible and hidden), visual impairments, and psychiatric disabilities. I have less experience working with persons who are deaf or those with significant cognitive or intellectual disabilities. Nonetheless, I believe that the core approach to the understanding of clients with disabilities lies in eliciting the appropriate information from clients and using that information to derive collaboratively a case formulation that incorporates the disability to the proper degree—neither overemphasizing nor minimizing the disability.

Having said how different various disabilities are, I want to make the reverse point as well—there are incredible similarities in experiences across different types of disabilities. Some of these similarities include experiences with medical professionals (both positive and negative), the need to pay attention to varying energy levels, management of stigma, being reduced to a category ("people with disabilities"), underestimation of abilities, and discrimination.

D-AT is not a prescription for treatment or a manualized set of procedures. Rather, it is a template for gathering information, systematizing the information, and understanding the disability in the context of the individual (and family) in order to develop a case formulation that guides treatment. Treatment flows from the proper understanding of our clients (i.e., case formulation), and D-AT is designed to help with that understanding.

Overview of the D-AT Template

Disability-affirmative therapy has two main components. First, it involves a series of nine areas to be explored with a client (or family) with a disability. These nine areas are designed to cover the various aspects of disability experiences for the specific individual (or family). The goal of this exploration is to derive a case formulation that neither overinflates nor underestimates the role of disability in the person's life and presenting problems. Too often disability is seen as such a *defining characteristic* (Wright, 1983) that it overshadows other important aspects of an individual, and all of that individual's problems are seen through the lens of disability. The purpose of D-AT is to help clinicians, together with the client, focus the lens appropriately to view disability in the proper perspective.

The second component of D-AT is the stance of the therapist. This stance comes from disability studies, tenets of gay-affirmative therapy, feminist therapy, the independent-living movement, and the importance of the specific culture of the client(s). The stance involves taking a constructivist view of disability—that is, disability is a social construct, and adopting the World Health Organization's biopsychosocial model of disability (see Chapter 6). Disability is viewed as a naturally occurring phenomenon that will always exist.

A good fit between the therapist's case formulation and the client's self-understanding is important for achieving positive outcomes in therapy (Wampold & Imel, 2015). D-AT should facilitate this mutual understanding of the key aspects of disability experiences and the role of these experiences in the client's current functioning, presenting problems, and relationships. D-AT is not a theory of therapy but a process for understanding a given client. As such, it does not supplant the clinician's own theoretical orientation. D-AT can be thought of as a clear plastic template laid over the common factors of therapy and the tenets of the specific theoretical approach. There may be lots of writing on the template, indicating that much from the disability perspective has to be incorporated into the theory. Alternatively, it might be relatively blank, leaving a clear view of the theory underneath. In either event, the template gets incorporated into the theory, much like cocoa might be mixed into a vanilla batter, transforming it into something different.

Clinicians might need templates other than D-AT. For example, cultural factors will be important in learning about a person's disability (c.f., Bryan, 2007), as is true for overall understanding of any clients. Therefore, it is necessary to view disability within the cultural context and not to allow disability to be so overriding that other variables such as gender, age, ethnicity, religion, sexual orientation, and socioeconomic status are overlooked. None of these can be considered in isolation. My image of this process, to go back to the template idea, is that each factor is an overlay on the others, developing an ever more complex view of the client.

It is possible that D-AT fits more readily with some theories than others. This is as yet an untested empirical question. However, throughout this book I have kept in mind feminist therapy, cognitive behavioral therapy, psychodynamic theory, family systems therapy, and medical family therapy.

D-AT does not dictate how to treat the client—what interventions to apply; the order of interventions; when, how, or if to use any specific technique; how to modify homework; what the goals of therapy should be. These aspects of treatment are guided by the clinician's own theoretical orientation and training. To be a good D-AT therapist one first needs to be a good therapist. Therefore, the common factors in therapy, a solid therapeutic relationship and ongoing monitoring of progress are assumed.

The chapters in this book are structured according to the nine components of D-AT. Then we take all of these components (think of them as eggs, flour, sugar, chocolate, butter, and milk, i.e., ingredients) and combine them to make a "cake" in which the separate ingredients synergistically combine. I begin this discussion with an extended case example (Chapter 3), used throughout the book to illustrate the nine components of D-AT, that involves intersectionality of identities (the client is gay, of low socioeconomic status, White, religious, with an early-onset disability).

Readers who are familiar with my earlier book (Olkin, 1999) will find that background helpful, but it is not essential to understanding of this book. When I wrote my earlier book I was just beginning to develop D-AT. The main focus there was on helping clinicians less familiar with disability to begin seeing disability in a new way, from an insider's perspective. This book is the first full laying-out of the principles and practice of D-AT.

The nine areas of D-AT discussed in this book are as follows:

1. The developmental history of the individual (and family) and how disability affected the history;
2. The current sequelae of disability, with an emphasis on pain, fatigue, sleep, and falls;
3. Models of disability(moral, medical, social, biopsychosocial) of the individual, the parents, the partners, and the therapist;
4. Disability in the context of other demographic and cultural variables;
5. The disability culture and community, and the client's knowledge of and interface with this culture and community;
6. How disability is affecting the person's current social interactions;
7. The experiences of microaggressions and the person's responses to these experiences;
8. The management of affective prescriptions (mourning, cheerfulness, bravery) and prohibitions (anger);
9. Current intimacy (sexuality, partnership relationships) and disability within the context of those relationships

What Do We Know about Psychotherapy with People with Disabilities?

Most empirical literature about therapy with people with disabilities is from rehabilitation psychology (an area recognized as a specialty by the American Psychological Association and the American Board of Professional Psychology). This makes sense, as disability and chronic illness are the focus of this specialty area. Rehabilitation psychology interventions are frequently provided after the acute onset of disability, when the person is an inpatient. Thus, in the hospital setting, interventions are typically short term and focused on the initial adjustment to the disability. Since rehabilitation psychologists frequently represent the first therapeutic contact with the person with a newly acquired disability, it is vital that they understand and incorporate the principles of D-AT into all of their interventions. Laying the groundwork for those with a newly acquired disability to understand the changed social world they are entering is perhaps one of the most important interventions that rehabilitation psychologists can provide.

In non-acute settings, rehabilitation psychologists focus on the long-term adaptation tasks imposed by disability or chronic illness. D-AT is particularly relevant to outpatient psychotherapy, is not specifically geared toward the acute-onset phase (though some clients will have been newly diagnosed), is focused on living well with a disability, not necessarily short term, and addresses disability in the course of treatment that may itself be focused on the disability to varying degrees, from none to primarily. Having said that, I believe the D-AT template will also be very useful for students in rehabilitation psychology as well as those in clinical and counseling psychology. Practicing clinicians may find that the addition of the D-AT template helps their understanding of clients and families with disabilities. Also, instructors of courses on psychotherapy, diversity, and disability may want to incorporate some of this material into their classes.

In the book I have included a chapter (Chapter 2) on what is known about outpatient psychotherapy with people with disabilities, from both the qualitative and quantitative literature. Many who have written about disability have helped shape my own ideas regarding D-AT. References throughout the book will help students and researchers find other useful materials related to their practice. I have also included a few measures throughout the book that I developed with colleagues for specific studies. Some are more well-validated than others. I include them here in the hope of interesting others in conducting large-scale studies to validate the measures and in generating more research in specific areas using these measures. Lastly, for those interested in reading more of my work, I have included an appendix with a list of my disability-related publications.

Definition of Terms

PERSONS WITH DISABILITIES VERSUS DISABLED PERSON

The language used to describe people influences the way we think about them. Whether a woman is called a chick, broad, gal, lady, girl, or woman both reflects and shapes the social interaction and power dynamics inherent in that interaction. In the United States the move has been toward using "people-first" language, that is, *person with a disability*. In the United Kingdom "identity-first" language has been adopted, that is, *disabled person*. Some have adopted the term *diffability*—a combination of the words *different ability*. There are valuable arguments for all of these ways of describing a person with a disability. In this book I use people-first language, for this reason: most of the U.S. media never abandoned older language to describe people with disabilities and have not adopted people-first language. Thus, when journalists use what seems to be identity-first language, it is not because they are adhering to a well-thought-out rationale, but rather it reflects ignorance of the disability rights movement. When a newspaper or magazine prints terms like "the disabled," it does not reflect awareness of identity-first language, but rather a failure to have caught up with use of people-first language. Thus, if I use identity-first language here, it would seem that I am sanctioning the use of older language in the media without forcing journalists to confront the language they use. Once they catch up in awareness of their language and its consequences, we can then be ahead again and move to identity-first language. (Also note that the *APA Publications Manual* encourages people-first language. For good discussions of the issues related to language of disability see Dajani, 2001, and Dunn & Andrews, 2015.)

IMPAIRMENT, DISABILITY, AND HANDICAP

The World Health Organization (WHO) (http://www.who.int/en/) uses different terminology to refer to various aspects of health. An *impairment* is any loss or abnormality of psychological, physiological, or anatomical structure or function. A *disability* is the functional limitation from the impairment (i.e., any restriction or lack of ability to perform an activity in the manner or range considered typical). A *handicap* is the disadvantage for a given individual in society that results from the disability. To use myself as an example, my impairment is muscle paralysis due to polio. My disability is mobility limitations. My handicap is inaccessible venues (a physical handicap), stigma by other people (a social handicap), having to pay out of pocket for housing modifications (an economic handicap), the frequency of use of handicapped parking placards by people without disabilities (a legal handicap), and the dearth of representation of people with disabilities in government (a political handicap).

ABLEISM, DISABLISM, INTERNALIZED ABLEISM

Ableism is prejudice against persons with disabilities and discrimination in favor of able-bodied people that disadvantages those with disabilities. It might be deliberate (e.g., an airline refusing to make its website compatible with screen readers for the blind) or inadvertent (putting merchandise in front of the handicapped dressing room) or even well-meaning (putting in a wheelchair area in the back of a lecture hall), but nonetheless restricts the choices or access for persons with disabilities. Ableism encompasses the bias that able-bodied is normal, typical, and desired, and therefore disability is aberrant, deviant, and undesirable.

Disablism is the rendering of persons with disabilities at a disadvantage due to environmental designs that assume able-bodied norms. It includes the presumption that everyone is able-bodied and creates environments (both built and social environments) that are inaccessible to people with disabilities. Further, it devalues those with disabilities and silences their voices as irrelevant or illegitimate. It might also be said to extend to the language used by the media and in everyday speech, in which disability is equated with negative outcomes: a *disabled* car blocked traffic; what you just said is *insane*; a *crippled* tanker spilled oil; at closing time of the bar we'll be left with fatties and *blind* girls.

Internalized ableism is internalized oppression, or the adoption of negative beliefs and attitudes about one's own group—in this case, people with disabilities—and believing that group to be inferior. Often the goal of someone with a great degree of internalized ableism will be to disassociate with the group (of people with disabilities) and try to "pass" (be accepted as non-disabled) in the mainstream group.

The intent behind the word *disablism* is to have an equivalent term for prejudice against disability, as racism and sexism are to ethnicity and gender. The following definition, from the website http://www.prettysimple.co.uk, amends a previous definition from SCOPE, a disability organization in the United Kingdom, that focuses on people with cerebral palsy:

> [Disablism is] discriminatory, oppressive or abusive behavior arising from the belief that disabled people are inferior to others, or through not acknowledging that disabled people are equal and taking reasonable measures to protect their rights accordingly.

However, it should be noted that the equivalency of disablism to racism, sexism, or homophobia is not a perfect alignment. As Tom Shakespeare, a noted disability writer in the United Kingdom, notes:

> Disabled people undoubtedly suffer the burdens of social exclusion, devaluation, poverty and discrimination, and these processes can be very similar to the exclusions which other oppressed groups experience. But the obvious difficulty about making a parallel between disabled people and black people, women or gays and lesbians, is that there is an intrinsic *disadvantage* associated with many forms of impairment, whereas there is no intrinsic physical or mental problem about having a different colour skin, being a woman, or having same-sex desires and relationships. (Shakespeare, 2004)

This is an important distinction, as some people mistakenly believe that to espouse the social model of disability (disability as social construct) means to ignore the reality factors of impairments that impose various conditions. To use myself as an example, when I hold something in my teeth because my hands are occupied with crutches, which in turn I am using because of mobility limitations, it is not that I have freely adopted a disability cultural norm, but rather have accommodated to a physical necessity. To achieve equity with the able-bodied population, people with disabilities may need resources not now available to them. Thus, as Shakespeare argues, elimination of barriers and discrimination are insufficient remedies; there must also be a reallocation of resources.

AFFIRMATIVE

The term itself means "agreement" or "yes." The term is used to describe gay-affirmative therapy, and I use it similarly to describe disability-affirmative therapy. The essence of an affirmative therapy is the notion that the otherwise-stigmatized aspect of a person (being gay; having a disability) will be thought of as a positive and not a deviation from a mainstream (heterosexual; able-bodied) norm—a difference, not a deficit. The issues of stigma, power, oppression, and discrimination and their effects on the individual or family or community are of necessity a part of the case formulation. Frequent goals are empowerment, reduced internalized stigma, and stigma management.

AGENCY AND EMPOWERMENT

As stated by McDaniel, Doherty, and Hepworth (2014), "*Agency* means active involvement in and commitment to one's own health care . . . and activation of the individuals and families to meet their needs related to health, illness, and the health care system, to contribute to their community" (p. 13). *Empowerment* is the act of helping clients recognize, strengthen, and utilize their own agency.

MICROAGGRESSIONS

For *microaggression* I use the definition put forth by Sue (2010): "everyday verbal, nonverbal, and environmental slights, snubs, or insults, whether intentional or unintentional, that communicate hostile, derogatory, or negative messages to target persons based solely upon their marginalized group membership" (p. 3).

RESPONSE TO DISABILITY, ADAPTATION TO DISABILITY, ADJUSTMENT TO DISABILITY, AND ACCEPTANCE OF DISABILITY

Although these terms may seem very similar, there are some important distinctions (Dunn, 2015). *Adaptation* and *adjustment* both imply a pre- and post-disability. If the person has a congenital or early-onset disability, there is no adjustment or adaptation, as the disability has always been a part of the self, and persons with congenital disabilities tend to have higher acceptance of disability scores than do those with later-onset disabilities (Dunn, 2015). Later-onset disabilities require some readjusting of the self, including identity, body image, functioning, and values (Dunn, 2015; Wright, 1983). As Dunn (2015) notes: "Psychosocial adjustment occurs when the person is satisfied with his or her own person-environment relation so that any physical losses or bodily changes are not preoccupations and the individual constructively focuses on abilities and what can be accomplished" (p. 29). Factors to consider are degree of independence, ability to actively problem-solve in daily living, awareness of assets as well as limitations, positive self-concept and self-esteem, sense of personal mastery, ability to navigate one's social and physical environments, and actively engaging in social, vocational, and leisure activities (Dunn, 2015). Wright (1960, 1983) has defined *acceptance* as the incorporation of the disability into the self-concept. This does not mean resignation, but a realistic and non-devaluing response that allows for the fact of impairment and its concomitant disruption to some daily life activities. In my view, it is possible to achieve acceptance of disability at one time in life and lose it at another time. I generally prefer the term *response to disability*, which implies ever-changing circumstances of re-evaluation and readjustment as one ages, changes social situations (e.g., high school versus working life), and shifts self-identity and self-concept (allowing for growth).

QUALITY OF LIFE (QOL)

This term is often used to judge the outcome of response to disability (Crewe, 1980). The WHO defines health as "a state of complete physical, mental, and social well-being and not merely the absence of disease" (Bech, 2012, p. 4). Similarly, QOL is not merely the absence of problems or distress. QOL is a multidimensional concept (Atwal, Spiliotopoulou, Colman, et al., 2014); it has variable meanings (Veenhoven, 2013) and thus variable ways to measure it. There are objective measures of QOL (e.g., indicators of health, income, education, neighborhood crime, pollution, housing, community resources) and subjective measures (e.g., life satisfaction; happiness; social, family and work life; positive and negative affect) (Sirgy, 2012), as well as measures for specific areas of life (e.g., health-related QOL). One useful definition is a tripartite model, comprising three domains: "intrapersonal functioning (subjective well-being, life satisfaction, perceived health), interpersonal functioning (satisfaction with family life, peer relations, and social activities), and extrapersonal functioning (performance of work activities and/or recreational pursuits, living arrangements, financial status)" (Livneh & Martz, 2012, p. 51). Elsewhere QOL has been described as a "successful restructuring of previously disrupted psychosocial homeostasis and attainment of an adaptive person-environment (reality) congruence.... QOL is considered to be linked to more positive self-concept and body image, as well as to an increased sense of control" over the disability, as well as "negatively associated with perceived stress and feelings of loss and grief" (Livneh & Antonak, 2005, p. 13).

CONCLUSIONS REGARDING LANGUAGE

Therapists often try to adopt the language a client uses, to show tracking and mirroring. However, there are reasons for clinicians to use language carefully with their clients with disabilities. Language is a form of intervention, a way of reframing reference points. If a client says she is "suffering from MS pain" and the therapist refers to her as "a woman with MS who sometimes experiences pain," the therapist is doing more than changing his or her language; the therapist is initiating a dialogue about the place of MS and pain in the woman's life. However, I would not want therapists to become tongue-tied out of fear of using the wrong words. If, as a therapist, you were to blurt out "autistic child" instead of "child diagnosed with autism spectrum disorder," the world (and the therapy) will not end. You can correct yourself the next time, and different language will become more habitual. Furthermore, it will change how you think about disability.

Discussion Questions

1. What makes a therapy "affirmative" (as in gay-affirmative or disability-affirmative)?
2. If all therapy is individualized, what is the rationale for a book devoted to clients with disabilities?
3. What are the two main components of disability-affirmative therapy?
4. At this point in history in the United States, would you advocate for people-first or identity-first language for disability?

2   What Do We Know about Outpatient Psychotherapy with Persons with Disabilities?

IN THIS CHAPTER I describe and evaluate the current state of professional literature on outpatient psychotherapy with clients with disabilities. This discussion excludes rehabilitation literature that focuses on persons in the acute-phase post-disability onset, on inpatient settings, or on very specific outcomes (e.g., vocation). The focus here is on general clientele that any therapist might see in private practice, community clinics, college counseling centers, veterans' clinics, Kaiser clinics, or similar facilities. The chapter is organized first by the type of studies—qualitative and quantitative. Each section follows its own outline, as the two sets of literature are organized very differently. For the qualitative literature the outline is as follows: (a) perspectives of people with disabilities in treatment, (b) lived experiences of people with disabilities that can inform treatment, (c) providers' perspectives on therapy with people with disabilities, and (d) three interrelated studies. The quantitative literature is simultaneously both legion and sparse. This paradox stems from the prolific literature on specific disabilities (e.g., multiple sclerosis), usually in rehabilitation settings or in group therapy, and often focused on a specific skill (e.g., coping), while there is very little about general outpatient psychotherapy with a variety of disabilities. A thorough search would require entering a series of impairments separately and searching for individual, couple, or family therapy with persons with each of those impairments. That is not what I did for this chapter, because I was looking for underlying principles that would apply across different disabilities. In addition, there are many articles on specific cognitive approaches (e.g., acceptance of pain) and positive outcomes, such as well-being or quality of life. Again, that was not my intent in this chapter.

Qualitative Research Studies

To address the contribution of qualitative research to therapy with persons with disabilities, I searched three journals (*Rehabilitation Psychology, Journal of Counseling & Development*, and *Disability Studies*—i.e., the main journals from APA's Division 22, the American Counseling Association, and Disability Studies), from 2012 to 2013, to examine search terms and then conduct an online literature search, in summer 2013 (using terms [*disab** or *handicap**] and [*therap** or *intervention* or *clinical* or *counseling* or *social work* or *community* or *outcomes*]). The search was difficult because there was not much to find, so I kept going back to be sure—one does not want to assert an absence of literature only to be proven wrong. I identified about 50 articles that seemed even tangentially relevant to clinical issues. Before discussing here the implications of those articles, some observations are relevant. First is the array of journals necessary for conducting a search to find relevant articles (from *Contemporary Nursing* to *Exceptional Children* to *Scandinavian Journal of Occupational Therapy*). Some journals, such as *Rehabilitation Psychology*, rarely publish qualitative research—I had to go back to 1994 to find one study applicable to the topic. Journals were from a variety of disciplines, making it unlikely that a clinician, even one who often works with clients with disabilities, would come across relevant articles unless conducting a deliberate and difficult search. The second observation is that almost three-quarters of the articles came from countries other than the United States. One benefit of qualitative research is that it gives direct voice to the lived experiences of people with disabilities. When the frequency of qualitative studies declines, those voices are less heard. If we are to learn about therapy with such persons, it would seem that this would be the first group to ask. Many studies asked professionals rather than end users. In this review I have given preference to studies that directly asked people with disabilities about their experiences. The most relevant of studies reviewed were those about experiences of people with specific disabilities who had participated in a treatment. The second set pertained to the experiences of people with disabilities living with chronic conditions, in which there are implications for clinicians. The third set focused on providers' perspectives. The fourth set comprises evaluations of or recommendations for program protocols. And lastly is a series of three studies by the same authors regarding exercise and fatigue in persons with MS. Although these studies could have been separated into the sets just described, they are discussed together, to show how multiple perspectives on one issue can converge into a more meaningful whole.

One study of therapy with people with disabilities involved an analysis of four videotapes from family sessions with people with intellectual disabilities (Pote, Mazon, Clegg, & King, 2011). This study from the United Kingdom found that vulnerability and protection were key themes of the therapy. Protection was from the disability itself and its consequences, from peers and abuse by others, from sensitive topics, unfairness, and inequality. But it was not just the person with the intellectual disability who was concerned with protection; each person took the role of protector and protected, spread across the family members in fluctuating waves. The themes of vulnerability and protection were the focus of therapy 25% of the time. One method of protection was to reframe statements. When family members did this they took a positive statement and reframed it as negative, whereas therapists did the opposite, going from negative to positive. The authors recommend that protection should be normalized for families with a member with an intellectual disability, so that there can be open discussion of protection—who does it, how it works, the types of protection, whom it protects. This level of detailed analysis of sessions would be invaluable with individuals and families with other types of disabilities. Protection may be a construct important in the work with clients with disabilities.

PERSPECTIVES OF PEOPLE WITH DISABILITIES IN TREATMENT OR RECEIVING SERVICES

There were 20 articles in this area, 6 from the United States. It is hard to draw overall conclusions from the studies because they included such a wide range of disabilities: stroke, diabetes, traumatic brain injury (TBI) or other neurological impairments, intellectual disabilities, hand osteoarthritis, multiple sclerosis (MS), spinal cord injury, chronic pain, cerebral palsy, lower amputation, psychiatric disabilities, and unnamed disabilities in children. Nonetheless, two themes do stand out. The first theme is the isolation experienced by families when a member receives a diagnosis, and the second related theme is the benefit of meeting with other similar families. Thus, group treatments, whether focusing on creating art (Beeseley, White, Alston, Sweetapple, & Pollack, 2011), receiving education on diabetes (Due-Christensen, Zoffman, Hommel, & Lau, 2011), or learning new skills after an acquired brain injury (Nilsson, Bartfai, & Lofgren, 2011), had an added benefit of addressing the isolation and making clients feel less alone. In addition, families frequently mentioned the value of learning concrete information from similar families (e.g., Carlson, Armitstead, Rodger, & Liddle, 2010; Knis-Matthew et al., 2011; Schreiber, Benger, Salls, Marchetti, & Reed, 2011).

The nonspecific factors of therapy would be expected to be as important for therapy with people with disabilities as they would be for people without disabilities. But there were nuances to the relationship aspects that were more unique to disability. For example, persons with intellectual disabilities mentioned the value of being able to talk about their problems and highlighted the relationship as the key aspect of therapy (Pert et al., 2013). Because persons with intellectual disabilities might not receive patient listening from many people in their lives, therapy provides a significant supportive experience. Similarly, adults with psychiatric disorders emphasized the importance of going from being a *diagnosis* of a disorder to being a *person* with a psychiatric disorder (Ridgeway, 2011). The parents of children with disabilities valued commitment from the professionals that indicated that their children were more than *cases* and the work was more than a job (Blue-Banning, Summers, Frankland, Nelson, & Beegle, 2004). It would seem that the common experience of being reduced to a disability in daily life means that the relationship with the practitioner takes on extra resonance.

Communication with practitioners was a major theme throughout the studies. In focus groups with 70 family members of children with disabilities, specific practitioner behaviors were suggested (Blue-Banning et al., 2004). Parents did not want professionals to sugar-coat or hide information or use jargon, and they valued privacy and tact. They were sensitive to blame and appreciated positive comments, as well as indications of valuing the child as a person rather than a diagnosis. Behaviors important to all consumers were important here as well, such as being on time, using honorifics and last names, and being courteous, but these behaviors may be extra important given the amount of time families of children with disabilities spend with professionals. Conversely, being handed information or dismissed because there was no cure available left consumers dissatisfied and with unanswered questions (Hill, Dziedzic, & Ong, 2011).

Some important considerations for therapy emerged from other studies. Interviews with nine adults with neurological impairments on a rehabilitation ward in Taiwan identified institutional barriers to independence (Chang & Wang, 2012). For example, the patients thought that nursing staff preferred to push them in wheelchairs rather than wait while they walked slowly with a walker. The authors concluded that "the primacy of biomedical-oriented rehabilitation ideology, insurance reimbursement policies, and cultural values associated with family caregiving" countered moves toward independence in activities of daily living (p. 538). In another study on persons with neurological impairments (TBI), preferences for home versus day-hospital settings for rehabilitation with an occupational therapist were assessed in interviews with 14 adults who had received treatment in both settings (Australia; Doig, Fleming, Cornwell, & Kuipers, 2011). Both the adults with TBI and the occupational therapists preferred the home setting and felt it was more beneficial to rehabilitation outcomes. Rehabilitation activities in the home bypass the need for generalization of learning from a medical setting to the natural environment.

Two studies related to people with intellectual disabilities used short-term cognitive behavioral therapy (CBT) for anxiety and/or depression. In the first study researchers in the United Kingdom (Douglass, Palmer, & O'Connor, 2007) conducted two interviews with six adults with intellectual disabilities and anxiety and the person who attended therapy with them (one person did not have a significant other to bring). All clients felt therapy had improved their coping skills, and significant others felt they had a greater understanding of the individual's difficulties than prior to participation in the group. Results of the Glasgow Anxiety Scale showed a decrease in anxiety for three clients, but a slight increase for three clients. However, for those showing increased anxiety on the scale, this was contradicted in the interviews. This discrepancy is important; clinicians should always use multiple outcome measures with people with intellectual disabilities, looking for convergence of data. The second study was also in the United Kingdom, using interviews to assess responses to CBT for anxiety and/or depression between the fourth and ninth sessions. Participants valued the opportunity to talk about problems and were able to identify areas of positive change but, interestingly, thought these changes would not be sustained.

A helpful study illustrated some difficulties people with disabilities might encounter in receiving psychological treatment in the United States (Hampton, Zhu, & Ordway, 2011). Access to health services for women with MS, spina bifida, or spinal cord injury (SCI) were addressed in six open-ended interview questions. Most (91%) of the 23 women (10 were women of color) expressed a need for services (64% had a psychological diagnosis of depression or anxiety). Although 48% had HMO insurance and 27% drove a car (i.e., eliminating two major impediments), results indicated numerous perceived barriers. The women affirmed the need for psychological services, but identified three main obstacles: (a) lack of expertise about disability among mental health service providers (and some mentioned "bad attitudes" on the part of therapists), (b) lack of choices for selecting psychological services, and (c) inaccessible environments in which services were available. Their major strategy to cope with problems was to use informal support, but socialization had decreased since disability onset, owing to loss of friends who had pulled away, inaccessible houses and other environments, and lack of accessible transportation. This study highlights the need and desire for services, as well as the lack of training of mental health professionals about disability.

The reliance on others who are not service providers was echoed in a study in Canada with 22 adults with stroke, MS, or SCI in a six-session self-management group (Hirsche, Williams, Jones, & Manns, 2011). Interviews with participants indicated multiple factors that accounted for program outcomes, but one consistent factor was common experiences among the group and learning from peers.

Three studies on pain indicated mostly positive outcomes. Cognitions and beliefs about pain are key variables in outcome (Van Huet, Innes, & Whiteford, 2009), and biopsychosocial approaches in a primary care setting can effect gains in adults with pain (Martensson, 2001). This echoes results from much of the quantitative literature, but the Van Huet et al. study also found a variety of strategies used by persons with chronic pain. Such variability is demonstrated in a very different study in Ireland, on responses to phantom-limb movement therapy to address phantom-limb pain. Although the number of participants was only four, there were individual differences in ability to use motor imagery to reduce pain, and outcomes were quite different across the four participants. The authors concluded that phantom-limb pain is a multidimensional disorder. This idea of multidimensionality is critical in going beyond the diagnosis or disability to the person with the disability and in not merely taking treatments off the shelf, but matching them to the individual and viewing progress as a process that is neither straightforward nor quick (Van der Riet, Dedkhard, & Srithong, 2011).

The last study reviewed here had results that seem so obvious once stated and are bolstered by the evidence. Ten Korean American parents of children with disabilities were interviewed (in Korean) about their experiences with White therapists working with them on child management issues (Park, 2012). The core result was that parents were not likely to follow the therapists' suggestions, and 6 of the 10 parents felt they did not have a good relationship with the therapist. The problems were linguistically and culturally related. For example, therapists suggested withholding enough food and drink at meal time to reserve these for primary reinforcers for behaviors. This seems so culturally obtuse on the part of the therapists that I cannot help but wonder if the presence of disability in the children overshadowed cultural variables. Again, as was culturally normative, most mothers did not discuss their disagreements with the therapists in therapy. Interestingly, the mothers referred to the therapist as a "teacher" when the therapist was effective, and as "the person" when the advice was not effective.

LIVED EXPERIENCES OF PEOPLE WITH DISABILITIES
THAT CAN INFORM THERAPY

There were 15 articles reviewed for this section, 5 from the United States. As in the previous section, a wide variety of disabilities and issues were covered.

Several studies focused on the experiences of people with disabilities in social and leisure activities (Berger, 2012; Hjelle & Vik, 2011; Kramer & Hammel, 2011; Lawlor,

Mihaylov, Welsh, Jarvis, & Colver, 2006; Liddle et al., 2011). An interesting study from Norway examined wheelchair users' experiences with participation in society (Hjelle & Vik, 2011). The six participants in a focus group asserted the importance of being engaged in others' lives, work, leisure activities, and public or disability rights service. However, being out in public subjected them to others' comments and stares. The authors describe the variability of experiences, from positive to negative, as "climbing up and sliding down the participation ladder" (p. 2479). Two studies on children with cerebral palsy (one in the United States, the other in England) suggested that for these children competence was about the ability to engage in an activity, not about the skill level or how independently they could perform the activity (Kramer & Hammel, 2011). According to 13 parents of children with cerebral palsy, there were numerous barriers to full participation that were related to mobility equipment, transportation, lack of information, and negative attitudes and staring by others (Lawlor et al., 2006). Finally, a study in Norway focused on driving after TBI and identified distinct phases (learning about driving restrictions and application to oneself, being on hold while awaiting permission and learning new skills, and returning to driving), each with its own issues relevant to therapy (Liddle et al., 2011). The 15 participants felt strongly that they wanted the opportunity to show what they could do in simulated driving rather than having a medical team make the decision for and without them about a return to driving. A study in the United States on older adults with later vision loss who were in otherwise good health found personal, environmental, and emotional barriers to their participation in leisure activities (Berger, 2012). The author recommends advocating for increased access, discussing with clients ways to conserve energy, and helping clients practice assertiveness.

Five studies show how the person with the disability and parents or professionals might view the same situation differently. Six children with cerebral palsy and their parents were interviewed in a study in Canada that focused on the value of walking (Gibson et al., 2011). Parents thought that being a good parent included trying everything and maintaining hope, and thus wanted their children to walk. The children, by contrast, equated walking with exercise and found it less functional than alternate means of transportation. In the United Kingdom 12 persons with psychosis thought that the side effects of medications and symptoms of psychosis were equal—that is, they equally affected their quality of life (Hon, 2011z); thus going off medications did not seem like a bad decision, but merely trading one set of symptoms for another set. In the third study, for 16 Chinese-Australian women with breast cancer who had undergone a mastectomy, concerns focused on continuing to be able to be a good mother and wife, not on sexuality or attractiveness (Kwok & White, 2011). This article also discussed the misinformation held by some of the 23 women (e.g., that stress can cause cancer, that it is a White woman's disease), the cultural insensitivity of many resources, and thus the primacy of friends in giving and getting information.

Assistive technology can be an important aspect of disability. In one study, for 24 lower-limb prosthetic users, functional independence was emphasized as a key goal by service providers, but psychological benefits were valued more by the prosthetic users (Schaffalitzky, Gallagher, MacLachlan, & Ryall, 2011). Quality of life was how service providers thought about changes in functioning with prosthetic use, but users gave specific examples (e.g., "I can still live at home"; "a wheelchair would be more stigmatizing"). Services providers thought about safety, but users saw falling as embarrassing. These differences in language can guide therapists in framing ideas in therapy. For example, rather than saying, "Being able to visit more friends would improve your quality of life," one could say, "If you could go up three steps with a railing you could visit your best friend at his house."

Two studies focused on persons in either the hospital (So & Pierluissi, 2011) or long-term care (Wang, Mihailidis, Dutta, & Fernie, 2011). For 28 English- or Spanish-speaking hospitalized older adults in one study in the United States, the patients perceived that staff discouraged them from walking; the doctor did not suggest exercise, and staff were not keen on patients traipsing up and down the hallway (So & Pierluissi, 2011). Although a key to independence in care facilities is the ability to get around independently, staff may be reluctant for residents, especially those with dementia, to use power chairs. A study of five older adults with cognitive impairment who were using smart wheelchairs that provide collision feedback showed that 5 hours of training yielded positive outcomes (Wang et al., 2011). The article has a good list of seven principles to follow in making assistive technology useable by people with cognitive impairments (Wang et al., 2011, p. 802), and these suggestions could help therapists make their materials more user-friendly.

A perennial issue for persons with disabilities is underemployment, so understanding what makes vocational success more or less possible for people with specific disabilities is important. A Swedish study of employed people with fibromyalgia found that "adjustment of the work tasks and work environment were the main factors [that] influenced whether the women with fibromyalgia could work or not" (Mannerkorpi & Gard, 2012, p. 1). Interestingly, cutting down from 8 to 4 hours per day did not achieve an appreciable difference in stress or fatigue. Work demands, especially unclear roles, were still a prominent problem. Therapists may need to be creative in helping clients with disabilities maintain employment, going beyond standard reasonable accommodations to individualized solutions.

An important study on partner violence against physically disabled women augmented previous data from quantitative research (e.g., Nosek, Howland, Rintala,

Young, & Chanpong, 2001). The earlier study had shown similarities in the incidence of abuse of women with and without disabilities, but differences in the length of abuse and the relationship to the abuser. A qualitative study focused on the pattern of abuse and its relation to disability onset (Copel, 2006). In interviews with 25 women (ages 36–55) the pattern that emerged was different from Walker's (1977) three-phase cycle of violence in that there was no honeymoon phase after violent episodes. Instead, there was a period of avoidance, followed by a return to superficial normalcy. An especially disturbing finding was that for 21 of the 25 women the first episodes of abuse coincided with the onset of the disability and the changes in role functioning resulting from the disability. Furthermore, some abusive behaviors were unique to disability, such as hiding or destroying medications or insurance cards or disabling assistive technology. Barriers to leaving the abuser included lack of accessible shelters and reliance on others for assistance with activities of daily living. In all cases the abuse stopped only with the dissolution of the relationship. Copel (2006) makes several excellent recommendations for therapists, key among them being the need to inquire specifically about abuse. But she notes that "there is a lack of research and clinical information about the type of counseling that the women with disabilities received and how a particular counseling approach contributed to the women leaving the abuser" (p. 127).

Several authors have recommendations for clinicians that emanated from specific studies. These include ensuring that the ability to engage in leisure activities does not get overlooked (Berger, 2012; Kramer & Hammel, 2011), asking about positive sequelae of disability (Karlen, 2002; Kwok & White, 2011), and being both comfortable and skilled in discussing spirituality in therapy (Specht, King, Willoughby, Brown, & Smith, 2005).

PROVIDERS' PERSPECTIVES ON TREATMENT FOR PEOPLE WITH DISABILITIES

Eight articles were reviewed for this section (two from the United States), the two most relevant to therapy being by Pattison (2005, 2010), from the United Kingdom. She focused on how counseling can be inclusive for people with intellectual disabilities. She conducted a survey of 396 counselors (2005), most of whom were in private practice, and did semi-structured interviews with 15 of them. The interviews yielded six indicators of inclusive counseling, or counseling appropriate for people with intellectual disabilities: that counselors 1) take a proactive approach (e.g., increase awareness that counseling for people with disabilities is appropriate, have accessible materials); 2) focus on the relationship with the client (be warm, friendly, patient, and nonjudgmental); 3) have policies that are inclusive; 4) make initial assessments inclusive; 5) are flexible and creative in their approach; and 6) go outside their practice to raise awareness among others and to get further training. Pattison notes that too often therapy or medications are used to address the goals of other people who are bothered by behaviors of the person with the intellectual disability, rather than for the person's own goals. In a follow-up article Pattison (2010) gives strategies for reaching out to adolescents with intellectual disabilities. These include simplifying language on all materials, checking frequently for understanding, repetition, emphasis on main points, awareness of nonverbal communication, and more mirroring of clients.

Two articles focused on training professionals to work with people with developmental disabilities. In the first study, in the United States (Russo-Gleicher, 2008), master's level social workers (MSWs) who work with this population were asked about the rewards of the work, what other MSWs should know, what opportunities there were in the field, and what coursework and fieldwork would have been useful. The 24 MSWs (21 White; 18 working in nonprofit organizations), many of whom felt they had fallen into this work through happenstance, stated that developmental disabilities were often overlooked and that they really had no specific preparation for this population. They noted that students have little exposure to clients with disabilities and there was little connection between the classroom and the fieldwork. Their message and recommendations to others working with people with developmental disabilities were that such people are appropriate for therapy; the work is very rewarding, but the focus should be on small achievements; and people should remain living in the least restrictive environment possible. They also cautioned MSWs to see the person, not the diagnosis, a theme that echoes the studies reviewed in a previous section.

A study in Australia (Iacono et al., 2011) used DVDs of children with cerebral palsy to train students in health care. The authors had 241 students complete a five-question attitude scale (Interaction with Disabled People Scale) and conducted focus groups with 10 students and 10 tutors. The scale showed no pre–post differences, but the authors posited that the scale focuses mostly on comfort level with people with disabilities, which may not be affected without direct contact. However, the qualitative analysis showed that students had paid rapt attention to the DVDs, thought they were better than paper vignettes, and helped decrease focus on the disability and increase focus on the person.

Authors from Sweden examined published articles on physiotherapy (PT) interventions for children with cerebral palsy (Larsson, Miller, Liljedahl, & Gard, 2012). From the 21 articles reviewed they identified three paradigms: (a) making it possible—that is, function based, the PT as collaborative, based on a biopsychosocial model; (b) making it work—that is, impairment based, PT as coach leading the goals, intervention, and evaluation, who instructs the family, based on the biomedical and biopsychosocial model; and (c) making it normal, which is also impairment based, the PT as authoritative expert and based on the biomedical model. The authors concluded that the paradigm of disability drove the intervention approaches, thereby influencing the entire process, including relationships with the children. This has clear implications for therapy in that the paradigm of disability also would be expected to drive the therapy process. In a related article from Australia, 24 physiotherapists were interviewed by phone about fall prevention in persons with disabilities. There was tension between what the therapists felt was the correct program and what they thought the consumer would adhere to. The paradigm of disability might influence the expectations therapists have for the capabilities and outcomes for clients. In another study from Australia, 23 professionals in health and disability services at four agencies were asked about their definitions of wellness for children with disabilities (Breen, Wildy, Saggers, Millsteed, & Raghavendra, 2011). There was no consensus, but an important finding was that it was the organizational culture of the agency that determined the definition. Again, paradigms drive everything.

The last study reviewed here focused on overinvolved parents of children with developmental disabilities (van Ingen, Moore, & Fuemmeler, 2008). Before turning to the results I think it is important to examine the premises of this study. First, it was conducted in the United States, where a high value is placed on independence of children. Second, the concept of overinvolvement usually gets applied to parents of children with disabilities, not to parents of children without disabilities, and we should question why this is the case. And third, in this study overinvolvement and making things difficult for the professionals were conflated. Interviews with professionals about the parents they viewed as being overinvolved yielded three domains of behaviors: cognitive, emotional, and relational. Some behaviors identified included parents thinking they need to be involved in every decision and parents' distrust of providers, both of which may have some bases in reality for parents of young children with disabilities. Other behaviors were those that would be troublesome for any parent, such as exhibiting anger and frustration, being inconsistent and demanding, and rarely being satisfied. These behaviors do not imply overinvolvement but rather difficulty; I suspect that if the children did not have developmental disabilities the parents would simply be labeled difficult. There is something about the paradigm in which disability is viewed that allows professionals to connect parents' behaviors with the disability of the child in a way that may be quite inaccurate.

PROGRAM EVALUATIONS AND PROTOCOLS

There were four studies reviewed here, with one from the United States. Two studies described online treatments for depression (Bendelin et al., 2011; Montero-Marin et al., 2013), and both would be very helpful for practitioners thinking of designing or using an online intervention. A third study, from the United Kingdom, described the gap between training (in this case in solution-focused therapy) and learning (Smith, 2011). The MSWs, who were working with adults with intellectual disabilities, found that they easily slipped back into old patterns of behavior and perceived conflicts between what they learned in the 2-day workshop and the organizational culture in which they worked, which seemed to encourage a more directive and task-focused stance. As in the previous section, paradigms of thinking about people with intellectual disabilities directly affected the work.

The fourth study was the only one to be published in *Rehabilitation Psychology* (Schwartz & Rogers, 1994). The purpose of the study was to teach coping flexibility to people with MS who participated in an 8-week course on coping with chronic illness. The description of the course would be useful to other practitioners. It covered dealing with feelings about the illness, teaching new methods of setting goals, developing strategies to compensate for cognitive impairments, and improving communication with so-called caregivers. The authors note the difficulty of getting primary care physicians to refer clients with disabilities for therapies that have not been proven effective; there are few proven therapies for clients with disabilities, as most randomized controlled trials omit people with disabilities (Olkin & Taliaffero, 2005). One implication of this study for therapy, however, is that coping flexibility, not just the number of coping strategies used, seems to be better for coping with long-term problems such as chronic illness or disability.

THREE INTERRELATED STUDIES

Three studies from New Zealand examined the relation between MS-related fatigue and exercise. The first study (Smith, Hale, Olson, & Schneiders, 2009) focused on how exercise influenced fatigue in 10 persons with MS (eight females). Results came from analysis of interviews with the participants in an 8-week exercise program. Five themes were identified: listening to your body, perceived control over fatigue, reaching the edge (of limits), the nature of tiredness (good tired or too much), and exercise outcomes. The authors stressed *listening to your body* as critical for persons with MS. The second study then asked nine women with MS how fatigue affected exercise participation (Smith, Olson, Hale, Baxter, & Schneiders, 2011). Interviews with the participants showed that perceived control over fatigue was influenced by seven factors. The authors recommended asking exercise participants about their *perceived control over fatigue*. In the third study healthcare providers of exercise programs for people with MS were asked about their beliefs related to this exercise (Smith, Hale, Olson, & Schneiders, 2013). They described their beliefs about *the nature of fatigue* and barriers to exercise, including interdisciplinary conflicts. The authors stressed the importance of more *active listening* to clients with MS.

Taken together, these three studies underscore the complexity of the relations among MS-related fatigue, beliefs (by the person with MS and by healthcare providers), and exercise, concluding that listening to one's body is critical. (Though it might be noted that for some disabilities or symptoms the person might need to learn to ignore some aspects of the disability. Only body symptoms that are signals to change behaviors require attention.) Both clients' and providers' beliefs about perceived control over fatigue levels influenced behaviors. Also, differences between treatment providers in different disciplines need to be addressed to remove barriers. The three related studies provide a composite picture that promotes understanding of an important issue for people with MS. A quantitative study might have used multiple regression analysis to assess factors influencing exercise in people with MS, but beta values would be less informative than these qualitative results. The evidence shows not only that the variables are related but, more importantly, *how* they are related.

Quantitative Studies

As stated previously, there is paradoxically both a lot and very little in the quantitative literature on outpatient psychotherapy with people with disabilities. The very little amount that is useful has to do with the question of what empirical quantitative studies can tell us about the direct experiences of clients with disabilities or their outcomes in therapy. The abundance of relevant material comes from circling the topic to find other studies that can inform therapy and from including studies on specific disability populations. Many of these come from the fields of rehabilitation or health psychology and are not reviewed here because they were often specific to one type of chronic illness or disability and mostly did not directly inform general outpatient psychotherapy.

Unlike the sequenced outline for the section on qualitative literature, here I present the quantitative literature chronologically. Although my intent was to be as inclusive as possible, I have omitted articles specific to psychotherapy with persons with intellectual disabilities or Deafness, as those are very specialized subsets which most therapists are unlikely to encounter unless working in disability-specific settings (in which case one presumes they had more specialized training in these populations). Much of the literature is opinion, theory, or case studies, with just a few empirical studies. Readers will note a change in tone and perspective from earlier to later works.

Regarding empirical work on outpatient individual, couple, or family therapy including client(s) with disabilities, there is remarkably little on the topic. Many questions have never been addressed, including (a) whether people with disabilities, or with certain disabilities, are more likely than others to seek therapy; (b) how many therapists in private practice have accessible offices; (c) whether mental health agencies offer in-service trainings on disabilities; (d) whether and how psychotherapy is (or should be) modified for persons with specific disabilities; and (e) the degree to which presenting problems include the disability and in what ways, to name just a few. One thing is clear: there are not enough clinicians with disabilities to provide services to clients with disabilities, thus cross-cultural therapy (able-bodied therapist and client with a disability) is the norm (Andrews & Lund, 2015). Furthermore, trainees with disabilities are unlikely to be mentored by psychologists with disabilities (Lund, Andrews, & Holt, 2014). Thus clinicians need to educate themselves (which is one purpose of this book).

An early review of the history of psychotherapy with people with physical disabilities (Grzesiak & Hicok, 1994) was written predominantly from a psychoanalytic perspective. Disability is compared to the themes of trauma and loss. A second analytically oriented article (Langer, 1994) continued the theme of mourning and loss with disability, including vignettes with three adult males. A third paper reviewed both the theoretical and empirical literature on psychotherapy for depression in older adults with disabilities and included different models of treatment (Landreville & Gervais, 1997). That article ends with a call for more outcome studies, a call that is still resoundingly relevant 20 years later. However, I would note that the issues regarding aging and then acquiring an age-related disability might be very different from those regarding aging with a pre-existing or congenital disability. Responding simultaneously to aging and to new disability at a phase in life when there is a higher incidence of death of friends and perhaps retirement undoubtedly holds more issues that could lead to dysphoric mood. All three of these articles promulgate the perspective of disability as loss or deficit.

An article on therapeutic relationship issues in working with children and adolescents with physical disabilities (Gordon, Zaccario, Sachs, Ufberg, & Carlson, 2009) presents five cases studies. The approach is psychodynamic, and the focus is on transference and countertransference and what might necessitate breaking the therapeutic frame. The cases illustrate "the complex clinical dilemmas" (p. 113) of working with this population. In a similar vein, a chapter on Jungian and psychoanalytic therapy with adults with congenital physical disabilities discusses ruptures in bonding and early traumatic experiences (Asper, 2010). The author acknowledges that disability does not necessarily lead to psychological problems nor to a predisposition toward them. Part of the goal of this book is to address the common view of predestined negative outcomes for those born with disabilities and to help clinicians take an affirmative perspective.

One of the few insider articles (i.e., by a person with a disability) discusses the factors affecting psychotherapy with clients with physical disabilities. Balter (2006) offers suggestions for therapists to be more informed and sensitive, discussing factors that can impede the therapeutic relationship. She notes that challenges in this therapy may differ from those in work with non-disabled clients. Importantly, the tone of this article is in marked contrast to some of the earlier writings just cited, in that it puts the responsibility on the clinician to be culturally informed and sensitive, rather than focusing on the intrapsychic mechanisms of the client with a disability.

One publication is actually a collection of articles by various insiders (Erickson Cornish, Gorgens, Monson, Olkin, Palombi, & Abels, 2008). The overriding concept is ethical practices with clients with disabilities. The first section (Erickson Cornish, Gorgens, & Monson, 2008) posed the question of what constitutes ethical practice with persons with disabilities, and what knowledge, skills, and attitudes are necessary for disability cultural competence. The authors note that it can be hard for practitioners to integrate disability into conceptualizations of diversity, for two reasons: difficulties in acknowledging 1) one's own able-bodied privilege and 2) one's own vulnerability to disability. They specified particular areas of requisite knowledge (e.g., laws, office and internet accessibility, barriers to psychological care, biases, models of disability, developmental issues, partnering and parenting issues, modifications for assessment and intervention) to avoid common mistakes. They further promote skills in advocacy, social justice for persons with disabilities, consultation, and interdisciplinary resources. Finally, they emphasize that attitudes of empathy and compassion must be accompanied by high expectations.

In the second section of that collection (Olkin, 2008), I posed specific discussion questions related to attitudes, knowledge, and skills, emphasizing that attitudes alone are insufficient without knowledge and skills. Increasing skills in turn increases trainees' confidence, making them more effective clinicians. But I also noted that instructors and supervisors are probably untrained in disability issues, as only 7 out of 210 APA-accredited programs have a required course on the psychosocial aspects of disability.

The third section (Palombi, 2008) followed up this point by noting that inadequate training leads to clinical treatment errors. Palombi provides a case vignette in which a client's disability is not incorporated into the case formulation, which oversimplifies the client's problem as one of lack of confidence without acknowledgement of the myriad disability-related barriers. Ignorance of disability issues in therapy can lead to further marginalization of clients with disabilities. Palombi posits that ethical services require (a) a broader definition of diversity, (b) multicultural models that include factors related to disabilities, (c) more exploration of attitudes toward disability, (d) education regarding disability issues, and (e) infusion of knowledge and skills related to disability into service, supervision, training, consultation, teaching, and research. She also would include knowledge and skills in civil rights, social justice, and public policy, barriers impeding full participation of people with disabilities. She suggests that psychologists should lead the way in advocating for people with disabilities and acquiring or teaching these skills, not follow years behind attitudes and research.

In the final section of Erickson Cornish et al.'s collection (2008) Abels (2008) notes that ethical competence includes viewing clients as more than just the disability but as comprising multiple identities. He raises questions about a clinician's own disability status, which can be helpful if the therapist has a disability (as it might increase knowledge and skills) or harmful (when the clinician is struggling with a new impairment and might be adjusting ways of practicing). Abels cautions against the automatic assumption that disability leads to depression or that presenting problems are about the disability in a causal link. The "spread effect" (Wright, 1983) occurs when all deficits (whether real or imputed) are seen as being due to the disability. He offers an example of a microaggression that takes the form of a compliment, calling clinicians' attention to the fact that sometimes well-meaning positive statements are perceived as slights. If a client points out barriers in the clinician's building or in treatment, these might profitably lead to praise for the client's self-advocacy and thanks to the client for the education regarding accessibility. Abels notes that finances are often a challenge for people with disabilities, and therefore discussion of therapy fees is an ethical obligation. He makes the excellent point that privacy issues may be paramount for people with disabilities, as a visible disability often invites boundary violations in public. And lastly, he cautions that "avoidance through silence" (p. 496) perpetuates ineffective treatment and incompetence.

An affirmative tone characterizes another article on cultural competence in psychotherapy with people with disabilities (Artman & Daniels, 2010). Again, the focus is on what the therapist can do as well as on conceptual models of psychotherapy and cultural competence. These include critical areas of awareness, knowledge, and skills, as well as practical information about accessibility (in the broader sense) and resources.

I include here a reference on group therapy because it directly challenges psychoanalytically oriented group therapy to counter the marginalization of persons with disabilities (Watermeyer, 2012). The author notes that psychoanalysis has sometimes lacked political awareness regarding people with disabilities, which he views as an oppressed and systematically disadvantaged minority. He links disablist discrimination to unconscious countertransference responses in the therapist that are evoked by impairment.

A personal account traces how the author's understanding of disability shifted and suggests the same might be happening within psychotherapeutic circles (Frankish, 2013). The author recounts his personal practice of disability psychotherapy and concludes that he has shifted from a position of "doing to" to "doing with," an approach much more in keeping with the tenets of the disability independent living movement. However, another article continues the pairing of disability with Freud's notions of melancholia and mourning (Bartram, 2013), describing psychotherapy with an adult with a disability as well as the parents of a young child with a disability. This idea that disability is a loss that must be mourned (what Beatrice Wright [1983] called the "requirement of mourning" with which people with disabilities are saddled) is so pervasive in the literature and impervious to the failure of empirical studies to find mourning normative that it is alarming to see such a recent article continue this line of thought.

There are some books (e.g., Wilson, 2003) and some chapters on therapy with people with disabilities (e.g., Cobb & Warner, 1999) that I am not reviewing here. Some are quite good, even standards in the field (e.g., Mackelprang & Salsgiver, 2015; Marini & Stebnicki, 2012). However, for this chapter I was searching for evidence-based documents on general outpatient psychotherapy with clients with disabilities, and although those books cite studies, most studies on evidence-based therapy exclude people with disabilities (Olkin & Taliaferro, 2005). In fact, the lack of empirical work is quite striking. Also absent are works using CBT specifically for psychotherapy with clients with disabilities in general outpatient settings (i.e., not in specialty clinics or agencies, usually those geared toward specific disability populations, such as intellectual disabilities or autism spectrum disorders). Although many CBT approaches are standard for aspects of disability such as pain, stress management, coping strategies, and illness beliefs, the articles tend to be specific to one type of disability (not surprisingly, as evidence-based therapy tends to focus on efficacy more than effectiveness; Wampold & Imel, 2015). Furthermore, CBT articles often focus on changes within the person (or group of people) with particular disabilities, often to the exclusion of the discriminatory environments and attitudes that affect people with disabilities. An exception to this approach is an article by David (2009) that discusses how to integrate issues of oppression into CBT (for all oppressed groups, not just those with disabilities).

As the notion of microaggressions (Sue, 2010) has come to the forefront of discussions about marginalized groups, their impact on individuals with disabilities has been largely ignored. There is documentation of the negative health effects of microaggressions for people of color, women, and people who are gay, lesbian, or bisexual (Sue, 2010). However, there are only two studies related to microaggressions and persons with disabilities. In the earlier study, Timm (2002) developed a 40-item Disability-Specific Hassles Scale (DSHS; hassles were so labeled before the term *microaggressions* had become commonplace). Her methodology of developing items was to ask eight people with various disabilities, both hidden (e.g., learning disabilities) and visible (e.g., spina bifida), to keep a daily journal documenting disability-related hassles. This not only helped generate items for a scale but yielded a serendipitous finding. The participants were astonished at the number of daily hassles they would routinely have overlooked had they not been asked to keep track of them. It seems that one coping mechanism in the face of numerous daily hassles is to barely register their occurrence.

The data (Timm, 2002) from 235 people with disabilities (ages 18–64; 72% females; 86% White; 80% living in the United States; 74% with a physical disability) who completed the DSHS showed good reliability (Cronbach's alpha = .91). The average number of disability-specific hassles in the previous month was 14, and 10 hassles were endorsed by over 50% of the respondents. Factor analysis of the DHSH yielded six factors: environmental infrastructures, imposed helplessness/avoidance, violation of personal space/privacy, depersonalization-minimizing, depersonalization-aggrandizing, and violation of civil rights. One of these factors (depersonalization-minimizing) predicted psychological well-being as measured by the Perceived Stress Scale (Cohen, Kamarck, & Mermelstein, 1983).

In the second study, Richard Keller and colleagues (Keller & Galgay, 2010; Keller, Galgay, Robinson, & Moscoso, 2009) conducted semi-structured interviews in a group format with 12 participants. They designated five types of microaggressions: invalidation, patronization, ascription of intelligence, desexualization, and exoticization (Keller et al., 2009). Those results were presented at the annual convention of the American Psychological Association but not published. In a later publication based on the same study (Keller & Galgay, 2010), the authors reanalyzed the data and found patterns of microaggressions that fell into eight domains.

One difference for people with disabilities compared to other types of oppressed groups is that built environments contain microaggressions, through the creation of spaces that are inaccessible or are only accessible through alternate routes. For example, encountering a building with a heavy door, a sidewalk with no curb cut, or a separate accessible entrance that goes past the garbage cans and through the basement can have effects similar to those produced by interpersonal microaggressions, as they remind the person with a disability of his or her minority status and separateness. The stigma associated with the built environment comes from the segregation of people with disabilities from others.

In my research with women with disabilities and their experiences of microaggressions (Olkin, Hayward, Schaff, & VanHeel, 2016), 27 women with disabilities readily apparent to others completed questionnaires online then attended one of five focus groups. All of the women were over 18 years of age (mean = 56); 26% were women of color. Income was bimodal, with about five doing very well and others below the poverty line. Questionnaire data showed that two of the four most frequently experienced microaggressions were also two of the four most bothersome microaggressions: someone downplays the effects of disability on your life, and your right to equality is denied (discussed further in Chapter 9). This suggests that women with disabilities experience a high rate of at least two very bothersome microaggressions.

Conclusions and Moving Forward

Given these works on microaggressions, it would seem that one implication for treatment of individuals with disabilities would be to incorporate discussion of microaggressions and their management into the therapy. If people with disabilities experience a high rate of microaggressions and those microaggressions are bothersome, then it follows that clients will have developed ways of coping with these microaggressions. Coping can take many forms, and the flexibility of coping might be an important goal (i.e., not tilting at every windmill). The issue of microaggressions and its managements is incorporated into disability-affirmative therapy (D-AT).

Often in the professional literature, disability is treated as the single demographic variable (though perhaps paired with gender). It is less frequently examined in conjunction with sexual orientation, ethnicity, and religion, among other variables. Thus, this book contains a chapter devoted to intersectionality of demographic variables (Chapter 7) and includes some of my own research on gay men with disabilities.

No discussion of my thinking about disability would be complete without acknowledging Beatrice Wright and her seminal book (Wright, 1983). In particular, her concept of value-laden beliefs (Wright, 1972) underlies all of D-AT. Although written specifically for rehabilitation psychology, these beliefs apply equally to outpatient psychotherapy. (For a list of those values and their D-AT equivalents see Table 2.1.)

I would be remiss if I did not acknowledge the work of those authors focusing on other marginalized groups. The term *disability-affirmative therapy* was borrowed from gay-affirmative therapy. Works on White privilege, inherent bias, and stigma as well as countless writings from disability studies have all helped shaped the template I outline in this book.

Of course, the entire field of rehabilitation psychology has informed much of my work, although I was not trained in that specialty. My training was in counseling psychology (with less of a focus on pathology and more on strengths and optimal development), family therapy (thinking in systems), and disability studies (which includes fields outside psychology, such as sociology, medical anthropology, and literature). Lastly, as a person with a disability, I have my own lived experiences, as well as those of my students and clients, that have helped shape my development of D-AT. But I continue to grow and learn, and I suspect that as soon as this book is published I will want to refine it in accordance with some new information or experiences.

TABLE 2.1

COMPARISON OF VALUE-LADEN BELIEFS AND DISABILITY-AFFIRMATIVE THERAPY (D-AT) COROLLARIES

#	Value-Laden Belief (Wright)	D-AT Corollary (Olkin)
1	Every individual needs respect and encouragement; the presence of a handicap, no matter how severe, does not alter these fundamental rights.	Therapy requires the core foundation of an empathic, nonjudgmental, and authentic relationship, which is not altered by the presence of a disability.
2	The assets of a person must receive considerable attention in the rehabilitation effort.	D-AT examines areas of strengths, growth, and effective coping.
3	The active participation of the client in the planning and execution of his or her rehabilitation program is to be sought as fully as possible.	Therapy is a collaborative process in which the client actively participates.
4	The client is seen not as an isolated individual but as part of a larger group that includes other people, including family.	Disability affects not only the person but also his or her partner, children, parents, siblings, and other relatives. Communities also may be affected.
5	Because each person has unique characteristics and each situation its own properties, variability is required in rehabilitation plans.	D-AT requires an exploration of nine areas that inform the case formulation and thus individualize the treatment plan.
6	Predictor variables, based on group outcomes in rehabilitation, should be applied with caution in individual cases.	Evidence-based therapy, inasmuch as it is normed on able-bodied populations, should be applied with caution and modified as appropriate for individuals with differing needs and capabilities.
7	The significance of a handicap is affected by the person's feelings about him- or herself and the situation.	The person's beliefs and values and self-esteem will influence the way in which his or her disability affects the person, more than will the objective degree of impairment.

(Continued)

Table 2.1 (*Cont.*)

#	Value-Laden Belief (Wright)	D-AT Corollary (Olkin)
8	The severity of a handicap can be increased or diminished by environmental conditions.	Disability is a social construct, that is, the degree of handicap varies with the environment, tasks, and the political, economic, and social system in which it is located.
9	It is essential that society as a whole strive continuously and persistently to provide the basic means toward fulfillment of the lives of all its inhabitants, including those with handicaps.	D-AT is not only about how we treat our individual clients but also about strong advocacy on behalf of all people with disabilities, as well as being change agents for a more equitable world and reallocation of resources.
10	Provision must be made for the effective dissemination of information concerning legislation and community offerings of potential benefit to persons with handicaps.	Clients, especially those with newer onset of disability, cannot be expected to be experts in their legal or economic rights; therapists must take some responsibility for helping clients navigate their world and guide them to the disability community and culture, as appropriate.
11	Involvement of the client with the general life of the community is a fundamental principle guiding decisions concerning living arrangements and the use of resources.	Proximity is not the same as inclusion; D-AT strives for full inclusion of people with disabilities in all aspects of the community.
12	In addition to the special problems of particular groups, rehabilitation clients commonly share certain problems by virtue of their disadvantaged and devalued position.	D-AT addresses the commonalities across many types of disabilities that result from being part of a stigmatized and oppressed group.

Discussion Questions

1. Why do you suppose most of the qualitative studies on therapy with people with disabilities come from outside the United States?

2. Where do the perspectives of patients and consumers with disabilities and professional staff differ, and where do they overlap?
3. What are some of the barriers to outpatient treatment for people with disabilities?
4. How might ethnic-cultural factors, in addition to disability, affect the expectations for therapy and the therapeutic relationship?
5. What recommendations for therapists might come directly from the studies in Chapter 2?

3 A Case Example: "Sam"

THE FOLLOWING CASE is taken (with permission) from an actual client. The rationale for using a real person rather than an amalgamation of several persons is that there is a psychological consistency within the story of a particular person that is hard to duplicate when borrowing from various sources. Additionally, actual stories contain elements that would never occur to the writer, because truth is often stranger than fiction. I include the case here as I refer back to it in several places throughout the book, in order to illustrate specific points and give clinical examples. Then, after outlining the elements of disability-affirmative therapy (D-AT), I revisit Sam and use him as an example to walk through the case formulation using the D-AT template.

Case Study
ID

Sam is a 57-year-old White gay male who had polio at age 2. He wears a full leg brace on one leg, walks with Canadian crutches, or uses an electric wheelchair or scooter. He retired at age 50 and lives in a condo he owns with his husband of 10 years, a Korean man 10 years younger than him. He smokes marijuana daily, to the dismay of his husband, Eddie. They sometimes attend church together on Sundays; Sam is ambivalent about his involvement in the church.

CONTEXT

Sam was referred after 15 sessions by a male therapist—the therapist and Sam agreed that disability issues were paramount in the treatment and a therapist more knowledgeable about disability was warranted. (In retrospect, it seems odd that the referral was made after so many sessions; I believe the therapist felt unprepared to treat this client.) When Sam called he stated right away that he needed a therapist with disability knowledge. He then asked if I would take Medi-Cal insurance, and when I declined he began to rant at me that I was not able to handle his disability ("If you're the expert and you can't handle it what good are you?"). I stayed steadfast, and within a few minutes he said "I might as well kill myself," and hung up. I was unable to call back as I did not have his phone number. After 10 minutes, he called back and apologized and we scheduled the first appointment.

PRESENTING PROBLEMS

At the initial session Sam bombarded me with information: names of several doctors he was seeing, including a psychiatrist for medication; pages of tables with all his medications, dates/times he took them, and symptoms; and action plans. He told me his diagnosis was probably bipolar, that he also had attention-deficit/hyperactivity disorder (ADHD), and possibly posttraumatic stress disorder (PTSD). He acknowledged his outburst with me on the phone and said it was good that I set limits; now he knew he couldn't do that with me. He said that he "goes off" on people, gets angry and yells, and has even been thrown out of places. He maintained that this "works" in the sense that it gets him what he wants. However, it is usually followed by guilt, shame, and obsessive thoughts.

The Medi-Cal insurance issue raised on the phone had been misconveyed to me; he was not really asking whether I take Medi-Cal insurance. Instead, he wanted a standard insurance form to be completed for his records, and he was paying out of pocket. I helped him complete the form, which I then photocopied, dated, and gave him after each session.

For about the first year of therapy Sam would often enter saying that he was having an "episode" (of extreme irritation or anger) or that he was depressed. He continued to believe he had bipolar disorder until I told him I had never seen any signs of mania currently or in his past, and I didn't believe the anger outbursts were due to mania. He did have major depression, superimposed on dysthymia with childhood onset. He cried frequently in the session, and when he got overwhelmed with emotions he would start making rapid hand movements and get confused, forget what we were talking about, withdraw, then say, "What am I supposed to be doing now?" rather plaintively or in a sharp business-like tone.

Sam's relationship with Eddie changed over the course of treatment, seeming somewhat precarious and insecure at first, then resulting in a commitment ceremony and then marriage, by which time they had been together for over 15 years. The relationship was one area discussed in treatment. Another area was the fact that Sam smoked marijuana about 14 times per day, although this was not a concern to him. Over the first year of treatment he cut down his drinking from about three drinks per night down to one glass and reduced marijuana frequency to six times a day. After about 1 year in therapy he started to acknowledge the effects of marijuana on his thinking and memory and set a date to quit, though he ultimately never quit. The following dialogue is from early in therapy:

> SAM: But I need it [marijuana] to reduce my pain! I can't be in pain all the time.
> RHODA: Give me an idea of how much pain you feel. On a scale of 1 to 10, with 10 being the worst you can imagine, how much pain do you feel right now?
> SAM: About a 4.
> RHODA: And on most days?
> SAM: I don't know. (Getting whiny) It can be a 7 or 8!
> RHODA: And it gets to a 7 or 8 *with* marijuana.
> SAM: Now you sound like Eddie. He's always trying to get me to quit.

CURRENT LIFE CIRCUMSTANCES

Sam and Eddie live in a two-story condo, with a chair lift to the second floor and an elevator to the ground level. The condo is rather inaccessible due to messiness (attributed to Eddie). Additionally, Eddie owns or babysits many dogs, which create too much mess and chaos for Sam. Once, Eddie hid the fact that one of the dogs was pregnant; it had a litter of four, which Eddie tried to sell for $1,000 each. Although Sam saw this as just another of Eddie's many schemes, they were in fact creative entrepreneurial plans by someone who was often unemployed.

Sam retired earlier than expected due to disability-related fatigue and weakness. He had been a project manager, traveling all over the world. His spreadsheets (e.g., of medications) were a way of staying connected to his work self and to manage his anxiety. Eddie had been intermittently unemployed, working for minimum wage, getting new jobs, getting promotions. As Eddie found more solid employment he had less time to spend with Sam, which was difficult for Sam. Sam learned to reduce his temper with Eddie and found that Eddie in turn responded more favorably.

Sam's social circle comprised Eddie's large family, gay or lesbian couples, and a gay male who also had polio.

SAMPLE QUOTES FROM THERAPY

Following are some statements Sam made early in therapy. They show his antagonism towards various institutions and his attempts to force others to be more disability-aware.

"If you won't do this for me then you're just part of the problem. The medical establishment won't listen, they won't take my disability into account."

"I gave him the book and he wouldn't read it!" (Bruno's book on post-polio; the "him" refers to many people.)

"They're a bunch of old suburban women who don't know what they're doing, want to control everything, in your face, scolding." (About a polio support group; unconsciously also about me, a suburban woman around Sam's age.)

"They don't want to change" (said in a whiny voice, about the Episcopal church he attends).

HISTORY

Sam was the youngest of three boys from a small town in the Midwest. Both parents (now deceased) graduated from high school and were Baptists. He was raised on an isolated rural farm, with no indoor plumbing or central heat; in the winter they would turn on the oven and open the oven door.

Sam's earliest memory is of being in the hospital at age 2 (from polio), trying to escape from his crib and getting caught in a bed sheet. He hung cradled in the sheet and fell asleep; he has no memory of being rescued. Two other memories from this time include being pushed into water in the hospital; he believes he was held underwater. He also remembers being home at Christmas but feeling very anxious and sad because he had to go back to the hospital after Christmas was over.

Shortly before we began therapy Sam had a fight with one brother and his wife about where to go out to dinner. The fight escalated as Sam got more unreasonable. Both of his brothers stopped speaking to Sam for some time. Then a rapprochement occurred among the brothers, and Sam traveled to attend one brother's anniversary party, an important concession on Sam's part. Nonetheless, when Sam's brother and his wife bickered, Sam found this hard to tolerate, and it reinforced his belief that arguments never resulted in resolution.

Sam came out as gay at age 20, first to one brother (also gay), and then to his parents. He moved to California to be a part of the hippie and gay communities. In his early twenties Sam got throat cancer; surgery and radiation led to complete recovery, but being hospitalized again was very traumatic for him. In his mid-twenties he fell in love for the first time, and they planned to go live abroad. Sam left first, and once there got a "dear John" letter. He felt abandoned and heart-broken in a foreign land and resolved not to fall in love again. Although he does love Eddie, he says he's never felt the same about anyone since his first love.

Sam was part of a church that had a heavy front gate that was often closed, making it impossible for Sam to enter. He got into numerous fights with people at the church over accessibility and over church doctrine. After about 6 months of therapy he switched to his current Episcopalian church, but he still got into occasional fights about liturgy.

Twice I have seen Sam get extremely upset, helpless, and infantilized over something that happened during the week. The first time was when he attended a church retreat and they asked participants in a workshop to lie on the floor. Sam refused—lying on the floor created flashbacks of polio experiences. He was able to recover and leave the situation. The second time, he was getting cataract surgery and didn't think the anesthesiologist was listening to him about (what he believed were) problems with anesthesia for persons with polio. He pulled the IV tube out of his arm, sat up on the gurney, and started shouting. A nurse took charge, cleared the room, calmed Sam down, and got a different anesthesiologist. Sam felt and acted like he was fighting for his life.

> RHODA: Sam, you were able to stop what was happening that you didn't like.
> SAM: He wasn't listening to me!
> RHODA: Yes, but you ultimately had the power.
> SAM: I had to really scream and pull the tubes out!
> RHODA: Is there anything else you could have done that might have stopped what was happening?
> SAM: What do you mean?
> RHODA: [Laying down on the floor, and using his description] I'm lying here on the gurney, and there's an IV in my arm. The surgeon hasn't come in yet, and there are two nurses hovering around. The anesthesiologist is busy and doesn't seem to be listening to me. Tell me what I can do.
> SAM: [Like a 5-year-old] I don't knnnooooowww!
> RHODA: Sam, watch. Suppose I try this. "I am withdrawing my consent to this surgery!"
> SAM: That would get their attention.
> RHODA: Is that something you could do?
> SAM: I don't know. [He is substantially calmer now.]

MENTAL STATUS EXAMINATION AND EXAMINATION DATA

Sam is a nice-looking man, about 5 feet 10 inches, who usually dresses in a button-down shirt, slacks, and leather jacket. He's quite masculine looking, but looks older than his age, and often quite tired and worn. Sam can look quite fierce, like a cartoon face of someone who is angry, with furrowed brow and a dark look. Rantings often start with a little-boy voice, whining ("If he would just read the book!") or generalizing about a "they" ("The church says it wants to change but they won't do the things they need to do to change"). He almost always asks me how I am when he enters. He has a routine when he arrives: walking in, he puts his crutches on the floor, takes off a backpack, takes out his water bottle, takes off his glasses and puts them down, finds a pen, arranges himself on the chair, loses his glasses or water or pen, then finds them again. At the end of sessions much of this routine is repeated in reverse.

A neuropsychological evaluation was done shortly after Sam retired, at the request of Sam's then therapist, at his peak of depression and agitation. Wechsler Adult Intelligence Scale (WAIS) scores ranged from 30th (performance) to 88th (verbal comprehension) percentile, i.e., remarkable variability. Sam indicated feelings of worthlessness, self-criticalness, loss of interest and pleasure, pessimism, indecisiveness, irritability and agitation, poor concentration, excessive worry and rumination, low frustration tolerance, and increased sleep and fatigue. The report noted use of alcohol and marijuana, and intellectualizing or externalizing as defenses. The diagnosis was Depressive Disorder NOS (still *DSM-IV*), with mild cognitive deficits, and Global Assessment Functioning (GAF) score was 45. However, there were several reasons I did not believe the WAIS to be valid, including the use of alcohol and marijuana on a daily basis, the extreme emotional dysregulation at the time, and inconsistency between the report and the level of job he had held successfully for many years.

Sam's intellect showed when he talked about his previous work, when he remembered and made connections between things we had talked about in the past, and when he talked about computer systems he has developed to track projects. But his memory, concentration, and motivation were all significantly dampened by his daily marijuana use. He reduced his use from about 16 times a day to 7 times a day after about 2 years of therapy. With my urging he set a date to quit 6 months hence. On the quit date Sam stopped smoking marijuana and gave all remaining stash to a friend. Abstinence lasted about 2 months, until Sam had a particularly bad week and he resumed smoking about five times a day. And ultimately he decided he did not want to quit smoking marijuana; the level remains about 6 to 12 times a day. He has been quite unempathic to Eddie's insistence that Sam not take marijuana in the car with them; Eddie undoubtedly believes that he—an immigrant, a gay male, and an ethnic minority—would be in big trouble if stopped by the police. Vacations and car trips have been sullied with arguments over this.

Sam is notable for his seriousness, with little sense of humor about himself, difficulty with empathy, and selfishness, all of which he admits to freely. When I talk about empathy (a topic he barely tolerates and doesn't know why on earth we are discussing) he says with irritation: "Didn't I always tell you I was selfish?"

Functioning level at intake was quite low (about 31 in the older GAF model), then reached about 40 after just over a year, then at least 60 by the end of year three, with indications of continued improvement. (Coda: GAF was up to 81–90 after 5 years, and therapy was tapered to once a month.)

Diagnosis in DSM-5

> 296.32 Major depressive episode, recurring, moderate; currently in partial remission
> 300.4 Pervasive Depressive Disorder, early onset
> 305.30 Cannabis Use Disorder, moderate
> 301.83 Borderline Personality Disorder (initially; potentially resolved by year three)
> *Medications:* Provigil, Ambien (prn), Vicodin (prn), Cymbalta

RELATIONSHIP

Initially my response to Sam was to feel overwhelmed and exhausted after each session. Some of this came from awareness of his inner rage, much of it from feeling I had to be on my toes, one step ahead of him, at all times. Mistakes were costly. For example, I mentioned I was doing a study of pain in individuals with post-polio. He took this as a reason to go to a polio support group and try to recruit subjects for me. He entered the meeting late and immediately tried to commandeer the meeting to talk about my study. The female leader tried to keep control of the meeting but met with escalating resistance from Sam. When Sam yanked a chair, hitting the hand of a woman with arthritis, security was called and Sam left. A few days later I was at a polio meeting and two women who had been to the meeting with Sam gave me their versions of what had happened. Interestingly, both of them seemed to feel compassion for Sam, saying, "it is hard to be Sam." At the next session I told Sam what I'd heard about the incident. He said he almost didn't come to the session, was enraged at me, thinking I had set him up, had sent him to do a task that would be impossible, that I was another one of those women criticizing and scolding him. I acknowledged and accepted his rage, apologized for any way I might have contributed to events, expressed sadness that he felt I would set him up, and wondered why he thought I might do so.

When Sam alluded to sexual preferences he couldn't discuss with me I didn't force the issue. A few months later he finally told me about his experiences with men he met online for one-time sexual encounters. This was significant in that he was allowing me to see all of him, to be present and complete in therapy. In his view, this risked my rejection of him, and thus my acceptance of all parts of him was an important model. Nonetheless, there were many times I felt very critical of Sam. His lack of empathy could be breathtaking, and after about 20 minutes, sometimes I would notice my posture, my tone of voice, and my content being harsh. I would have to take a deep breath, pull back, and get into his world view. This helped me be more accepting of him. But his trouble with empathy meant that sometimes in the moment he couldn't tolerate much empathy from me, though in the long run it seems to have helped.

Sometimes I would choose to disclose something about myself as a person with childhood-onset polio. For example, one time I told him I had recently been to a party, and that when I entered, two women instantly offered to bring me a plate of food, and someone got me a chair; I said these things felt good to me. He said he could never do that, let people help him. When I asked how it was to hear these things about me he said he felt hopeless, alienated—he could never get to where I am about disability. I worried out loud that as he read my book (*What Psychotherapists Should Know About Disability*) this would be hard for him, as it would highlight the contrast between where we each are in our relation to our disabilities.

During the third year of treatment, Sam's depression significantly decreased. But solidifying the gains was hard. Return to daily marijuana use was part of the problem, but so was the fact that Sam had no experiences of joy to draw on. He had been significantly deprived of true experiences of unmitigated pleasure and unambivalent closeness. On the weeks when he felt better he believed he could change and learn these, but when he was more fatigued or sad he felt hopeless about his own abilities and sometimes talked about not wanting to live out his life like this. Surprisingly, he was not actively suicidal throughout therapy, with the exception of the time he thought I had set him up. He looked forward to coming to therapy, finding it helpful even when painful. It was apparent that he thought about the things we talked about quite a bit. After a few years he was able to tolerate increased confrontation. For example, we discussed whether he would marry Eddie, and I challenged his rather superficial reasons for not doing so, pushing for the underlying fears, which he finally expressed. Although the session ended on a somewhat antagonistic note, that week he spoke with Eddie, who readily agreed to marry, which they did not long thereafter.

CASE FORMULATION

This is a man who thinks there are two choices in life—to be the abuser or the abused, perpetrator or victim, and he'd rather be the former. In aid of this he developed an angry persona that is quite formidable. As the son who ruined his mother's life (as she told him), who was not protected from the mom by his father, whose mom forced him to do all the things nondisabled children do (and to do them better), whose brothers resented how much time and attention he used, he learned early that who he was—a boy with a significant disability—was unacceptable. Then, as he recognized his homosexuality he came out rather rapidly but introjected the idea of basic badness. So, in total he is, by his own definition, a selfish, gay, disabled male, and the package is totally unacceptable. Therapy is the one place in which all of these parts of him are known. He continued to believe that no one would accept him with all of these aspects, and that I only do so because it's my job. Thus he hides parts of himself from everyone (e.g., from his friend with a disability his own negative feelings about disability, and from his gay friends how disabled he is). When all these parts come together in therapy, he feels overwhelmed with sadness and despair. As he has recently experienced brief moments of well-being and happiness for the first time, his despair sometimes increases as he loses these moments again.

Sam's thinking style is dichotomous (e.g., abuser/abused; I'm getting better/I'm no better at all; my mother loved me/she totally failed me). He has no internal model of play, joy, or happiness (life on the farm was work). His disability pervaded his childhood but was not allowed to be discussed openly. His parents had to carry him upstairs to bed at night and down again in the morning, but he was supposed to be as capable as any other boy, if not more so. He internalized this dichotomy and now "hides" his readily apparent disability.

TREATMENT

Sam had been in previous therapy, for 10 years with one male therapist and with the referring (male) therapist for 15 sessions. Termination with the first therapist was abrupt; it occurred after the therapist sent the police to Sam's home after a suicide threat. Sam was enraged that the therapist intruded on him in this way, feeling it was his right to commit suicide if he wanted to, but also asserting that he would never really kill himself, which the therapist should have known ("He never really knew me at all!"). He complained that the therapist's office was inaccessible (up several steps) and that the therapist never did anything about this and didn't read "the book." The second therapist had a more accessible office, and Sam gave him a book about polio to read, but didn't seem to make a connection with the therapist (who didn't read the book). Sam then asserted that anyone who didn't have a disability could never really understand him. When he first called me he was excited at the idea of seeing a therapist with a disability, but leery of seeing a female therapist and terrified at the idea that, because I have a disability, I might actually understand him—all of which was unacknowledged and probably unknown by Sam at the time.

Sam's initial goal for therapy was to "feel better." He was somewhat obtuse about exploring what "better" meant besides the fact of feeling better. He did say he would need to change his thinking, thus the language of CBT fit him well initially. Some of his automatic thoughts could be challenged directly. For example, he asserted that he "had no friends," yet I had heard him name many people, so I took out a piece of paper and asked him to list the people in his life. There were at least 14, and I gave him the list. I have reminded him of the list frequently when he asserts his aloneness, and now he is able to say that he *feels* alone because at times it is so hard to be with or contact or reach out to other people. One of the therapy mantras has been that *feelings are not truth*.

Other thoughts and beliefs were approached more gingerly because they triggered schemas. His core schema was that he was in danger of ceasing to exist (represented nonverbally by the toddler hanging from the crib, helpless and unable to free himself). He also believed he was defective. These two schemas conflict: he is fighting to save a man who is not worthy of saving. Sam feels that he is selfish, and that he is fundamentally flawed and unworthy of love because he is gay and disabled. Over the course of therapy we slowly shifted focus. In the first year we focused on functioning, automatic thoughts, countering depression both cognitively and behaviorally, and accessing his social circle more. In the second year, as functioning improved and depression lessened, we moved to his core beliefs. Rather than challenging them, I accepted them as the way Sam feels. Since he was unacceptable to his family, even until recently to his brothers, it is no wonder that he has felt unacceptable to himself. But when I would point out how he learned to feel fundamentally bad, he would despair that he is so damaged from not getting what he needed from his parents that he cannot get better. When I would talk about self-acceptance or self-care, he literally had no idea what I meant and would get confused. When he talked about needing to do *A* before he can do *B*, I would remind him he has been talking about doing *A* for 2 years. He started to acknowledge that he needed to turn thoughts into actions, but typically sabotaged action (e.g., he believed he needed to feel better before he could quit smoking marijuana, and I would assert that he had to quit smoking regardless of how he felt).

In the third year of therapy, as the depression lifted significantly and he experienced more pleasure in life, Sam enlarged his circle of friends. He left the house almost daily; doing so greatly improved his mood. His angry outbursts were greatly diminished. However, he would slip back into his dichotomous thinking when his mood worsened, and he would worry again about being abandoned (by Eddie, sometimes by me). A fall that injured the leg most affected by polio set him back emotionally, and therapy by phone was necessary to remind him of the coping strategies he had previously mastered to stave off a major depression.

Sam and his friend with polio read my book aloud together over the phone, then discussed it. Sam both was drawn to and afraid to read the book. He underlined: "The vulnerability comes from trying to meet able-bodied standards despite the disability." This encapsulates how he was raised by his mother, who his cousins called "Sarge" because she barked out orders. Discussing this line led to a conversation about accepting himself as a man with a disability. The following from a session in the third year of treatment shows how difficult this continued to be for him, even as his mood improved and his thinking was less emotion-focused:

> SAM: Maybe I'll go to Denver for the [Democratic National] Convention. I have a friend there who's given me an open invitation. I really shouldn't be talking about going to Denver; I want to go to Thailand and see my friend there. But I don't know if that's realistic now [he starts scratching his arm, a sign of anxiety].
>
> RHODA: What is unrealistic about it?
>
> SAM: I could die there (in Thailand). My friend's mother died there and he thought the hospital was at fault.
>
> RHODA: You don't feel confident that if you got ill in Thailand that you would be taken care of.
>
> SAM: No. It takes so little time [for an infection in his foot to become really bad]. I have to be put on the right antibiotic or I could die. But that was my dream, to retire and visit friends all over the world.
>
> RHODA: You retired early *because* of your disability, and now you're retired *with* a disability.
>
> SAM: [Teary] Maybe I just can't do it anymore. Maybe it's not realistic to go to Thailand.
>
> RHODA: If you gave up the idea right now, would you feel a sense of relief?
>
> SAM: Yes. [Pause; more teariness; scratching more at arm] I don't want to be a disabled man. I can't look in the mirror from the chest down. I don't like what I see. [He abruptly stops picking at his arm and sits upright.] What were we talking about? I forget the thread.
>
> RHODA: We're talking about self-acceptance, a topic we've come back to many times.

Discussion Questions

1. What are the key disability events in Sam's history that might prove important in treatment?
2. What microaggressions does Sam experience frequently?
3. What factors in the relationship are going to be most challenging, and how might you handle them?
4. What is the evidence to support (or refute) a diagnosis of borderline personality disorder?

4   D-AT I: Current Disability Status—Disability Sequelae and Their Management

AS THE THERAPIST, the place to start your inquiry with a client with disability is about the current status of the client. Just as you might start with the current symptoms of depression before moving to the history of depression, you want to understand the current disability symptoms, the disability course, and expected outcomes. Of key importance are experiences of pain and fatigue, if sleep is affected, danger of falling, the degree of uncertainty about the future course, and whether the disability implies a shortened life expectancy (Olkin, 1999).

    Recall from Chapter 1 that different words are used to describe medical conditions: impairment, handicap, and disability. The *impairment* is the actual medical condition. For Sam this is polio with leg weakness. The *disability* is the direct result of the impairment. For Sam that would be limited mobility, wearing of a brace on one leg, use of an electric wheelchair, and inability to climb stairs or stand for more than a few minutes. And lastly, the *handicap* is about the interaction of the person with the disability and the built environment and other people—that is, the psychosocial consequences of having a medical condition, the ways in which one is disadvantaged in socioeconomic, education, political, financial, and interpersonal arenas (World Health Organization, 2001). Thus when people refer to themselves as a *person with a disability* they are talking about the effects on functioning, not the medical condition. For the past 30 years or so the disability community in the United States has adopted people-first language, that is, *people with disabilities*. (But recall from the definitions in Chapter 1 that in the United

Kingdom the preferred term is *disabled persons*, and there is a movement in the United States toward this "identity-first" language; Dunn & Andrews, 2015).

Given the terms just defined, how would you go about asking a client about the disability? There is no one right way to ask, and it is better to ask than to get so caught up in politically correct language that you don't inquire. You could be straightforward: "What is your disability?" You might ask: "What are your disability issues at this time?" or "Can you tell me about your disability?" In each case you might use the term *disability* until you hear the language the client uses. For example, if a client said, "I have cerebral palsy" you could say, "I know that cerebral palsy varies widely from person to person; what does the cerebral palsy involve for you?" But here some knowledge on your part about cerebral palsy (CP) will be important in your follow-up questions. If the person did not mention any learning disabilities, you could inquire about that specifically, because there are often some cognitive impairments associated with CP (Rosenbaum, Paneth, Leviton, Goldstein, & Bax, 2007). On the other hand, if I had asked Sam whether there were any cognitive impairments related to his polio, he would have been deeply insulted. Polio does not affect cognitive functioning the way CP does (Bruno, Cohen, & Frick, 1994), and the question would have shown that I didn't know about polio. Furthermore, it would be indicating the spread effect (Wright, 1983)—that is, the assumption that the disability affects all aspects of the person, which is probably an assumption that Sam encounters frequently. By asking the question I would be, in his view, mistreating him in the same way others do, and thus therapy would not be a different or reparative venue. But suppose you did not know whether polio involved cognitive impairments? My suggestion would be to err on the side of caution, not ask about cognitive impairments yet, and go do some homework on the specific impairment before the next session.

There are less helpful ways to ask about a disability. The question "What did you do to yourself?" implies some personal responsibility for incurring the condition. As medicine moves toward greater mind–body connection and health habits are more clearly related to medical conditions (e.g., people with more plaque and gingivitis are more likely to have a heart attack; Pihlstrom, Michalowicz, & Johnson, 2005), there is a slippery slope to blaming individuals for their disability. Thus some people with disabilities may feel particularly sensitive to intimations of blame. The way in which the inquiry about the disability is phrased can reinforce the idea of blame (e.g., "What did you do to yourself?").

Current Symptoms

Once you learn about the nature of the disability, you need to understand its symptoms, probable course, and effects on daily life (see Box 4.1). Do not think of this as an inventory to be completed in one session. The questions are delicate, and

> **BOX 4.1**
> **POTENTIAL QUESTIONS ABOUT THE DISABILITY**
>
> What is the nature of your disability?
>
> When were you diagnosed?
>
> How were you diagnosed? (e.g., Invasive tests? Prolonged wait for answers? Misdiagnosis?)
>
> How have the effects changed over time?
>
> What was your/your partner's/your children's/your family's response to the diagnosis?
>
> How does it affect you in your daily life?
>
> Do you experience pain? (Where, how often, how severe? How often does the pain prevent you from doing things you want or have to do?)
>
> Do you experience fatigue? (How often, how severe? How often does fatigue prevent you from doing things you want or have to do?)
>
> Have you fallen in the past year? Do you do things to avoid falling (Restricting activities? Installing grab bars? Sitting in the shower?)
>
> Do you have weakness in any parts of your body?
>
> Are there activities you used to do that you can no longer do? (What are they? How do they get done? If they were fun activities, what have you replaced them with?)
>
> What aspects do you find most troubling?
>
> What is the probable course of the condition over time? (Over the next 5 years)
>
> Are there any expected changes to your life expectancy because you have this condition?
>
> What are the positive aspects associated with your disability?
>
> If you could wave a magic wand and no longer have the disability would you want to? Why or why not? How would your life be different, if at all?

the answers can be emotional. Have them in mind, and ask them when they are an organic part of the sessions. However, if this does not happen naturally (by about session four), you can ask permission to ask more questions, much as one might ask permission to do a mental status exam: "Would you mind if we took some time today for me to understand the particulars of your disability more fully?"

PAIN

If pain, sleep disturbance, interference with activities of daily living, fatigue, and/or loss of pleasurable activities are part of the disability package, then they probably are an important part of the treatment. Treating people with disabilities often requires some knowledge of simple techniques for managing stress, exertion, fatigue, and pain. These might include mindfulness, yoga, tai chi, journaling, distraction, as well as cognitive restructuring about pain beliefs (Ehde & Jensen, 2004). You don't have to be a pain management specialist, but you should have rudimentary knowledge of these low-cost techniques, along with some facility in cognitive restructuring skills.

Pain is multidimensional (Robinson & O'Brien, 2010). Accordingly, there are numerous ways to assess pain (e.g., Hawker, Mian, Kendzerska, & French, 2011). Often in medical settings patients are asked to report their pain on a scale from 1 (low) to 10 (high), or some other version of a verbal rating scale. Other methods use faces with various expressions, or a color analogue scale (from blue = no pain to red = intense pain) or mechanical analogue scales (e.g., with a dial, such as a volume control) (e.g., Closs, Barr, Briggs, Cash, & Seers, 2004). Such scales can be useful but may not be the primary way that clients describe pain. A study on pain indicated that one way clients prefer to talk about pain is in terms of how the pain affects their plans for the day (Zelman et al., 2001). Zelman et al. found that people with pain preferred the terms *manageable* or *tolerable* pain, rather than *acceptable* pain. With manageable pain the person was able to take the edge off the pain (with or without medication at a level that minimized side effects) and perform valued activities, did not feel dysphoric or irritable, and was able to socialize.

Another way to think about chronic pain is like a computer program that is running in the background but slows the computer down. To use myself as an example, on a daily basis I experience pain that is just outside conscious awareness. This is pain that is normal for me, it doesn't affect my daily activities, it is not giving me new information, and thus there is little reason to pay attention to it. Nonetheless, it takes up part of my cognitive space, and I am continuously monitoring the pain, continuously assessing whether it changes by either increasing, changing location, or altering in type, in which case it might indicate that I should change my behavior (rest, elevate, ice, etc.) or investigate the cause. If I tune into my body I become aware of my pain. This is important, as some clients with chronic pain may resist exercises that focus inward (e.g., mindfulness) because they can increase awareness of pain. However, learning how to make the pain recede is a valuable skill, so it can be helpful to encourage clients to continue with the exercise past the initial teaching of it. It also is helpful in that the client can practice the exercise while aware of pain, that is, practice state-dependent learning, so that the exercise is more likely to be used when the client is in greater degrees of pain.

Clients may have activities they enjoy doing but that increase their pain. They may nonetheless judge the risk–benefit ratio in favor of the activity. For example, carrying groceries from the car to the house may increase lower back pain, so one might explore alternate ways to accomplish this without having back pain. However, gardening may likewise increase back pain but be judged worthwhile. Although steps can be taken to reduce the degree of pain and avoid injury (e.g., raised garden beds, using stools with wheels), the degree of pain increase is balanced against the joy of the task. Each person has to grapple with the risk–benefit equation for him- or herself.

Pain at low intensity can be quite unmanageable if it continues for some time, much like a toothache would become less tolerable over time, even if the intensity stayed static. Thus when we talk to clients about pain, we have to be aware of the nuances and extremely personal nature of pain and learn about its meaning, influence, and position in a person's life. There is no one right way to ask about or describe pain; see Box 4.2 for a form containing various ways to describe pain. Furthermore, acceptance of chronic pain has become an increasingly reported goal for clients (McCracken, Vowles, & Eccleston, 2004), with a subsequent focus on retention of functions and activities rather than on reduction of pain.

There are several medical methods for addressing pain that therapists should be aware of. In addition to medications (see next section) there are regional analgesia techniques, which reduce pain by blocking neural pathways. Such methods include transcutaneous electric nerve stimulation (TENS) units. TENS units work through four electrodes attached around the area of pain; the unit sends out stimulating pulses across the surface of the skin and along the nerve strands. It feels rather like thousands of ants crawling across an area of the skin and is best used when sitting still. A treatment of less than an hour can provide relief for one or several days. However, TENS units don't work for everyone, cannot be used on all parts of the body, and sometimes stop being effective. But it is a noninvasive procedure with no side effects that a person can use at home. More invasive procedures might include injection of anesthetic compounds or corticosteroids or intramuscular injection of lidocaine (Robinson & O'Brien, 2010). Most interventions reduce pain by about 40% and total erasure of chronic pain is unlikely (Turk & Winter, 2006).

MEDICATION

Medication can be a complicating factor in therapy. There are medications prescribed for people with various disabilities that can affect cognitive abilities. Pain medications, antispasmodics, and muscle relaxers are examples. Medications for pain control include over-the-counter nonsteroidal anti-inflammatory drugs (NSAIDs) (e.g., Advil) but also opioids. Opioids are not effective for everyone (Robinson & O'Brien, 2010) or every type of pain, have considerable side effects, and are potentially addicting. What can be difficult for the clinician is knowing if and how much a medication or a cocktail of medications is affecting a client. Furthermore, decisions about whether any particular medication or combination of medications is

BOX 4.2
DESCRIBING YOUR PAIN EXPERIENCE

Pain can be difficult to describe to another person. Pain is subjective, and there are many ways to try to describe pain. Below are several methods of describing your pain to another person. Using these different methods will help me understand your experience better. Please feel free to make changes or notes on each of the scales if it helps to better describe your pain.

You may be experiencing more than one site or type of pain. For some of the questions you will be asked to respond to the pain that is *most* troublesome to you. For other questions you will be asked to describe *all* of the pain you typically experience.

A. *Using a pain scale to describe pain intensity.* For this question please consider *all* of the pain you experience in a typical week.
   0 = No pain
   1 = Very mild, almost unnoticeable pain
   3 = Mild but noticeable pain, such as the beginning of a headache
   5 = Moderate and very noticeable pain, such as a throbbing headache
   7 = Considerable pain that takes your attention, such as a migraine
   9 = Almost unbearable pain that commands all of your attention
   10 = The most pain you can imagine or have ever experienced

B. *Using words to describe the type of pain you experience.* For this question please describe the pain that is *most troublesome* for you. Check all that apply.

____ Achy	____ Electric	***Use your own words:***
____ Acute/sharp	____ Itching	_____
____ Burning	____ Numbness	_____
____ Shooting	____ Throbbing	_____
____ Hot	____ Pins and needles	_____
____ Tingling	____ Crippling	_____
____ Angry	____ Dull	_____
____ Chapped	____ Excruciating	_____
____ Heavy	____ Irritated	_____
____ Inflamed	____ Raw	_____
____ Swollen	____ Stabbing	_____
____ Vice-like	____ Stiff	_____
____ Tender	____ Swollen	_____

C. *Using a picture to describe pain location:* Please place an X on *all* of the parts of the body where you experience pain on a daily or weekly basis. If you wish, you can write a word next to the site that describes the type of pain (such as the words used in section B).

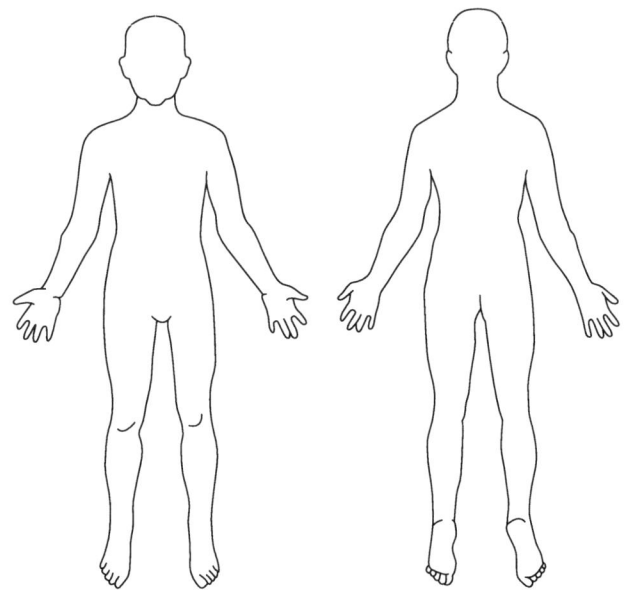

D. *Using a scale to describe the effects of your pain.*

    1 = I am not really aware of the pain unless I choose to focus on it. I can go about my daily activities. The pain is very manageable.

    2 = I am not really aware of the pain until I focus on it, but it is affecting my mood. Others might notice my mood or behavior has changed slightly. The pain is manageable.

    3 = I am aware of the pain enough that I do some things to accommodate the pain (e.g., shift in chair, take off shoes, stretch, walk around, stop walking). However, I can still go about my daily activities. The pain is still manageable but there is risk of it becoming less manageable.

    4 = The pain is very present, and I have to alter my daily activities to accommodate the pain. I might go home early, rest, change position, put on or take off a brace, use an assistive device more, take medicine to reduce the pain. The pain is unmanageable because it affects my activities too much.

    5 = The pain is commanding most or all of my attention. I am stopping my daily activities to make efforts to cope with or reduce the pain. The pain is unmanageable because it is all I can think about.

a. Put a mark on the line that describes the most pain you are experiencing *today*.

|———————+———————+———————+———————+———————|
1   2   3   4   5

b. Put a mark on the line that describes the most pain you experienced *yesterday*.

|———————+———————+———————+———————+———————|
1   2   3   4   5

c. Put a mark on the line that describes what is *most typical* for you when you going about your daily activities (i.e., there is nothing unusual that you are doing that day that you don't do most days).

|———————+———————+———————+———————+———————|
1   2   3   4   5

E. *Your pain history.* Over your entire lifetime, what has been your experience with pain?

What has been the most pain you ever experienced? What were the circumstances of this experience?

_____
_____
_____
_____

How did your parents/family respond if you or a sibling was in physical pain?

_____
_____
_____
_____

> What messages about pain did you learn from your family (e.g., suck it up; lie low until it passes; soldier on; pamper yourself; suffer in silence; make sure others know you are in pain, etc.)?
> _____
> _____
> _____
> _____

warranted is mostly outside a therapist's expertise. However, the therapist may be the only one aware of all the medications prescribed by different doctors. Thus therapists have a responsibility to assess and possibly address medication issues in treatment.

Some therapies for depression and anxiety seek to not only ameliorate immediate symptoms but also reduce risk following termination of treatment (DeRubeis, Siegle, & Hollon, 2008; Hollon, Stewart, & Strunk, 2006). Pharmacological treatment of these disorders does not have the same post-treatment risk reduction. Furthermore, use of medication for depression and/or anxiety during therapy may dampen the effects of treatment in two ways: the mood state may not be present during treatment, such that there is no state-dependent learning, or the client may attribute the changes made during therapy to the medications rather than to changes the client has made. Many clients with disabilities will be on such medications.

It is easy to find oneself concerned that medication side effects are interfering with treatment but without the knowledge or authority to suggest changes. But this doesn't mean the therapist is powerless. A clinical example here might help:

> Walter is a married, African American father of a young child, in couple's therapy. Due to arthritis, diabetes, high blood pressure, moderate depression, and leg injuries from combat overseas, he is taking aspirin as a blood thinner, blood pressure medication (lisinopril), a benzodiazepine (Xanax), an antidepressant (Zoloft), NSAIDS (ibuprofen), sometimes a nasal spray corticosteroids for increased inflammation (budesonide), Arava (a disease-modifying drug for arthritis), and Fortamet (for diabetes); he has Vicodin to use as needed for pain relief. Thus his list includes aspirin, ibuprofen, Lisinopril, Xanax, Zoloft, budesonide nasal spray, Arava, Fortamet, and sometimes Vicodin. The prescriptions are written by three different doctors, one of whom is the primary care physician, who knows the complete list of medications but is not well versed in antidepressants, pain medications, or some of the specialty medications. Sometimes Walter seems slowed down during sessions, with slightly slurred

speech, or eyes closed, or not quite tracking. When asked about his medications he insists he needs all of them. When asked specifically about Vicodin he says, "I hardly ever take that," but his wife says he is not always aware of taking it and that he takes it several times a week. She believes he is impaired more by the drugs than by the underlying disorders and that he should stop taking several of them. Walter dismisses this as her "anti-medication rant."

It can be hard to know how to start with this list of medications. The first step is to slow down and not appear too eager to do away with any medications—in the case just presented you would be seen as the wife's ally in her anti-drug stance. Second, you have a fair amount of homework to do in looking up each drug and seeing its uses, contraindications, and possible side effects. Then you need to think about the drugs in combination. WebMD has information about drug interactions, and on Medscape one can enter two medications and get information about whether there are interactive effects (but one can only enter two medications at a time). A pharmacist, a psychologist trained in psychopharmacology, or a psychiatrist also are good sources.

All of these resources are about educating yourself, not about how to address the issues with your client. That is the trickier part of the equation. Use of over-the-counter and prescription medications is often driven by beliefs about medications, beliefs that generally are not articulated or even conscious for the client (Mann, Ponieman, Leventhal, & Halm, 2009; Petrie, Perry, Broadbent, & Weinman, 2012). Some questions from medical family therapy are useful here. In medical family therapy it is understood that each person, each family, and each culture has beliefs and practices around illness, disease, disability, medication, and treatment, and that these beliefs affect current practices (McDaniel, Doherty, & Hepworth, 2014). Box 4.3 lists some questions that might be useful to ask clients to help explicate their beliefs and practices about illness, wellness, and medications.

Since medications are a common part of life for people with disabilities, clinicians will be treating clients who have varying stances and practices regarding medications, from eschewing them altogether to taking dangerous cocktails. There is no one right way to handle issues of medication with any particular client; what I am offering here is a process for figuring out what to do. Part of this process has to include asking yourself, the therapist, the questions in Box 4.3, because your own beliefs will affect how you view any client's behavior. To go back to Walter, do you think of him as seeking relief unrealistically, as a substance abuser, as a patient who is doing a good job of being compliant with his doctor's prescriptions, or as someone who just needs to try yoga and mindfulness and get off all these medications? Then you have to check your beliefs at the door and figure out what is in the best interests of Walter.

BOX 4.3
QUESTIONS ABOUT ILLNESS AND MEDICATION BELIEFS

What illnesses did you have as a child?
What happened in your family when you were ill? How did everyone react?
Were there family remedies that were used (e.g., prayer, chicken soup, hot baths, cold compresses)?
Was it ever a fun thing to stay home from school sick? Did your parent(s) let you stay home? Did they send you to school anyway? What would they say about staying home/going to school?
Were there specific things your parent(s) did when you were sick (e.g., read to you, change your sheets, fluff your pillow, let you watch TV, give you special foods)?
How quick were your parent to give you medications?
What were the beliefs about what caused the illnesses (e.g., viruses, stress, poor habits, a cold wind, tempting fate)?
Were the beliefs of your family consistent with your culture? Which were the same; which were different?
Who in the family took medications regularly? What did they take? For what reasons? What were you told about this?
What are your beliefs about prescribed medications? Over-the-counter medications?
What are your beliefs about complementary medicine (e.g., acupuncture, massage, mindfulness, yoga)?
What does "wellness" mean to you?

SUBSTANCE USE AND MISUSE

Discussion of medications leads us to consider medication misuse and other substance use. There are some legal issues to consider here: persons misusing alcohol are protected by the Americans with Disabilities Act (ADA), those misusing legal substances *may* be protected by the ADA, and persons misusing illegal substances are *not* afforded such protection. Substance abuse alone does not make someone eligible for Supplemental Security Income (SSI), though Medicaid, under the Affordable Care Act (ACT) (2010)[1], will cover addiction treatment (https://www.addictioncenter.com/rehab-questions/medicaid-and-medicare/). These legal parameters may be especially important when seeing clients with disabilities. Bear in mind that the prevailing model of alcoholism is moving away from the disease model (a categorical model) to a continuum that varies along a spectrum of severity (Bombardier & Turner, 2010).

---

[1] The ACA is under review by congress at the time of publication.

Disability and substance use are linked in several ways. First, substance use contributes to a higher probability of disability (through accidents related to driving, shooting, boating, skiing, swimming, diving, and other sports). Second, certain disabilities are more prevalent among particular genders and age groups, which in turn have higher rates of substance use disorders. A prime example is spinal cord injury, with its higher prevalence among young adult males (82%; http://www.sci-info-pages.com/facts.html). Third, substance use prior to disability is the best predictor of substance use post-disability (Bombardier & Turner, 2010; Greer, Roberts, & Jenkins, 1990). Fourth, beer and alcohol companies are major contributors to disability charities. Alcohol ads might say in small type "drink responsibly," but alcohol is implicated in a large percentage of disabilities, especially traumatic injuries (e.g., traumatic brain injury and spinal cord injury) (Bombardier & Turner, 2010). Fifth, substance rehabilitation centers may not be accessible to persons with various disabilities, especially those who are deaf. Thus people with disabilities and substance use disorders may be less likely to find treatment.

Finally, medications prescribed for disability symptoms are particularly subject to misuse and addiction. For example, *hydrocodone* (e.g., Vicodin, Lortab) may be prescribed for pain, leading to abuse, currently at an all-time high in the United States (http://www.rehab-international.org/hydrocodone-addiction/facts n.d.). Use of *benzodiazepines* (e.g., Valium, Klonopin, Ativan, Halcion; mostly used for anxiety but also used to decrease muscle spasms) is a depressant of the central nervous system. It is particularly dangerous (even fatal) when mixed with other substances, including alcohol. Benzodiazepines account for a high rate of addiction and hospitalizations, and the rate is increasing; the rate for hospital admissions for opioids is rising even faster (Camenga, Gaither, Leventhal, & Ryan, 2015). (According to a report by the Substance Abuse and Mental Health Services Administration (SAMHSA), over 33,000 people received treatment for addictions to both hydrocodone and benzodiazepines in 2010. *Zolpidem* (the active ingredient in Ambien and Zolpimist, which are sleep aids) is easy to overuse. If sleep is not restful the person might take a second pill, leading to overmedication. In 2005–2006 zolpidem overmedication accounted for almost 22,000 emergency room visits; this rate jumped to over 42,000 by 2009–2010. Unlike with other drugs of misuse, individuals most likely to be seen in emergency rooms with zolpidem overdose are female (68%) and older (45 to 54 years of age) (https://www.samhsa.gov/newsroom/press-announcements/201408110215, 2015). Just over 22 million people used *marijuana* in the past month in 2014. Cannabis is still the most frequently used illicit drug in the United States (https://www.drugabuse.gov/publications/media-guide/

most-commonly-used-addictive-drugs, 2016). (Alcohol is the most abused drug in the United States; Bombardier & Turner, 2010.)

In one study, 79% of practicing rehabilitation psychologists reported working with clients with disabilities with co-occurring substance use disorders (da Silva Cardoso, Pruett, Chan, & Tansey, 2006). However, rehabilitation staff are likely to underestimate the frequency of substance abuse among their clients. One study found that rehabilitation staff estimated a rate of 22% of patients had substance abuse problems, when the actual rate was significantly higher (Basford, Rohe, Barnes, & DePompolo, 2002). An earlier study found that women with disabilities were more likely to abuse drugs than were women without disabilities; this difference was true for almost every major drug category (Li & Ford, 1998). Women with disabilities are also more likely than men with disabilities to be victims of substance use–related violence (Li, Ford, & Moore, 2000). The authors of this study found that specific disability factors put women with disabilities at higher risk of being victims of substance use–related violence, including acquired disability, multiple disabilities, and chronic pain. And being the victim of substance use–related violence in turn was associated with a higher likelihood of substance abuse by the victim. Higher perceived discrimination and lower acceptance of disability may increase vulnerability to substance use for both men and women with disabilities (Li & Moore, 2001). Adolescents with disabilities are particularly at risk for substance use (Hollar & Moore, 2004).

There may be many reasons for the increased risk of substance use disorders among people with disabilities. Clearly, from this discussion it would seem that ready access to addicting medications and misuse of them is one reason. There may be more than one prescribing physician (e.g., a primary care physician, a neurologist, and an orthopedist) involved, each unaware of the other medications being prescribed. Additionally, substance use may be a response to frequent stressors associated with disabilities. Unemployment is higher among people with disabilities; with unemployment the day is less structured, there are fewer restrictions on behavior, and greater isolation, all risk factors for substance use disorders. Rates of childhood sexual and physical abuse are also higher among children with disabilities (Olkin, 1999), which is another risk factor for substance abuse. Enabling by the family and/or care providers may be implicated if they are reluctance to confront the person abusing medications (e.g., because of pity or fear or hostility).

According to Fiske's (2011) model of dimensions of stereotypes, there are two dimensions (warmth versus cold, and competent versus incompetent), yielding four possible quadrants. Each quadrant tends to elicit different emotions from others (Fiske, Cuddy, Glick, & Xu, 2002). People with disabilities are viewed stereotypically as warm but incompetent, and people who abuse substances are viewed as low on both warmth and competence. This combination of disability and substance abuse in one person can result in a perception of the person as profoundly incompetent, leading to yet greater stigmatization and blame.

In sum, people with disabilities are a high-risk group for substance misuse and addiction, as the medications they are likely to use are frequently prescribed and highly subject to misuse and addiction. These drugs are dangerous alone or in combination. Treatment options may be limited by inaccessibility (both physically and psychosocially). Such persons are likely to be highly stigmatized for both the disability and the substance use.

Assessment of alcohol and substance use should be part of routine intakes. The CAGE questionnaire is the most efficient method that still yields useful results (Ewing, 1984). The four questions are as follows:

1. Have you ever felt you should **C**ut down on your drinking?
2. Have you ever felt **A**nnoyed by someone criticizing your drinking?
3. Have you ever felt bad or **G**uilty about your drinking?
4. Have you ever had a drink first thing in the morning to steady your nerves or to get rid of a handover (**E**ye opener)?

Other methods of assessment are discussed in Bombardier and Turner (2010), along with basic treatment recommendations. What is key is to do the assessment of substance use as a routine part of D-AT.

FALLS

Falling is an issue for those with disabilities (Novack, Sherer, & Penna, 2010), as well as older individuals. So it can be a very pronounced issue for people with disabilities as they age. What makes falls different for people with disabilities than for those without them is the degree of damage and, therefore, incapacitation that can result from even minor falls (Novack et al., 2010). Furthermore, because circulation in extremities is often affected by the disability, healing takes longer than for those without disabilities. To use the case of Sam (see Chapter 2) as an example, when he broke his leg, he was mostly housebound for about 6 months because the healing time of limbs affected by polio was significantly lengthened.

There are two aspects to falls that are important to understand: depression and fear of falling (what has been called post-fall syndrome; Murphy & Isaacs, 1982). Both of these aspects tend to have a bigger effect on people's lives than do actual falls (Cumming, Salkeld, Thomas, & Szonyi, 2000; Legters, 2002; Vellas, Wayne,

Romero, Baumgartner, & Garry, 1997). In the case of fear of falling, it is not necessary to have experienced an actual fall to develop a fear of falling (Friedman, Munoz, West, Rubin, & Fried, 2002). That fear leads to changes in behavior, such as reducing mobility, the number of trips outside the house, or travel. When activities are reduced, this can lead to depression (Gagnon, Flint, Naglie, & Devins, 2005; van Haastregt, Zijlstra, van Rossum, van Eijk, & Kempen, 2008). In fact, there is a robust correlation between depression and falls that is true across many types of disabilities. Of course, with correlation we cannot conclude that either causes the other, only that they are related. But a plausible sequence would be: falling → increased fear of falling → reduction in activities → reduction in socializing → depressed mood → further reduction in activities and socializing → increase in depression → increased fears due to a depressive lens, in a cyclical fashion.

The clinical implications are several. First, persons with disabilities should be routinely screened for depression in primary care settings. (Probably everyone should be, but that is outside my purview.) Second, fall training (how to fall) and fall prevention should be a part of treatment, whether in primary care or occupational or physical therapy. Third, fear of falling should be evaluated and addressed by clinicians so that the putative cycle with depression is arrested. Fourth, depression should be seen as a possible risk for actual falls. And fifth, prevention of falling can be discussed in therapy because there are psychosocial (and financial) aspects to fall prevention. For example, it may involve someone adopting use of assistive technology (discussed further later in the chapter), installing grab bars and ramps and handrails, or making the home more accessible in other ways. These all involve financial expenditure, from a small amount (grab bars) to very large amounts (e.g., renovating the bathroom to make it wheelchair accessible). Thus ideal solutions may not be options for everyone. For those on government assistance (e.g., SSI, SSDI, Medicare), getting even simple devices can take a year, and Medicare is more apt to pay for restorative than for compensatory care (Carlson & Ehrlich, 2006). Some assistive technology may be covered by insurance (private or government), such as a wheelchair, but not others (such as the lift that puts the wheelchair into the car, and the adapted car). Prevention is generally less costly than post-injury treatment, but, regrettably, it is mostly not covered by medical insurance. Increasing coverage for fall prevention and more assistive technologies is a policy change that would actually save money in the long run. Universal design of housing (e.g., ramps instead of front steps, accessible bathrooms, wide doors) would decrease the costs to individuals with disabilities who have to make the changes themselves. These sociopolitical and financial factors will affect the discussion within therapy about fall prevention.

Sandra is a 14-year old girl with cerebral palsy who uses a manual wheelchair. She is unable to walk and has limited arm strength. She comes from a low-income family with three children. Her mother provides most of the caregiving support that Sandra needs, including lifting her from the chair to the couch, into bed, and onto the toilet. Sandra could be more independent if she had an electric wheelchair. According to her mother, Medi-Cal (as Medicare is called in California) will not pay for an electric wheelchair unless the family has a van to put the chair in. However, the family cannot afford a van. The issue is getting more pressing as Sandra grows and weighs more, making it more difficult for her mother to carry and transition her.

SLEEP

It has become increasingly clear that sleep is important in many ways for all individuals. A poll of sleep hours of children found that 32% of 6- to 11-year-old children slept less than 9 hours a night (National Sleep Foundation, 2014), a finding that was even more pronounced among older children: 71% of 12- to 14-year-old children and 90% of 15- to 17-year-old teens slept less than 9 hours a night. Pain is a significant factor in sleep problems (National Sleep Foundation, 2015). Although need for a specific number of hours of sleep has not been established and varies across individuals, the average number of hours of sleep for Americans is 6.8 hours (Jones, 2013), which is less than the 8 hours usually recommended.

Too little sleep is associated with a number of problems, including overall poorer health, motor vehicle crashes, industrial accidents, hypertension, diabetes, depression, obesity, and increased mortality (Centers for Disease Control and Prevention, 2015). Factors known to interfere with sleep to assess in treatment include use of alcohol, caffeine, and nicotine (which reduces sleep and REM time; Davila, Hurt, Offord, Harris, & Shepard, 1994; Jaehne, Loessl, Bárkai, Riemann, & Hornyak, 2009), daytime napping, too little exercise, exercise too late in the day, and sleep hygiene habits.

It is easy to see from this list how these problems would be compounded for people with disabilities, who already might have issues of cognitive and physical fatigue and pain. For those with disabilities lack of sleep can contribute to cognitive and physical fatigue, emotional problems, and increases in the experience of pain. Additionally, medications can affect both duration and quality of sleep. Reduced activity level is another factor in problems with falling or staying asleep, and those with disabilities might have reduced activities due to physical limitations (stairs in the front of the house), broken equipment, fatigue, or fear of falling. Also, pain can interfere with sleep, and reduced sleep can increase perceptions of pain. Some clinicians believe that the first treatment for chronic pain is addressing insomnia (Smith & Haythornthwaite, 2004; Vitiello, Rybarczyk, Von Korff, & Stepanski, 2009). Thus, for many reasons, sleep is an important area to explore with clients with disabilities. Notably, however, some of the standard solutions for sleep problems may need modifications for these clients. For example, the standard sleep hygiene recommendation of getting out of bed if awake for more than 15 minutes may require assistance or be difficult. Use of particular medications for insomnia may be contraindicated because of disability factors or interactions with other medications. Some individuals may watch TV in bed (which is discouraged for good sleep hygiene) so that they are physically resting while watching or to elevate their feet. But most suggested remedies will work, such as specific bedtimes, pillow use and placement, sound machines, relaxation training, and addressing counterproductive cognitions.

The quality of sleep is as important as the number of hours. Estimates of the prevalence of sleep apnea vary widely. One site puts the estimate at about 4% of men and 2% of women (Nabili, 2015). Another site states that the rate increases with age, being about 3% for men ages 20–44, 11% for men ages 45–64, and rising to 18% for men ages 61 or older (Phillips, 2015).

Sleep apnea is associated with being overweight in a bidirectional fashion— increased weight can lead to sleep apnea, which in turn makes weight loss more difficult. But there are many risk factors besides weight, including age, enlarged tonsils or adenoids, frequent alcohol use, smoking (both genders), and being postmenopausal and not on hormone replacement (for women). Although snoring during sleep is one sign to check for sleep apnea in adults, this is less the case for children; many more children snore than have sleep apnea, and daytime fatigue is not usually the presenting problem (Carroll & Loughlin, 1992; Chan, Edman, & Koltai, 2004). Also, the relationship of weight to sleep apnea is not found in children as it is for adults (Mallory, Fiser, & Jackson, 1989). However, sleep apnea may be more common in children with specific disabilities, such as Down syndrome (Marcus, Keens, Bautista, von Pechmann, & Ward, 1991; Shott et al., 2006) and severe cerebral palsy (Kotagal, Gibbons, & Stith, 1994).

Signs of possible sleep apnea include daytime sleepiness or fatigue, dry mouth or sore throat in the morning, headaches in the morning, night sweats, restlessness during sleep, snoring, waking up feeling like one is gasping for air or choking, and trouble getting up in the mornings (WebMD, n.d.). As can be seen from this list, these symptoms can be caused by many things, including the disability itself, so parsing out sleep apnea has to be done with a sleep study. But clinicians should be alert to the possibility of sleep apnea, because a client with a disability may attribute all symptoms to the disability, overlooking other (treatable) disorders. For example:

Jonathan was a divorced 52-year-old White male with multiple sclerosis (MS) who was about 25% overweight. He complained of daily fatigue and often curtailed his social activities to rest. He attributed his fatigue to the MS, and in fact, fatigue is the most common symptom in MS. However, he also reported vivid nightmares and sometimes found himself out of bed suddenly in the middle of the night. Since motor activity is reduced during REM sleep, this seemed odd that he would awake from a dream while standing out of bed. A recent exam had proved negative for any thyroid problems. The therapist suggested that Jonathan request a sleep study. He was reluctant, thinking it was a waste of time, but finally did have an overnight study at a sleep center. Results showed that he woke approximately 120 times/hour due to apnea (30/hour would be in the mild range; 120/hour is in the severe range). Jonathan received a CPAP machine to help him breath when sleeping. However, this raised many psychological issues for him. He worried no one would ever date a man with two disabilities, and the combination of MS and sleep apnea made him seem more "broken" to himself. Furthermore, he had unrealistic fantasies that treating the sleep apnea would erase all of his fatigue and he would feel like he did before the MS onset.

ASSISTIVE TECHNOLOGY (AT)

Many people with disabilities use or could use AT (Hendershot, Larson, & Lakin, 2003). There is a range of AT, from simple and common devices like compression socks, to slightly more specialized equipment such as grab bars and crutches, to more sophisticated and complicated technology such as lifts and electric wheelchairs. Adoption of any of these aids often carries significant psychosocial implications (Scherer, Sax, Vanbiervliet, Cushman, & Scherer, 2005). (For a good review of conceptual models of AT use, see Lenker & Paquet, 2003). Thus use of AT is often a topic in therapy. Since most AT is rarely displayed in places most people frequent, knowledge about what devices exist or differences across models of the same device is hard to come by. Which device or technology can address which physical or cognitive needs is not intuitively understood. It is thus useful for clinicians to find and keep mail order catalogues from various AT suppliers, as well as ads from disability-focused magazines, in order to keep up with what's available as well as new innovations. Readers might wonder if this is a clinician's role. But one feature of living with a disability is that the person gets split into body parts and functions, which in turn are treated by different healthcare providers with different areas of expertise. For example, the primary care physician will not know much about wheelchairs or scooters. Physical therapists can tell a client about compression socks, but not where to get cheap grab bars (much less ones that match the fixtures in your bathroom). The orthopedist knows about crutches, but not models of scooters. And none of the above will talk about all the options within a category, nor about the psychosocial factors involved in use of any devices or technology. Most of the devices sent home with patients released from a hospital are never even used (Johnston & Evans, 2005; Phillips & Zhao, 1993; Verza, Carvalho, Battaglia, & Uccelli, 2006). Therapy is the one place where all of the person—as a whole physical, cognitive, emotional human in relationships with other people—comes together. Thus it may well be the therapist who has to help a client locate and organize the information and make decisions.

At least one study suggests that persons with early-onset disabilities are more inclined to use assistive devices as adults than those with later-onset disabilities, even with the same level of functional impairments (Kaye, Yeager, & Reed, 2008). It could be that early adoption of assistive devices allows the device to become part of their self-definition or body image. Or it might be that early use demonstrates the utility of assistive devices, whereas the idea of using an assistive device for the first time later in life emphasizes the change in status without the benefit of knowing how much easier life can be with it. Use of assistive devices also varies with age, race, ethnicity, education, income level, and type and severity of disability (Kaye et al., 2008). Those less likely to use assistive devices are ethnic minorities, lower-income households, later disability onset, and disabilities that are cognitive or psychiatric (compared with physical or sensory). Persons with visual impairments are more likely to use assistive devices than those with other disabilities (Olkin, Abrams, Preston, & Kirshbaum, 2006).

The reactions of other people to someone who uses AT cannot be overemphasized (Jutai & Day, 2002; Scherer, 1996a; Shinohara & Wobbrock, 2011) and are a big factor in resistance to adoption of AT. For example, when I walk using crutches no one pats me on the head, and, curiously, no one does this when I use my scooter. But when I use my electric wheelchair this happens to me about once a month. Thus it is not just about being seated, or it would be the same in both the scooter and wheelchair; it is the social meaning of wheelchairs (permanent, disabled, not able to walk, infantilized) versus that of scooters (able to walk, using the scooter only to go longer distances, fully adult) that makes the difference. There is a value hierarchy of AT: One crutch is better than two crutches, crutches better than a scooter, scooter better than a manual wheelchair, the latter better than an electric wheelchair. But all devices or AT have psychoemotional baggage. For example, when I urged Sam to install grab bars in the bathroom after a fall, he frowned at me and changed the subject. When pressed, he said, "I'm not that old yet."

Virtually all people who have gone from being barely mobile (with or without crutches) to use of a wheeled device talk about the new freedom they feel and all the things they can now do that they couldn't do before (Scherer, 1996b). But that is after the fact, after the psychological shift that allowed the adoption of AT. Before adoption, it is hard to know this in advance or to see that the trade-off is worth it.

If you do not have a disability, you may be better at taking a neutral stance on the use of AT than I am. I use crutches, a travel scooter, and a wheelchair freely now (though I didn't always), so I have made the transition and realize the benefits of being able to do so much more than before. In doing therapy I find I want to pull clients along more rapidly when they are falling frequently or unable to go many places. But a neutral stance is important—few will come to use an AT being pulled by a rope. Timing, integration with other aspects of the client (e.g., a museum lover, a nature walker, a dog owner, a big-box store shopper), and sensitivity are required, and using motivational interviewing is suggested. Clients respond better to positive benefits (getting out to dinner, going to a park) rather than to avoidance of negatives (preventing fatigue or falls). Having them talk to other users of AT also can be motivating and help with the decision of which AT to use (Rackensperger, Krezman, McNaughton, Williams, & D'Silva, 2005; Ripat & Booth, 2005; Scherer, 1996a).

Sometimes sowing seeds over a period of months can be helpful. For example, I might ask, "Did you use the store's scooter?" but not pursue the topic further, then sessions later point out that the overfatigue experienced after an outing could have been mitigated by use of AT. It may be that I can do this because of my own visible disability and that this observation would be less palatable from an able-bodied therapist.

Another aspect to AT is that the use of AT makes the disability apparent to others. Sometimes persons with non-apparent disabilities use AT to make the disability apparent. This can help when trying to access accommodations, especially if others tend to question the need for the accommodation. Examples include asking someone to move from handicapped seating on a crowded bus, or going in the shorter wheelchair line at airport security. The person may find it easier to use items such as a cane or braces or other AT to legitimize their disability to others. This may solve one problem (legitimacy to others) but create other problems (feeling false to oneself or resentful of the need for validation from others).

> Jenny has osteoarthritis and limited mobility. She has a handicapped placard in her car, but often finds that when she emerges from the car someone questions her right to use the handicapped parking space. Many times when she drives places with friends in the car she warns them there might be a scene when they

park. Sometimes she takes a cane just to avoid the scene, but feels resentful and inauthentic when she does this.

The Course and Outcomes of Disability

Some disabilities are relatively stable, but often the course is variable, increasing, uncertain, or some combination of these. The course of the disability affects the ways in which people cope and respond to the impairment (Lynch, Kroencke, & Denney, 2001; Solomon, O'Brien, Wilkins, & Gervais, 2014; Wineman, 1990). Variability and uncertainty require very long-term and flexible coping (Rolland, 2003). Most autoimmune disorders, for example, are both variable and uncertain. Multiple sclerosis (MS) is a prime example. At diagnosis the person is told there is no way to predict the course of the disease. The relapsing and remitting type (the most common type) can have periods of extreme exacerbation (paralysis, perhaps hospitalization) and then remit completely. It might remit to a different and higher level of baseline, and thus move into the slowly progressive type. Even polio, thought for years to be stable, turned out to have a kicker about 30 years after onset, called post-polio syndrome, in which there is increased pain, fatigue, and muscle weakness. Not everyone with polio develops this syndrome, however—another uncertainty. Spinal cord injury, the injury itself remaining stable, carries a high risk for secondary conditions. And most disabilities will interact with the natural aging process, during which the disability can seem to progress. Thus uncertainty and unpredictability are significant factors in living with a disability (Livneh & Antonak, 2005). This uncertainty makes it difficult to construct personal meaning and a cognitive schema for the disability, what Mishel (1981) called "perceived uncertainty" (p. 258), and requires cognitive flexibility in responding to the disability.

The potential and probable outcome of disabilities will affect the person deeply. For example, ankylosing spondylitis, a form of arthritis of the spine, has a deteriorating but nonfatal course. Amyotrophic lateral sclerosis (ALS; often referred to as Lou Gehrig's disease) is both deteriorating and then fatal in about 5 years from diagnosis. Yet about 5% of people with ALS live much longer (Stephen Hawking is a prime example), but no one is able to say who will be one of the 5%. And the prospects change with new research and treatments. A prime example of this is HIV, which once meant a certain progression to AIDS, a then-fatal disorder, but now has a good prognosis with treatment.

As can be seen in these brief examples, receiving a diagnosis can be extremely stressful. First, most people do not know much about many of these disorders and thus may not know either the expected course or the probable outcome. They are very vulnerable at that moment of diagnosis to information they receive from the doctor. I have found that many of my clients report what their doctor said verbatim, especially the negative things, as illustrated in the following case study.

> Evie, a Latina married woman in her early thirties, had a period of pronounced fatigue, and some imbalance when she stood up or walked. She worked during the day and was enrolled in some night classes as a paralegal. When she complained to her doctor about fatigue he commented on her busy life and told her she needed to rest and relax more. When she started to fall, the doctor finally referred Evie to a neurologist, who ordered many different tests without telling Evie what he was testing for. She looked on the Internet, however, and knew that the possibilities were not good. After several weeks of tests she had an appointment to get the results. Sitting in his office, in front of his desk, with the neurologist behind the desk, he pronounced "You have multiple sclerosis. We don't know what type it is yet, we have to wait 5 years and see what the course of the disease is." She asked what to expect in the next few years and, in particular, if she could have children. The doctor responded, "You have MS— there goes your sex life." Evie left and sat in her car and cried. She did not know anyone else with MS, or if MS was terminal; she was not given any information about the National Multiple Sclerosis Society, and she thought she had no chance of becoming a parent.

Often the possibility of mortality from the diagnosed disorder is the first concern. Once that is resolved, then the level of impairment is the next issue. But the probable level of impairment often is not knowable, as discussed previously. Newly diagnosed individuals need space to set their own pace for information and input, even if, when, and how to tell others.

Cultural factors and language are critical factors that affect all aspects of the relationship with medical professionals, from help-seeking behaviors, level of trust, expectations, compliance with treatment, to outcomes (Bryan, 2007). Therefore, when a therapist is gathering information about the disability, it is important to bear in mind what might be idiosyncratic to a particular family versus what is normative in that family's culture. (For more discussion on culture, see Chapter 7.)

Words that are considered less pejorative by one culture are insulting in other cultures. Interpreters in medical settings need to perform both linguistic and cultural translation, knowing when to change words to and from English to be more sensitive. Just as "football" in most countries means "soccer" in the United States, other words might have literal translations that are technically correct but culturally incorrect. For example, the direct translation of the word for intellectual disability (ID) in some Asian Indian dialects is "empty brain" (Narayan, 2014). A direct translation might make the medical personnel concerned about the parents' attitudes toward their child with ID.

Coping

It should be obvious from the previous discussion of sequelae that a person with a disability has to cope with many factors that affect daily living. Generally, coping has been conceptualized as a way to ameliorate the effects of stressful life events (Lazarus & Folkman, 1984). There is a large literature on coping with chronic illness and disability. But generally, coping is divided into two strategies: *disengagement coping strategies*, which are passive, indirect, or avoidance oriented, and *engagement coping strategies*, which are active, direct, and goal oriented (Livneh & Antonak, 2005). Very often studies will link the former type with poorer outcomes and engagement coping strategies as more helpful (c.f., Jensen, Turner, Romano, & Karoly, 1991; Revenson & Felton, 1989). One study found that children with cystic fibrosis who experienced daily pain used problem-solving, acceptance, and self-encouragement to cope (Hubbard, Broome, & Antia, 2005). Problem-solving and self-encouragement are active coping strategies, and acceptance could be conceived as either disengaged or engaged coping.

How a person copes can affect interactions with other people. For example, an analogue study asked undergraduates to make decisions about awarding compensation to persons making a disability claim, varied by gender and coping style (MacLeod, LaChapelle, Hadjistavropoulos, & Pfeifer, 2001). Respondents were more likely to perceive disability and thus award compensation to those with a more disengaged coping style (catastrophizing, praying, hoping). Another study used interviews to assess coping in the person with MS, their healthy partner, and their children (Ehrensperger et al., 2008). They found that there was no correlation between the coping of the person with MS and the healthy partner, but there was a correlation between the coping of the healthy partner and the children.

These are just of few examples showing the complexity of coping styles. In the final analysis, what may be more important than the type of coping strategy used is flexibility in coping (Cheng, 2001; Cheng & Cheung, 2005; Cheng, Lau, & Chan, 2014; Fresco, Williams, & Nugent, 2006). Some factors are not within the person's control, do not require any action or decision-making. In such cases it may be more helpful to use disengagement coping. This does not preclude taking steps to ensure overall health (e.g., tai chi, or relaxation), which are aimed at general well-being.

Clinical Applications

This chapter covered a lot of ground: pain, medications, falls, sleep, assistive technology, the variable courses of different disabilities, and potential outcomes. Not every aspect covered here will be relevant with each client or family with a disability, but of course, as the therapist, you won't know that unless you inquire about each area. The danger is that this level of inquiry may appear to be an undue focus on disability, which is not right for all clients with disabilities. Conversely, not asking about these areas may fail to give a full picture of the person's experience with disability. So that is the conundrum—you need the information for a better understanding, but asking for the information can be misconstrued as undue focus on the disability. So how might you walk this fine line? I suggest waiting until the presenting problem has been stated and elaborated on. Then you can ask: "Do you think your disability plays a role in this problem?" The person might then say yes and can elaborate on how. The person might say no, and then you have to form your own opinion that concurs with the client or not. There are many things clients tell us that we question (e.g., how much they drink, about their perfect childhoods, or about being 100% anxious 100% of the time). We store these away and bring them up again as timing and the relationship and the topic make room for them. But just by asking directly about the disability, and asking the client to think about the role, the clinician is behaving differently from most other social contacts—being direct, not being afraid to address disability directly, and asking the client's view of its role without making assumptions about its centrality.

Discussion Questions

1. How might the information about current disability symptoms affect the therapy?
2. What are your personal beliefs about pain medications (over the counter, prescription, opioids)?
3. You have a client who falls frequently, sometimes resulting in injuries, but who does not want to use any assistive devices. How might you approach this with the client?

4. You are seeing a client who has a disability about which you know very little, but the client is in crisis and needs immediate assistance. How might the disability affect your immediate interventions?
5. A client with a disability mostly uses religious prayer and avoidance to cope with pain and depression. What are your reactions to this, and how might you handle this situation therapeutically?
6. What are two different ways to describe pain?

5   D-AT II: Developmental History—Disability, Medical, Educational, and Advocacy

MOST THERAPIES INVOLVE taking a history of the client. In cognitive behavioral therapy (CBT) the history might focus on the development of the presenting problem. The family therapist might focus on the stages of the family. In disability-affirmative therapy (D-AT) the developmental history includes the disability experiences.

About 10% of children in the United States have a disability (Fujiura & Yamaki, 2000; Newacheck & Halfon, 1998), although the estimate of disabilities in children varies greatly across different methods of data collection, ranging from a low of about 4% to a high of about 17% (see Halfon, Houtrow, Larson, & Newacheck, 2012, for a discussion and results of different collection methods). The most common causes found were respiratory diseases and mental impairments. But causes of disability are changing over time, in part because birth rates are dropping and women are having children at older ages; these women are at greater risk of having a child with congenital disability. Also, there is a 20% rate of poverty, another risk factor for disability, among families with children (Halfon et al., 2012). Consistently, higher rates are found for boys, older children, and single parent families. Families with lower incomes have the highest rates of disability in children, but surprisingly there have been greater increases in economically advantaged children between 2001 and 2011 (Houtrow, Larson, Olson, Newacheck, & Halfon, 2014). Children with disabilities are more likely to live alone with a single parent than are other children (Olkin, 1999). Rates of cerebral palsy (CP), to use one example, are 2.08 among individuals in the highest income levels and 3.33 in the lowest income levels. Lower birth weight (a risk factor for CP) is one reason, but even comparing across normal birth weights rates were higher in babies born into lower-income families (2.42/1000 versus 1.29/1000 in the higher-income families; Dolk, Pattenden & Johnson, 2001).

Premature births (Patel, Kandefer, Walsh, Bell, Carlo, Laptook, . . . & Hale, 2015) and traumatic brain injury (from abuse, motor accidents, gunshots, and other causes (Asemota, George, Bowman, Haider, & Schneider, 2013) are leading causes of disability and death in children and adolescents. Injuries do not always result in disability, but injuries requiring hospitalization often do (Barker, Power, & Roberts, 1996). Leading types of disabilities for children in the U.S. are neurodevelopmental or mental health (including epilepsy, speech problems, learning disabilities, ADHD, and intellectual disabilities; Houtrow et al., 2014). These disorders are on the rise, while physical health conditions (e.g., asthma, hearing or vision problems, bone or joint or muscle problems) are declining. Children younger than 15 account for 5% of blindness worldwide (50% in developing countries; Steinkuller et al., 1999). (See also Mathers, Fat, & Boerma, 2008, regarding rates of childhood disorders worldwide.) Unfortunately, child abuse (chiefly battering and shaking) is one cause of disability in children (DiScala, Sege, Li, & Reece, 2000). Three studies of mothers with disabilities found that in some instances childhood abuse either caused or exacerbated existing disabilities (Cohen, 1998; Conley-Jung & Olkin, 2001; Olkin, Abrams, Preston, & Kirshbaum, 2006). This suggests that studies of childhood-onset disability should include direct questions about abuse in the onset or exacerbation of the disability.

It is important not to confuse the disability per se with the experiences that might have developed from having a disability. The type of onset of the disability (congenital, early, traumatic), the childhood experiences (stigma, hospitalizations, ostracism), adolescence and developing body awareness, surgeries, friendship patterns, ability (or not) to play sports, and experiences of physical abuse—all of these may stem from the fact of disability but are not about the disability itself. For example, the onset of the disability might have necessitated hospitalization and thus separation from parents. There might have been a traumatic injury such as a fall, a gunshot, or a car accident. That traumatic event might have involved injuries to other persons, even family members. What can be seen in these examples is that the disability onset can be fraught with meaning and emotion. Thus it is important to ask about the story of disability onset. Many clients may have never had a chance to tell the story in one piece. There is a poignancy and emotional salience to the onset story, even those from many years past. And hearing about the story may give the therapist clues as to the themes that have reverberated throughout a client's life. For example:

> Teresa, now 45, had polio in Mexico when she was an infant. She walked more than a mile to and from school each day, but was exhausted. She then had to help her mother with chores around the house and preparing meals. When she thinks of her childhood she feels she was invisible, that no one really saw her needs, particularly how exhausted she was all the time. Now, as an adult working in a large company, she again experiences exhaustion. However, she has not asked for any accommodations, stating, "What good would it do?" She continues to feel unseen in terms of who she really is, and disempowered as a Mexican American woman with a disability. The therapist hypotheses that Teresa is waiting for someone to notice she needs help, much as a parent might do but her mother never did, and offer support. When she suggests this to Teresa, Teresa shrugs and says, "I want to be behind the scenes, not to make trouble. I don't want them to know how tired I am. They might fire me if they think I cannot do the job." It would seem that Teresa has internalized the invisibility—what was once imposed in her childhood is now imposed by herself.

Of course, there are many versions of the disability onset story, and it can be helpful to ask about it from different vantage points. For example, suppose a woman in her early twenties is diagnosed with multiple sclerosis (MS). Questions might include how she found out, what the doctor said to her at the time of diagnosis, the lag time between symptom onset and correct diagnosis, whether there were tests for other scary disorders, who accompanied her to doctor appointments, what she first knew (perhaps mistakenly) about MS and what she subsequently learned, who she first told and that person's reaction. Then the story might be sifted again for the perspective of any partner from that time, or the parents and siblings, or friends. Perhaps a partner left shortly after the diagnosis, or a parent insisted the woman come home, or she put off plans to have a child, or she lost some friendships, or she couldn't work for some time. It is these psychosocial aspects that will be put into the disability "suitcase," one that will be quite different for each person with MS.

Suppose this same woman with MS is now in her fifties; is the onset story still relevant? I maintain that it is, for many reasons. It might help her realize how far she has come, how much strength she had during a difficult time, which friends and family were there to be relied on. Or there might be lingering emotions, such as rage at a doctor's off-hand comment ("You might want to go on disability"). If she was left by a partner, there might be doubts now about whether a current partner will stay with her if the MS progresses. In other words, there may have been lessons from the onset story that she kept with her, and those lessons might be positive, negative, or some combination of both.

Consider the example of Sam (see Chapter 3). When he had polio his mother put him and his two older brothers into the car and drove for 5 hours to the nearest hospital.[1] Sam was left in the hospital, and for him the critical memory is of trying to escape from the crib and get home. He got caught in the sheet and hung there, cradled in the sheet. But for his brothers, their main memory is of the 5-hour drive home with their mother sobbing the whole way. And for his mother it was the uncertainty of whether her toddler might die, whether he would be in an iron lung, what the aftereffects of polio would be, and the separation from him that lasted weeks while she tended the other two children and ran the household and the farm. And where was the father? It is pertinent that Sam doesn't have the story for him, that he seems absent from this episode. The first polio-related memory of his father is his dad carrying him up the stairs to bed each night, and down the stairs again each morning.

In addition to the onset story, there are other aspects in the developmental history that are key to understanding the disability's place in a client's current life. Unfortunately, the rate of physical and sexual abuse of children with disabilities is at least twice that for children without disabilities (Hibbard & Desch, 2007; Olkin, 1999; Sullivan & Knutson, 2000). Rates of abuse of adults with disabilities are less clear, but the types of abuse, the duration of abuse, and the nature of the perpetrator may be different (Nosek, Foley, Hughes, & Howland, 2001). Regarding types of abuse, disability creates avenues of abuse and intimidation that do not exist for others (Nosek, Howland, & Young, 2013). Examples include removing the battery from a wheelchair, refusing to remove someone from the toilet, disabling the automatic door opener, manipulating medications, breaking an assistive device, and refusing to help with feeding. Furthermore, studies suggest the abuse of women with disabilities continues over a longer period than for women without disabilities (Nosek et al., 2013). This may be due to some degree of physical dependence on others. Although women with disabilities are just as likely as those without disabilities to be abused by partners, they are additionally vulnerable to abuse by attendants and healthcare providers (Young, Nosek, Howland, Chanpong, & Rintala, 1997). The perpetrator may include those most directly involved in the care and well-being of the person with a disability, including bus drivers of para-transit systems, personal aids or paid assistants, or persons in control of finances. Thus, just as it is important to know about

---

[1] It is important to remember that if Sam had been African American, the nearest hospital might not have taken him; hospitals were still segregated at that time. Thus the nearest hospital that would take an African American child might have been even further away, meaning the family might not have been able to visit at all.

abuse for all clients, there might be more specific—and even different—questions to ask clients with disabilities.

For many individuals with early-onset disabilities there were hospitalizations and surgeries, perhaps casts, physical therapy, and numerous doctor visits. Medical stripping was a common experience—this refers to the entrance into the hospital or examining room of a doctor at a teaching hospital, followed by a bevy of residents. The patient's blanket or clothes are removed, and the doctor talks to the residents as if the child were not there, using unfamiliar words, perhaps cursorily asking the child a question. The phalanx of medical personnel then departs. One resident may wink or smile or wave at the child, the sole acknowledgment of the child as a person.

Jack, a man in his thirties with cerebral palsy, went to a specialist at a teaching hospital to talk about possible surgery to correct his gait. The specialist asked about bringing in residents to observe the examination and discussion. Jack said okay but instantly felt young, powerless, and angry. He said little during the exam and did not ask the questions he had intended to ask. In therapy, Jack relayed the story and was mad at himself for agreeing to let the residents in. He recognized that this was reminiscent of earlier childhood experiences of medical stripping, which he previously had discussed with the therapist. "But what if I'd said no? Would the doctor have been angry? Might I not have gotten as thorough an exam, or been treated rudely? Does anyone really say no? How else are residents going to get training?" Jack remained ambivalent, but before the next visit to the same doctor the therapist and Jack rehearsed saying no when asked if residents could come in. And they made a list of questions for the doctor which Jack took with him to the appointment. Once he thought he really could refuse the resident request, he felt more empowered and then decided it was all right with him if they did come in. The list of questions helped him stay focused on the present and, thus, less infantilized.

Asking the client about surgeries is important, and about what they involved. It is important to know if the client believes the surgeries were successful, if there was pain, if there was another separation from family, if retraumatization occurred. Again, there are different perspectives on these events that can be useful to inquire about: Who told you about the surgeries? How far in advance? How did you react to the news? Who visited you or stayed with you? How long were you in the hospital? What happened after the surgery? What happened about school? What was it like going back to school afterward?

Additionally, it would be good to ask about braces or other assistive devices. As discussed in Chapter 4, this may become a topic in therapy. If someone used assistive technology (AT) as a child and subsequently rejected it, the person may not be aware of changes in AT models. For example, leg braces were once heavy and cumbersome steel and strap devices. Newer braces are likely to be molded in various skin-tones and materials that are lighter weight and less obtrusive. Knowing about childhood experiences with AT may help the therapist frame current discussion of the use of AT.

Another aspect of the developmental history is educational history. Of course, children with disabilities attending school prior to the passage of the Education for All Handicapped Children Act (now reauthorized as Individuals with Disabilities Education Act; IDEA) had very different experiences from those attending school post-IDEA.[2] But segregation still occurs in many ways. A student might go into a resource room for part of a day, or be in the "slow" group during one subject period. Even if the slow group is called the Yellow Group, students know where they are in relation to peers. And there can be social segregation as well—no one to eat lunch with, inability to join ball games at recess, last selected for teams. When these types of segregation occur in grade school, it can leave lasting marks on self-esteem; in high school it affects the budding sense of one's place in social groups.

There also are positive effects of IDEA, of course. Children with disabilities are learning early that they have legal rights, that they and others in the family have to be advocates. They start to learn about their own strengths and weaknesses and what accommodations are helpful. They might be used to self-identifying as a person with a disability, and both the disability and the accommodations may become routine—not "special" but rather ordinary needs. Younger clients often have many emotional responses to how and why they were identified. There may have been one parent who argued against the diagnosis, or a parent who failed to recognize symptoms and the need for assessment. School districts vary in how many students get tested and identified for accommodations—generally there is a relationship between gender and ethnicity and the odds of being identified as a student with a learning disability, as well as the sociodemographics of the school district (Coutinho, Oswald, & Best, 2002) or artificial caps set by the state (see Hebbeler & Spiker, 2016 for discussion of differences across states). The method of identifying learning disabilities also influences the proportion of children identified (Fuchs, Mock, Morgan, & Young, 2003). The meetings among school personnel and parents can be especially difficult for non-native English speakers. Furthermore, the expectations of what is to happen at the meeting vary by culture. For example, some parents may expect the school to be the experts

---

[2] Part of the impetus for passage of the Education for All Handicapped Children Act is that one million children with disabilities were not in school at all at the time because of inaccessibility and lack of services or accommodations.

and thus may not question the recommendations; conversely, the school may view such parents as uninterested and uninvolved. When working with families of children with disabilities, it is useful to be familiar with IDEA and to discuss with parents what will happen at the school meeting and the expectations of all parties. I often attend these meetings about my younger clients (without charge), but I understand that this might not be feasible or desirable for all therapists.

Advocacy skills are of necessity a part of most people's disability needs (Balcazar, Seekins, Fawcett, & Hopkins, 1990; Lynch & Gussel, 1996; Test, Fowler, Wood, Brewer, & Eddy, 2005). When children are young, the parents take on this role. This makes sense—they minimize the incursions into a young child's life by prescreening doctors, getting information ahead of time, and holding difficult discussions out of earshot. But at some point the role has to be transferred to the person with the disability. As the child develops, the parents may expect him or her to take on more of the advocacy role. But this transfer may be limited, either because the parents did not have advocacy skills themselves or they may not have taught advocacy skills to the child. When the older adolescent moves away from home, the task of advocacy falls to the adolescent, perhaps without adequate preparation. Families who are of a nondominant ethnicity may talk openly about racism, but families with a member with a disability may not have ever discussed disability discrimination. And those with onset of a disability as an adult may have no experience at all of self-advocacy. Colleges and universities appear to be places where students are encouraged to learn advocacy (Foley, 2006; Graham-Smith & Lafayette, 2004; Lynch & Gussel, 1996; Skinner, 1998). But not all post-secondary education sites have strong offices of disability services, and not all adolescents go to college (about 30% of Americans have a bachelor's degree; Snyder & Dillow, 2012). So advocacy may be a relatively new topic for clients with disabilities, and the skills involved may be unfamiliar. The therapist may be called upon to introduce concepts of self-advocacy, as well as teach specific advocacy skills.

Clinical Implications

The developmental history of any client is obviously relevant to the case formulation and treatment plan. It affects how the therapist talks to a client, what the parameters of the relationship are likely to be, the probable stumbling blocks, and expected outcomes. The disability history is not something separate from this developmental history, even for those with later-onset disabilities. The messages about disability are ubiquitous, and the relationship a person has to his or her own disability is affected by the messages of society, media, community, family, and self. The developmental history is going to reveal much about how the person relates to his or her own disability.

I cannot emphasize enough that therapists need to become educated about major disability laws, most notably the main aspects of IDEA and the Americans with Disabilities Act (ADA).[3] Although the therapist cannot give legal advice, it can be helpful to alert clients to some rights they have. For example, one client needed time off work to attend physical therapy twice a week, but was afraid she would be fired if she asked for the time. I was able to explain to her what constituted a disability under ADA, what a "reasonable accommodation" might be, and her responsibility to (a) identify as a person with a disability and (b) request a reasonable accommodation. However, it also was important to point out that laws did not guarantee that the law would be followed. Although many people with disabilities are of necessity well versed in major disability laws, for those more newly diagnosed or who have less access to information there may be lack of awareness of their rights or even that they are members of a protected class. If the therapist is equally unaware of these things, then the therapy will treat disability as if it were only an intrapsychic phenomenon and fail to address the socioeconomic and political realities affecting all persons with disabilities. Indeed, "it serves the interests of neither professionals nor their clients . . . to ignore people's need for political and economic changes while offering them only clinical treatment" (Biklen, 1988, p. 137).

Discussion Questions

1. What are some differences between those with early-onset or congenital disabilities and those who acquire a disability as adults?
2. Disability and poverty are correlated. What are the social and policy implications of this?
3. Do you think medical stripping occurs today? What are your thoughts about this? What actions might you take?
4. How might you introduce concepts of self-advocacy to a client for whom this is new?

---

[3] See "Key laws and social history," in Olkin, R. (1999). *What psychotherapists should know about disability.* New York: Guilford Press. Go to http://www.ada.gov/ada_intro.htm for the original ADA itself and http://www.ada.gov/pubs/adastatute08.htm for the law as amended.

6   D-AT III: Models of Disability

MODELS OF DISABILITY are about the mental construction of disability, the beliefs and values the person attaches to disability. The model reflects the beliefs about causes, appropriate remedies, and meanings of disability. As such, understanding the client's models of disability tells you how to talk to the client, what words to use, the beliefs about remedies, and virtually all aspects of the disability. Thus it is important to understand not only the client's framework, i.e., model of disability, but that of his or her family as well.

There are many versions of different models of disability, with as few as three models and as many as eight models. However, I think simplifying down to three models is sufficient to understand the main constructs and key differences across models (Olkin, 1999). These three models—the moral, medical, and social models—encapsulate the differing core constructs of disability. Each model has its advantages and disadvantages, its merits and its drawbacks, its benefits and deficits. First I will describe the three models, and images of disability in the media as they reflect these models, then offer a critique of the models, and conclude with the clinical implications.

Three Models of Disability

The three models are the moral, medical, and social models. Table 6.1 shows a comparison across the three models. The explanations that follow are relatively brief; the

TABLE 6.1

COMPARISON OF THREE MODELS OF DISABILITY

	Moral	Medical	Social
Meaning of disability	Disability is a manifestation of morals, sins, evil, lack of faith. Conversely, it is a test of faith, or given selectively to someone who can withstand it.	A defect in or failure of a bodily system or impairment in a body function. It is inherently abnormal.	Disability is a social construct. Problems arise from the mismatch between the person's needs and the environment and in the attitudes of others.
Moral implications	The disability brings shame to the person with the disability and his or her family. It affects marriageability and future prospects.	Something has gone wrong, is damaged, due to genetics, bad health habits, a medical procedure, the person's behavior, or an accident.	Disability is a normal part of the human spectrum of differences. Society has failed a segment of its citizens and oppresses them.
Sample ideas	"God gives us only that which we can bear." "It is my fate or karma." "It is my burden to bear."	Clinical descriptions of "patients" in medical terminology. Isolation of body parts or system functions.	"Nothing about us without us." "Civil rights, not charity."
Origins	Oldest model. Most prevalent worldwide. Is prevalent in specific cultures within the U.S.	Mid-nineteenth century, during the Enlightenment. The most common model in the U.S., it is a predominant model in psychology, many rehabilitation clinics, and journals.	Early 1900s, then dormant until about mid-1970s. The first televised demonstrations by people with disabilities were the beginning of disability activism.

(Continued)

Table 6.1 (*Cont.*)

	Moral	Medical	Social
Goals of intervention	Spiritual or divine, acceptance, forbearance	"Cure" or amelioration of the disability to the greatest extent possible	Political, economic, social, and policy systems, increased access and inclusion
Benefits of model	An acceptance of being selected, a special relationship with God, a sense of greater purpose to the disability An appreciation of life, of survival, of everyday.	Decreased shame and stigma compared to the moral model. Faith in medical intervention. Defined roles. The model promotes medical and technological advances.	Greater integration of the disability into self-identity. Promotes community and pride. The model depathologizes disability.
Drawbacks	Shame, ostracism, need to conceal the disability or person with the disability Blame of family members for causing the disability.	Paternalistic, promotes benevolence and charity. Services are for but not by people with disabilities. Expects passive compliance with professionals' advice or prescriptions.	Salient awareness of oppression. Feeling powerless faced with need for broad social and political changes Person can feel victimized. The effects of actual impairments are minimized, which are not social constructions.

TABLE 6.2

LANGUAGE ASSOCIATED WITH THE MORAL, MEDICAL, AND SOCIAL MODELS OF DISABILITY

Model	Language Example: Descriptive	Comments
Moral	Joe, who is wheelchair bound since he was afflicted with MS, can only feed himself dinner by using special utensils.	Note the use of emotionally laden words such as "wheelchair bound," "afflicted," "can only," "special." Joe's differences are not only emphasized but also a negative value is placed on those differences.
Medical	Joe, a patient who uses a wheelchair as a result of partial paraplegia due to MS, eats dinner using utensils that compensate for reduced grip.	Joe is described using precise medical terms and diagnosis such as "partial paraplegia" and "MS." Note, too, the idea of compensation for a failed bodily function ("reduced grip").
Social	Joe, a man with MS who uses a chair, eats dinner.	In this description Joe's action of eating dinner is more salient, people-first language is used ("a man with MS"), some shorthand from the disability community is used (a "chair" denotes a wheelchair), and there is omission of irrelevant disability factors ("special utensils"). Capability is more pronounced, rather than failure or inability.
Model	Language Example: Clinical	Comments
Moral	My son can't walk straight, he can't use his right hand well, so he can't cut his own food. We have to do many things for him; it's very hard.	The focus here is exclusively on problems, on what cannot be done, and how this negatively affects his relationships in the family (burden).
Medical	My son has right hemiplegia but his brain works okay. He's learning to be more independent.	The description is very medical. The word *CP* is avoided as it carries a stigma. The parent is quick to assure that it isn't a more stigmatized disability ("his brain works okay") and that the goal is increased independence (a very mainstream American value).

(*Continued*)

Table 6.2 (*Cont.*)

Social	My son has CP. We want to know how to help him make more friends and to be happy.	The diagnosis is given without concern for the connotations. The focus is on a quality of life (friends, happiness) and how the parents can help the son, not on what a burden he is.
Model	Language Example: Positives	Comments
Moral	"I stepped on a land mine when I was 12. Now every day I wake up in pain, and it reminds me to thank Allah that I am alive."	Where we might have expected this person to say "and it reminds me to curse the land mines" we instead hear a positive meaning ascribed to the pain.
Medical	"Everyone has something to cope with. There are incredible advances all the time, and I know I can cope with this."	Disability is seen as no different than the "burdens" others might have. There is hope and belief in a better future—cure or amelioration of the condition—and a belief in personal strength.
Social	"I got to go to summer camp, where all the kids had disabilities. It was great, the best thing. Disability was just normal, no big deal."	The person feels a sense of belonging and a place in which disability is a unifier, but also where it is relegated to the background for once.
Model	Language Example: Negatives	Comments
Moral	"It is my wife's fault that our son has this disorder. She had too much stress during pregnancy."	There is blame and ascription of a cause of the disability that lies with one person (the mother) and causes negative feelings toward that person.
Medical	"Doctors don't know anything, they can't help me, they just want to pass me around as a specimen."	There is hopelessness, a lack of collaboration with medical professionals, and distrust of motives.
Social	"It will never change, people with disabilities will always be at the bottom of the totem pole. I can't change the world, that's just the way it is."	Again, there is hopelessness, this time at the enormity of tasks to be undertaken and the belief that some group (those with disabilities) will always be at the bottom of the social pecking order because that is human nature.

reader is advised to also read the table, to really understand the models. Additionally, see Table 6.2 for examples of the type of language a person might use that would be consistent with each of the models.

MORAL MODEL

The moral model is the oldest and the most ubiquitous model worldwide. In this model the disability reflects character, deeds, thoughts, and karma. It may carry great stigma and shame if the disability is viewed as a manifestation of wrong-doing or evil. A family or person may be blamed for causing the disability through misdeeds, evil thoughts, past lives, or other wrong-doing. More positively, the person with the disability may be seen as a reflection of God's will, and the family as specially chosen to have the disability because of their ability to cope with, care for, or manage the disability. The disability may be a reminder of positive things, such as being alive, having survived, or being chosen.

Although we may think that the moral model is outmoded and relegated to developing nations, this is not the case. For example, two studies of immigrant populations in California—one group of monolingual Chinese-speaking parents of children with autism (Wong, 2007) and one group of Asian Indian, mostly well-educated parents of children with intellectual disabilities (Narayan, 2014)—found that both groups adhered primarily to the moral model. In my own clinical practice I have found that many clients with disabilities intellectually disavow the moral model but struggle with emotional, well-ingrained traces of the moral model. The language used in the moral model often contains emotionally evocative words.

MEDICAL MODEL

This is the main model in most journals related to disability and virtually all medical journals. In this view, a disability is an impairment in a bodily system or function. It is inherently pathological and the goal is to return the system or function to as close to normal as possible. Expertise (medical, physical therapy, etc.) resides in professionals with specialized training, and persons with disabilities are patients or clients who should adhere to the advice of those with expertise. The language used is clinical and often medical, and it may be incomprehensible to "patients" until translated into lay terms. Rehabilitation psychology has been moving from the medical model in the direction of the social model, although the settings in which rehabilitation psychologists work tend to be medically oriented. Psychology in general is still very entrenched in the medical model: disability is not just different but abnormal, and the needs of those with disabilities are "special." Disabilities are viewed separately; articles and chapters tend to be about one type of disability, rather than about similarities across disabilities.

SOCIAL MODEL

The social model, developed in the early 1900s, was mostly dormant from the 1920s to about the 1970s. It arose again with activism designed to force implementation of the new Rehabilitation Act (passed in 1973 but still not implemented in 1975). This activism borrowed tactics from the Civil Rights Movement, with sit-ins and protests at city hall (most effectively in San Francisco). In this model, which is a significant paradigm shift from the other two models, disability is a social construct. The mismatch between the needs of the person with the disability and the environment—not the impairment itself—creates handicaps and barriers. The attitudes of others and inhospitable nature of the built environment are the more oppressive aspects to disability and the most significant obstacle to full inclusion. Disability is not special but a normal part of the human condition in all societies and all times, and the needs of persons with disabilities are extensions of the needs of all human beings. The goals of intervention are political, economic, social, educational, financial; they are changes to society, rather than to the person him- or herself. This does not mean that people with disabilities do not need assistance, rehabilitation, medical intervention, or therapy but rather that those interventions are only a small portion of the total areas to be targeted for change. Persons with varying disabilities are grouped for the purposes of political and social activism. In literature in the social model disability often is discussed as a general construct, rather than having sections devoted to specific disabilities.

Models of Disability and the Media

Media is one source of information and images about disability. Movies both reflect and shape society's perspectives on disability (Black & Pretes, 2007). Many stereotypes are prevalent in movies depicting characters with disabilities: pitiable and pathetic; sinister, evil, criminal; better off dead; maladjusted and own-worst-enemy; burden to family and society; unable to live a successful life; and supercrip (an often derogatory term meaning a person with a disability who goes beyond usual human levels, such as a wheelchair user who climbs El Capitan in Yosemite). In their review of 18 films, Black and Pretes (2007) found that images of people with disabilities as asexual, incapable of gainful employment, or maladjusted, leading to self-destructive behaviors, were still prevalent; ongoing intimate relationships were rarely depicted.

However, there are hundreds of movies with characters with disabilities, as well as several good analyses of depictions of disability in the movies. In addition to Black and Pretes' (2007) article there are reviews by Byrd and Elliott (1985), Darke (1999), Kraayenoord (2011), Norden (1994), and Safran (1998). There is also a documentary that examines the images of disability in films, with an eye toward assessing if film has affected perceptions of disability (*CinemAbility*, 2013), and a documentary about the history of disability in the movies (*Diffability Hollywood,* 2016). In the next section I point out a few movies that depict particular models of disability.

MORAL MODEL

In media depictions of the moral model, disability is depicted in several ways. In one type of portrayal, disability is a fate worse than death. There are many examples of this in films in which a person chooses to die rather than live as a person with a disability, for example, Al Pacino in *Scent of a Woman,* or the female lead in *Million Dollar Baby,* or Sissy Spacek in '*Night Mother* (1986). A second type of depiction of the moral model is using a disability to connote evil and separateness from the rest of society. *The Phantom of the Opera* and *Star Wars* (Darth Vader) exemplify disability as evil; *Edward Scissorhands* is an example of how disability must be kept away from society because of its inherent dangerousness. A third way of depicting the moral model is to promote the idea that as disability impairs one sense of the person, it elevates another sense, much like the blind seers of ancient Greece. An example is *Rain Man* (1988), in which a man with autism is also a savant with numbers. This film compounds the misunderstanding of autism by failing to distinguish between the effects of the autism itself and the effects of having lived in an institution all of one's life. *Daredevil* (2003) is another example, in which a youth is blinded by exposure to hazardous waste, but his other senses then develop superhuman sharpness. In *Simon Birch* (1998), a 12-year old little person believes that he is on earth for a higher purpose, and shortly after it seems that he fulfills that role, by saving the lives of other children, he dies.

Another example is disability as tragedy. In *Notting Hill* (1999) guests at a dinner party are playing a game of who is more deprived. Of course, the wife in a wheelchair wins, and to seal the pathos the scene ends with her being carried up the stairs to the bedroom by her husband. Since the couple is obviously well off, one wonders why they have not installed a chair lift.

MEDICAL MODEL

The medical model of disability is shown repeatedly in movies through a basic plot device: person with disability is downhearted and despondent, able-bodied person befriends person with a disability, through the friendship the person with the disability learns to embrace life. Movies using this basic model include *Rust and Bone* (2012), *Long Ago, Tomorrow* (1971), *Musical Chairs* (2011), *As Good as it Gets* (1997), *The Bone Collector* (1999), and *Moonstruck* (1987).

A reverse twist on this basic plot is the idea that the purpose of people with disabilities is to help people without disabilities learn the meaning of life. For example, in *I am Sam* (2001), the female lawyer who helps Sam fight for custody of his daughter learns to be a better mother through her encounters with Sam. In *Riding the Bus with My Sister* (2005), Rachel rides the bus a few days every 2 weeks with her sister Beth, a woman with mild intellectual disability, and learns about herself and loosens up her narrow view of the world. In *Radio* (2003), a young man with a developmental disability becomes an inspiration to his coach and his community. In *Where Hope Grows* (2014), a basketball player who gets injured finds meaning in life after befriending a man with Down syndrome.

SOCIAL MODEL

The social model is depicted in an early film, *Coming Home* (1978; Jane Fonda, Jon Voight), in which a woman whose husband is fighting in Vietnam falls in love with a veteran with a paralyzing combat injury. It is notable for a relatively graphic scene of sexuality that doesn't shy away from the disability. In *Rory O'Shea Was Here* (2004), Rory is a young man with a disability who moves into a residential home for the disabled. He befriends Michael, who has cerebral palsy and barely intelligible speech. The two move into an apartment and hire an assistant. The film is notable in that it is people with disabilities themselves who make the discoveries (rather than an able-bodied person coming to the rescue). It also shows community living even with significant disabilities, how an assistant can make this possible, and friendship between two insiders. In *Murderball* (2005), which is about men with quadriplegia playing rugby in the Paralympics, it is again insiders showing another person with a disability what is possible when a recently injured man in rehabilitation starts to find joy in the game. In *The Waterdance* (1992), several characters in a rehabilitation unit deal with their newly acquired paralysis. It is more realistic about the effects on a pre-existing romantic relationship and shows men with disabilities who are not necessarily likeable, saintlike, or courageous. In *Extremely Loud and Incredibly Close* (2011), a 9-year old boy with autism spectrum disorder tries to come to grips with the loss of his father in the World Trade Center attack on 9/11. His autism is depicted in the context of a loving family, rather than as a burden to them, and is realistically portrayed. One of the more interesting movies from a social model is *Mask* (1985; Cher). Although the initial unveiling of the face of the teenager (Eric Stolz) with a facial skull deformity is a bit sensationalized, over the course of the film the audience reaction to his face becomes quite normalized. It is an outsider group (biker gangs) that takes him in without judgment, and his mother's unconditional love (again, he is not a burden) that allows him to cope with the bullying at school and disappointment in love. And in *Music Within* (2007), a man returns from war with a severe hearing impairment and fights to get laws to benefit Americans with disabilities. Often those with disabilities who fought in the independent living movement and on behalf of important laws get overlooked, so it is important that this film shows the role of impassioned people with disabilities. *Inside Moves* (1980) gets a special mention, not for the overall theme of the film but for the joke that pokes fun at the usual way disability is depicted. Roary, who has tried to commit suicide and ended up disabled, says "I've jumped from a building. I tried to commit suicide." The response is "Hey, you've got it all backwards. First you get crippled then you try to commit suicide!"

Although the films cited here have been used to illustrate the models of disability, readers should be aware that in reality films often have multiple points of view. There is the perspective of the main character(s), that of the ancillary characters, and that of the director; these are not always aligned. A film might show a resilient character (e.g., *Forrest Gump*) and still reflect a stereotyped view of disability that comes from the director. Nonetheless, films can help therapists and clients see how there are different models of disability and how those models shape the world of the person with the disability.

Critique of Models

Each model has merits and drawbacks, and none by itself is sufficient to capture the full range of experiences by people with disabilities. There has been criticism of the social model and of the idea of disability as just another condition of diversity (Anastasiou, Kauffman, & Michail, 2016; Owens, 2015; Shakespeare & Watson, 2002). These authors argue that there are differences in differences. Several points are to be made here. First, in the United States, perhaps the only group that has not be defined as experiencing discrimination based on difference is straight, able-bodied, healthy, heterosexual, and young White males born in the United States. In other words, over 80% of the U.S. population is part of the umbrella of diversity. This washes out important distinctions across groups (Anastasiou et al., 2016). Second, disabilities will always exist, as they are a natural part of the human race. No amount of intermarriage and procreation will ever eliminate disability. For example, the percentage of Jews in the United States is dwindling due to interfaith marriages. But two able-bodied persons can have a child with a disability, and two parents with disabilities can have able-bodied children. Genetic mutations, naturally occurring variations, accidents, and birthing difficulties will all contribute to the fact of disabilities. Even as some causes become more scarce (e.g., taking folic acid supplements early in pregnancy to help the spinal cord develop in utero, avoiding spina bifida in the offspring), other causes will not be eliminated and new causes will arise.

If disability is considered a social construct, and the problems of disability sociopolitical, this suggests that purely sociopolitical solutions exist to eliminate all problems of disability. As Shakespeare (2006) has argued, disabilities constitute "a complex interaction of biological, psychological, cultural, and sociopolitical factors which cannot be extricated" (p. 38). No amount of legal or political or economic or social changes will address or eradicate the real facts related to impairments. Although elimination of social exclusion and oppression are necessary conditions, they are not sufficient conditions to address the physical problems related to impairments, such as pain, fatigue, and weakness.

Disability is not tethered to gender, ethnicity, country of origin, sexual orientation, or religion. There is no place in the world where disability does not exist, nor any country in which disability is the norm. The origins of disability cannot be traced back to any country, time in history, migration movement, or race. In other words, disability has no natural home.

Most oppressed groups are fighting to be treated as equals. But people with disabilities need treatment based on individual differences. For example, there cannot be a standardized set of accommodations in special education. As laws mandate, those accommodations are based on *individualized* education plans. So although the grouping together of extremely disparate disabilities may serve some social and political advantages, it does not serve well in adjusting to individualized needs across disabilities. An example of this is in the concept of *least restrictive environment* for education. Most children with disabilities are advantaged by participating in mainstream classrooms. However, children who are deaf have been disadvantaged by this same principle; the reading level of deaf children is significantly below hearing peers upon graduation from high school, and deaf children perform better academically when attending deaf schools that use sign language (Gentry, Chinn, & Moulton, 2004; Johnson, 1989; Marschark et al., 2009; Schirmer & McGough, 2005).

There are other important differences between disability and other oppressed groups. Disability segregation is not only tolerated but legal. The built environment leads to segregation: there are separate entrances, water fountains, transportation systems, hotel rooms, theater seating, etc. for people with specific types of impairments. Although the concept of universal design can eradicate some segregation (e.g., by putting open captioning on films and having ramps and door openers on main entrances) other types of segregation are not as easily erased. The deleterious effects of segregation were noted in the famous case of *Brown v. Board of Topeka Kansas* in 1954, but segregation remains very much a part of the daily lives of people with disabilities.

Another key difference is the combined economic disadvantages: earning disadvantage and conversion disadvantage (Anastasiou et al., 2016). *Earning disadvantage* has to do with the high unemployment among people with disabilities, the greater difficulties of getting employment, and the decreased option to remain working as age and disability combine to affect the body. The *conversion disadvantage* has to do with the need to convert income into tangible assistance and a good living. A percentage of income goes directly into out-of-pocket payments for disability-related items, such as paid assistants, prostheses, shoe or clothing alterations, car modifications, back-up equipment, repairs of assistive technology, home modifications, and higher priced but more convenient items (e.g., prepared foods). For these two economic disadvantages to be addressed would require not social justice but distributive justice. In social justice everyone has an equal share of available rewards. The rewards one person gets do not influence in either direction the ability of the next person to get the same rewards. This is clearly not the case with disability, where distributive justice is a better model. In distributive justice the rewards for the person with a disability may affect the rewards available to persons without disabilities. There are numerous examples: the parking spot near the entrance reserved for those with disabilities means those without disabilities cannot use that spot; the early boarding of passengers with disabilities on a commercial plane means those passengers get first choice of seating and space in the overhead bins and those without disabilities do not; when a child in school has a severe peanut allergy, other children in the classroom may not be able to bring peanut butter sandwiches for lunch. In each of these cases the needs of the person with a disability impinge on the actions of and rewards for those without disabilities. Americans hold the ideal of equality, but when the rights of one person conflict with the rights of another person, this is a harder situation for people to accept.

Often court cases focus on the conflict between the rights of different categories of peoples. In a real-life example of conflicts between rights of different groups, my local newspaper ran articles about a man who serially sued small businesses for inaccessibility. Rather than focusing on the number of businesses that were inaccessible, the articles focused on the wealth accumulated by this one man and the damage to several small businesses. Within weeks the California legislature passed a law making it more difficult to sue for inaccessibility. The rights of people with disabilities were trumped by the rights of small business owners, in the media, in public opinion, and in legislation.

A few words of caution are in order here. As you learn about these models you might have a tendency to see one model as superior to the others. Often students want to believe they ascribe most to the social model, and that clients should as well. Remember that each model has its pros and cons. Also, there are no good measures of the models. Elsewhere I proposed questions to ask to help determine a client's model (Olkin, 1999), and these were refined in another study (Wong, 2007), but the measure has not been validated. (There is a Disability Personal Identity Scale, which is similar but not quite the same thing; Hahn & Belt, 2004.) And lastly, there are not sufficient data to say that ascribing to one model or another is related to better mental health. One study found that positive disability identity and belonging to the disability community was associated with less depression and anxiety in persons with MS (Bogart, 2015). In another study stronger disability identity was associated with higher self-esteem (Nario-Redmond, Noel, & Fern, 2013). But more data are needed, data that include persons with disabilities who reap the benefits of their particular model of disability.

Clinical Implications

As can be seen in the descriptions of the three models of disability, clients will differ in their belief systems, their language, and their affective responses—virtually every aspect of the response to disability, even whether it is considered a disability or not. But many clients' conceptualization of their disability will have elements of each of the models. Imagine six cups, each labeled moral, medical, or social model, and each model having a positive and a negative cup. Then each cup might be empty, a little filled, or full, independent of the other five cups (see Figure 6.1). Understanding of a client's model of disability requires evaluation of the positives (benefits) and negatives (drawbacks) of each of the three models, not just the one that appears to be most dominant. For example, Sam says, "I have no friends" (despite being able to list almost two dozen). Investigating this further yields his core belief that he is flawed because he is a person with a disability and will be shunned because the disability makes him fundamentally unlovable. This reflects the moral model. It suggests that in treatment we might work on decreasing the negative aspects of the moral model and increasing his benefits in the moral model or moving him more to the medical and/or social model.

Another variable in the model of disability a client holds has to do with self-disclosure of disability, particularly for those with hidden disabilities. It may be that there is a relationship of each model to disclosure of disability. (See Table 6.3 for a hypothetical relationship between positive and negative versions of the three models

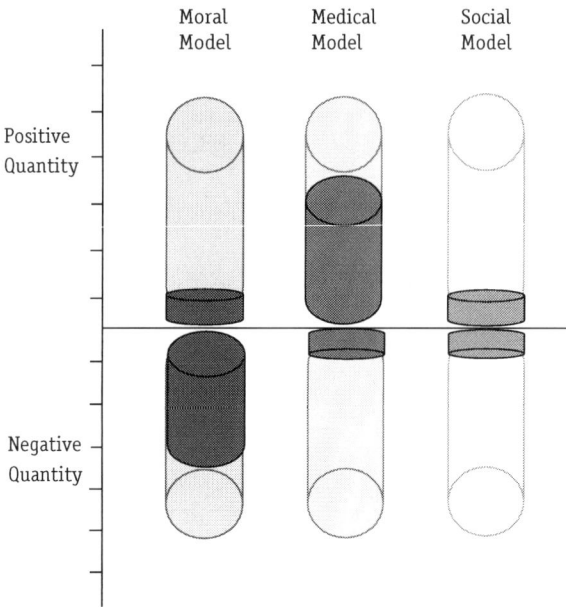

FIGURE 6.1 Hypothetical case showing degree of benefits and drawbacks a person has accrued for each of the three models of disability. This pattern suggests increasing the person's benefits from the moral model.

and disclosure of the disability.) Disclosure is related to other contextual variables as well. If the person with the disability has other characteristics that engender prejudice and discrimination, then disclosure of a disability—a highly stigmatize condition—may be even harder. But disclosure is not all or nothing—a person may disclose within his or her own community (e.g., in an ethnic neighborhood) but not in a community in which the person is a minority (e.g., in a graduate program).

A useful exercise is for therapists to evaluate their own model(s) of disability, with a goal of working toward embracing a biopsychosocial model (W.H.O., 2001)—expanding the social model to include responses to the critiques raised in the section above. There are several reasons for this being useful. First, a biopsychosocial model is the most free of blame for those with disabilities. Second, it is the least patronizing and most collaborative of the models. Third, disability issues are personal, familial, educational, economic, and political, and thus treatment should not be only personal. Lastly, the biopsychosocial model contains within it the idea that disability is a social construct and thus allows for that social construct to be either a moral or medical model construct, thereby allowing the therapist to hold the biopsychosocial model yet still talk with clients in the language of their preferred model.

In treatment, the client's or family's model of disability must be respected. Although the therapist holds the biopsychosocial model, he or she must never insist that clients do so as well. Rather, the goal in treatment is to help clients realize the

TABLE 6.3

MODELS OF DISABILITY AND HYPOTHETICAL PROBABILITY OF DISCLOSURE OF THE DISABILITY

Models of Disability	Positive or Negative	Issues	Effects on Disclosure
Moral	Positives	Relationship to God, being chosen, increased faith	Would disclose to select few (e.g., others with disabilities, family, faith group)
	Negatives	Shame, sin, stigma in the self and the family, adverse effects on marriageability	Unlikely to disclose
Medical	Positives	Clear role as patient, decreased stigma, encouragement to live "normal" life	Very select disclosure, as mostly trying to "pass" as "normal"
	Negatives	Patronizing, body divided into "good" and "bad" parts, little integration of disability into self-concept	Only likely to disclose in situations where something is needed (e.g., an accommodation)
Social	Positives	Integration of disability into self-concept, empowerment, identity with group, pride	Likely to disclose to most or all people
	Negatives	Victimization, problems of stigma and discrimination too large to manage	Likely to disclose in venues seen as safe

benefits of their model of disability and minimize the deficits. And the process of treatment must be framed within the client's model, or there will be a mismatch between therapist and client that will inevitably interfere with the therapeutic relationship and with the process and outcome of therapy.

A Clinical Example

Gupta and Lakshmi Singh immigrated to the United States for education and well-paid jobs. They have two sons, the youngest of whom (Devin) has an intellectual disability. Although both parents are well educated and have good careers, Lakshmi stopped working to take care of Devin. Devin attends school in a special classroom. The parents attend the individualized education plan (IEP) meetings together, but do not speak much, usually nodding assent to the suggestions made by school personnel. School staff erroneously assume that the Singhs do not speak much English and that this is the reason for their silence. Staff are unaware of the profound shame and guilt the parents feel for having a child with "empty brain," or the blame the father lays on the mother for bringing this on the family by eating the wrong things and being anxious during her pregnancy with Devin. Thus staff blame the parents for not following through with referrals for social groups for Devin and support groups for families of children with intellectual disabilities, not understanding the family's need to keep Devin out of the public eye. They are appalled when the parents use the language "retarded." The resource room teacher feels she is rescuing Devin from bad parents, who are not involved in the early intervention she knows is conducive to giving Devin greater independence.

This example illustrates that staff need to be aware of the model of disability the parents hold (the moral model). Additionally, they need to understand the meaning of intellectual disability, specifically in a boy, in Indian culture. Assumptions that parents do not speak much English, or do not care to be more involved, or are ignorant perpetuate a rift between the school and the family. For a therapist to avoid being in the same position as the school, the therapist (if the family ever would seek counseling, which they may well not) would need to be aware of the rift and its probable causes and speak to the family in the model they espouse. Unless the therapist can join with the parents in their worldview, he or she cannot be effective. It may seem difficult, even repugnant, to a therapist to hear how the father blames the mother, or how the mother blames herself, or how the mother has given up her career for her family's needs. But no good will come of insisting on a model the family does not believe in. Instead, the goal is to meet the family at their own starting point and then shift slowly to a more positive version of the moral model. For example, the mother may be willing to meet other Indian mothers of children with intellectual disabilities in a park, rather than in a clinical setting. The parents might be willing to read an article about causes of intellectual disability, or about models of disability, or about ways to help their son develop more skills in self-care. The goal of this reading is not to change their minds about the moral model, but to inch them toward less shame and guilt so that they might experience more agency in how they decide to care for their son.

Application of Models of Disability to the Clinical Example of Sam

Applying the models of disability to Sam illustrates how there can be dissonance for someone who is struggling with disability belief systems. Sam was raised with mixed messages. On one hand, he was expected to do everything any other boy did, not to complain or cry when he fell, and to behave to the greatest extent possible as if he did not have an impairment. However, the house he grew up in had two stories, and his father had to carry him upstairs to bed every night and downstairs every morning. The idea of shaping the environment to be more accessible was never discussed (and probably not financially feasible). Additionally, any emotional or social aspects of the disability were ignored, as if polio were a medical problem only. This gave the impression that polio was not something to be spoken about and, therefore, was shameful. Yet teasing from childhood peers, fatigue, and frequent falls all made the impairment salient for Sam, without any outlet for discussion or review. Sam internalized the moral model—*disability is shameful*—and the medical model—*I am a patient who must follow doctors' directions*. His coming out exposed him to the ideas of gay identity pride and civil rights, and he wanted to apply these ideas to disability. His exposure to the social model was furthered when he joined a disability support group, when he had a friend with polio who espoused the social model, and when he read my (1999) book. But the effect of this exposure was to make him feel guilty that he wasn't able to transcend his internalized shame and passivity about disability and embrace the social model fully; his head wanted to go there, but his heart was having a hard time following. Therapy helped him see how he was raised in the moral and medical models, which helped lessen the shame he felt for his own feelings and beliefs. Then exposure to the social model happened slowly, example by example. For instance, he had never traveled with his wheelchair, using crutches in the airport and waiting for an airport wheelchair to take him to the gate. This made him feel helpless, exhausted, and often enraged (e.g., when the wheelchair was slow to arrive). The idea of greater independence by using his scooter made him terrified that he would be left stranded and yelled at by security personnel at the airport. We had to go through what could happen step by step, from parking, to boarding the airplane, to getting the scooter at the other end of the trip. Throughout this process I had to remind him that he had a right to travel with a scooter, that he wasn't doing anything wrong. We rehearsed negative scenarios, though usually I had to play him, as he really did not have any internal models of an assertive person with a disability. These rehearsals calmed him down, and he was able to travel with his wheelchair. Similarly, we would brainstorm questions for him to ask a doctor before a visit, because he would become passive and frightened in doctors' presence. These are but two examples of translating a model into action, of taking theoretical ideas and making them concrete in everyday life. The issue wasn't that Sam didn't have the behavioral repertoire to do these things on his own, but rather that he didn't believe he had the right or the power. Once his mindset changed, his behavior followed.

Discussion Questions

1. What is your model(s) of disability? Fill in the "cups."
2. Think of a movie with a character with a disability (one not mentioned in this chapter). What was the director's perspective on disability? What was the main disability message of the movie?
3. What are some of the critiques of the social model of disability?
4. There are two students in class. One has a service animal, another has a dog allergy. How might you handle this potential conflict?
5. What are your own thoughts about disclosure of a hidden disability (a) at work, (b) in graduate school, (c) with friends, (d) with medical professionals?

7 D-AT IV: Context and Intersectionality—Interplay of Disability and Other Demographic Variables

DISABILITY IS OFTEN treated as is if it were both the most salient characteristic of a person and the only characteristic. For example, I had two graduate students with visual impairments, different as night and day, but who kept getting confused for each other. They were encoded in other people's minds as "the student with the visual impairment" and other variables were ignored. When a single characteristic spreads in this fashion to create an overall impression that minimizes other characteristics, it is called a *central characteristic* (Asch, 1946).

Disability is generally a central characteristic (Wright, 1983). In addition, when others are forming impressions of a person with a disability, not only is the disability central, but the presence of disability tends to spread to other unrelated characteristics (Dembo, Leviton, & Wright, 1956). *Spread* "refers to the power of a single characteristics to evoke inferences about a person" (Wright, 1983, p. 32). The presence of a disability is thus not only central to impression formation, it erroneously is allowed to define other unrelated characteristics. Thus a waiter might talk loudly to a person who is blind, as if the person were also deaf, or a younger person might patronizingly call an older woman in a wheelchair "honey," assuming the disability also implies either intellectual impairment or helplessness and youth.

It is obvious that other personal characteristics should not be so *overshadowed* (Mason & Scior, 2004) by the presence of a disability that they are ignored. As discussed in Chapter 6, regarding models of disability, disability carries quite different meanings according to the model of disability. But, additionally, we have to consider the social context, the ethnic community, the religious beliefs, gender variables, age, sexual orientation, socioeconomic status (SES), and education of the person. It is not possible to go over each of these variables in this chapter. Instead, I want to highlight some particular aspects that interact with disability in important ways. This includes education and SES, sexual orientation, and ethnicity.

Education and Socioeconomic Status

Disability and poverty are inextricably linked (Braithwaite & Mont, 2009; Emmett, 2005; Fitzgerald, 2007; Palmer, 2011). People with disabilities are much more likely than those without disabilities to live below the poverty line, to have government (versus private) insurance or no insurance, to have lower household income than that of their neighbors, and to be unemployed or underemployed. Chronic illness and work disability account for about half the defaults on mortgages (Huang, 2011; Robertson, Egelhof, & Hoke, 2008). Poverty is a risk factor for dropping out of high school (Chapman, Laird, Ifill, & Kewal Ramani, 2011). The data on disability as a risk factor for dropping out of school mostly show a higher rate of dropout (Dunn, Chambers, & Rabren, 2004; Leone et al., 2003; Scanlon & Mellard, 2002; Thurlow, Sinclair, & Johnson, 2002). Additionally, disability is associated with poverty and thus with more precarious school districts, both of which are risk factors for dropping out of high school (Chapman et al., 2011; Christle, Jolivette, & Nelson, 2007). Fewer students with disabilities attend college (Wagner & Blackorby, 1996; Wagner, Newman, Cameto, Garza, & Levine, 2005). Medical issues and health-related quality of life are associated with dropping out of college (DeBerard, Spielmans, & Julka, 2004; Jorgensen, Ferraro, Fichten, & Havel, 2009).

On the flip side, persons living in poverty are more likely to have disabilities (Fujiura & Yamaki, 2000; Grech, 2011). Reduced access to good dental, medical, and psychological health care is one causal factor in incidence of disabilities. And as discussed in Chapter 5, persons with disabilities face conversion disadvantage—the ability to translate income into better quality of life. Many people with disabilities have to pay out of pocket for ramps, grab bars, widening doorways, car lifts for scooters or wheelchairs, and other accommodations. Insurance, if the person has it, may exclude durable medical products, or it may cover the cost of a wheelchair but not a ramp to the front of the house. The net result is that families with disabilities not only have lower household income (Brault, 2012) but also higher out-of-pocket medical costs (Zaidi & Burchardt, 2005). Because of the higher costs of living with a disability, the devastating health effects of living in poverty, and the income disparities for those with and without a college education, post-secondary education for persons with disabilities is a vital asset. Furthermore, higher education is critical to getting jobs that do not rely on manual labor. Yet even persons with disabilities who hold advanced degrees are often under- and unemployed.

For example, I interviewed a blind man in his early fifties who was a licensed clinical social worker but who had never held any job that used his degree. I cite this one example as a stand-in for the countless persons with disabilities both I and my students have interviewed who similarly held masters or doctoral degrees but who were not in the workforce (Cohen, 1998; Conley-Jung & Olkin, 2001; Olkin, Loewy, Safron, Hall, & Crockett, 2016). Mothers with disabilities seem particularly likely to have stopped working outside the home, possibly owing to the synergy of barriers and difficulties of both parenting and working with a disability (Blackford, 1993; Doren & Benz, 2001; Farber, 2000; Kocher, 1994).

At the other end of the spectrum, so-called white collar jobs are more adaptable for people with disabilities. But the nature of the job isn't the only factor—social and attitudinal barriers may still exist in the professions, as has been noted for law (Jolly-Ryan, 2005), medicine (Mercer, Dieppe, Chambers, & MacDonald, 2003; Ouellette, 2012), and clinical psychology (Olkin & Pledger, 2003). (See Postar, 2011, for a bibliography of articles on law students and lawyers with disabilities). And in some fields where we might expect to see more professionals with disabilities because disability knowledge is an asset, we see very few; special education is one such example (Crutchfield, 1997; Hauk, 2009; Pope, Bowman, & Barr, 2001; Valle, Solis, Volpitta, & Connor, 2004).

As the jobs in service, technology, and information increase, education and training in skills essential to those jobs are important. The clinical implications of the importance of education are fairly clear: we have to help our clients with disabilities stay in school. There is a large literature on factors that enable students with disabilities to stay in K–12 and college (c.f., Getzel & Thoma, 2008; Knight, Knessel, & Markle, 2016; Roberts, Ju, & Zhang, 2016). Such factors include accurately tailored individualized education plans (IEP), assistance with developing specific academic and study skills, appropriate accommodations, and promotion of academic self-efficacy. This has to be true at all levels of education, from K–12 to doctoral degrees.

How can clinicians help children, adolescents, and young adults stay in school? There are many ways. In the earlier grades, therapists may need to get involved in the process of identifying disabilities (through appropriate assessments). Navigating the school system and its levels of assistance can be very daunting for parents. It can be helpful for the therapist to prepare parents for such meetings and even accompany the parents to the meetings regarding IEPs, as well as to have ideas about accommodations that would be useful. In middle and high school the social venue is critically related to the desire to stay in school or drop out. If the social atmosphere is rejecting, stigmatizing, belittling, isolating, or bullying, then going to school becomes onerous. Another possibility is that the student with a disability is rejected by many groups and thus joins whichever crowd allows entry, which may be the stoners and those who cut school. Middle school in particular can be brutal for kids with differences, because it is the peak time for conformity and fitting in. Emotional support, ego strength, and resilience are important tasks for therapy with those ages. A clinical example may help make some of these points.

> Ellen is a 15-year old girl with cerebral palsy who uses a manual wheelchair. She cannot transfer independently and relies on family for many of her activities of daily living. She was homeschooled during most of elementary school because of physical, learning, and social difficulties. Now she has returned to public high school but doesn't have friends. She tries to control her differentness by being goth, wearing all black, favoring Victorian style clothing, having piercings and a visible tattoo. But poor social skills and her disability mean she is a social outcast. Her future goals are to live in an apartment with other girls and be a veterinarian. The connection between her present life and what she would have to do to achieve this goal is tenuous for her. Doing math homework now and getting into college or living independently later seem separate to her.

Sexual Orientation

There is a higher rate of disability among lesbians and gay men; this remains the case even after controlling for covariates of disability (Fredriksen-Goldsen, Kim, & Barkan, 2012). Despite this fact, the literature on these multiple identities is scarce. Those clinicians serving lesbian and gay populations need to know about disabilities, and those serving people with disabilities need to know about lesbian and gay identities (Fraley, Mona, & Theodore, 2007).

Overall, there is more literature on lesbians with disabilities than on gay men with disabilities. I would posit several reasons for the focus on lesbians with disabilities. First, the women's movement and the disability independent living movement share many central constructs (e.g., a social model of construction of gender and disability). Second, inclusion is a key aspect of feminism, and thus lesbians with disabilities have been invited to the feminist table. Third, awareness of power and privilege are also part of the women's movement, and there is a logical link to awareness of able-bodied privilege. Fourth, there are issues that affect females more than males, such as sexual and physical abuse, that also are more likely to affect people with disabilities, so there are shared concerns. And fifth, lesbians with disabilities may be more successful in finding female partners than they might be in finding male partners, given the higher acceptability of physical variances among females than among males (Fallon & Rozin, 1985; Frederick & Haselton, 2007; McCreary & Sasse, 2000; Singh, 1993).

One of the more thoughtful writings on intersectionality discusses homosexuality, gender, ethnicity, and disability and the lack of attention to disability issues within gay culture (Greene, 2005). The author suggests that the omission of studies on disability within gay culture gives the impression that "heterosexism is the primary locus of oppression . . . or that the presence of a disability does not have a salient impact on the identity or the life of LGB people" (p. 384). Further, she notes that lesbian or gay persons with disabilities who require assistance from others for mobility literally may not be able to access the gay community, especially if the family does not approve of the sexual orientation. Finding other lesbians and gay males often involves visual and behavioral cues; these cues may be hidden from someone with a visual impairment or may be altered in someone whose disability affects their physical presentation (Asch, 1988; Greene, 2003). The tendency of able-bodied people to avoid direct contact with people with disabilities also could affect the ability of lesbians or gay men with disabilities to find each other.

There may be an important feature of lesbian and gay couples, particularly when one partner (or both) has a disability, which has to do with gender role flexibility. Heterosexual couples in which one partner has a disability tend to divide tasks on the basis of capabilities more than gender (Gordon & Perrone, 2004; Hafstrom & Schram, 1984; Peterson, 1979; Rolland, 1999). Similarly, same-sex partners cannot divide tasks based on gender and thus must find other ways to negotiate task sharing. Such tasks include parenting, and in fact there does seem to be more role flexibility among parents with disabilities (Kirshbaum & Olkin, 2002) as well as with same-sex parents (Goldberg & Perry-Jenkins, 2007; Weeks, Heaphy, & Donovan, 2001).

It is not a coincidence that many ideas in D-AT mirror those from gay-affirmative therapy (c.f., Harrison, 2000; Hunt, Matthews, Milsom, & Lammel, 2006; Laird & Green, 1996) and other multicultural writers (c.f., Falicov, 1995, 1998). For gay-affirmative therapy in particular, the person with the minority status (lesbian or gay) generally does not share that status with his or her parents, a situation that is usually the same for persons with disabilities. Thus the skills that other minority parents might teach their similarly minority children—such as self-advocacy, externalization of stigma, handling of prejudice and discrimination, learning which battles to fight and how to fight them—have to be learned outside the family (Linton, 1998). This means that therapy might well be one venue for this learning.

LESBIANS WITH DISABILITIES

The fact that there is more professional literature on lesbians than gay men with disabilities does not imply that there is much out there. Nor is there a lot on intersectionality (including other variables besides disability and sexual orientation; for an exception, see O'Toole, 2000). Furthermore, romance and dating is one of the least studied areas related to people with disabilities, with lots of questions remaining (Gill, 1996). These issues combined are problematic, because when there is scarce literature the existing articles tend to become gospel. Many are not empirical, and of those that are, samples tend to be predominantly or wholly White and middle or upper middle class.

In college, a gay student with a disability may be receiving services related to the disability while struggling with other aspects of identity, such as being gay, being a student of color (Harley, Nowak, Gassaway, & Savage, 2002), or even being a woman in a male-dominated field such as engineering. Integration of the self into a cohesive whole may be hampered by the multiple places in which the one woman feels ostracized or stigmatized. Gay and lesbian youths with disabilities possess multiple stigmatized identities and, despite very diverse needs, face similar stigma in many countries, notably the United States, Canada, Australia, the United Kingdom, New Zealand, Belgium, and Sweden (Duke, 2011). Lesbians with disabilities may still find they are viewed as less appealing as partners (Asch & Fine, 1997).

An early study on lesbians with disabilities noted that health professionals may hold negative attitudes toward both characteristics (O'Toole & Bregante, 1992, 1993). There is little known about the mental health needs and experiences of lesbians with disabilities (O'Toole & Brown, 2002). One study found that partners of lesbians with disabilities in rehabilitation often were not allowed access to medical records or information, were ignored, or garnered subtle negative reactions (Hunt, Milsom, & Matthews, 2009). Despite recognition of marriage between same-sex partners, such relationships still are not universally accepted in all parts of the United States.

An article exploring the experiences in counseling of lesbians with disabilities (Hunt et al., 2006) reported that 73% of those surveyed had sought mental health counseling. No such data exist regarding people with disabilities, and there is no empirical article about the counseling experiences of lesbians with disabilities, with the exception of Hunt et al. (2006). They note that there are several similarities for lesbians and persons with disabilities. Both live within assumptions of heteronormativity and being able-bodied. Both are subject to higher rates of sexual violence and abuse (Bradford, Ryan, & Rothblum, 1994). There are misconceptions and ignorance regarding the sexuality of both groups. And awareness of sexual orientation, and onset of disability, may both occur later in life—that is, both are groups that may be joined at later developmental stages. There are few role models for either group, much less for those in both camps. Lesbians with disabilities experience oppression related to gender, to sexual orientation, to being female, and perhaps for other things as well (e.g., ethnicity, religion, country of origin; O'Toole & Bregante, 1992). As a result, they may try to pass as either heterosexual and/or able-bodied (depending on the visibility of the disability). And they may have trouble finding mental health professionals who are knowledgeable and affirmative about sexual orientation and disability.

In their qualitative study using interviews with 25 White lesbians with disabilities, Hunt et al. (2006) they found three overarching themes: depression (reported by 10 of the women, even though not a direct question in the interview); perceptions of counselors (with five subthemes regarding satisfaction, effectiveness of counselor, counselor awareness, discrimination and bias, and counselor identity); and negotiating the counseling process (with three subthemes regarding coming out or self-disclosure, self-advocacy, and accessibility or accommodations). Regarding the counselors' identity, 12 women mentioned the importance of the counselor being self-identified as lesbian, but only 3 mentioned disability status and did not always agree on whether this was an important factor. Of note were the difficulties in basic accessibility. Even when the client disclosed a disability on the phone, the office might turn out not to be accessible. There were problems with alternate formats and testing/assessment for those with visual impairments, as well as financial barriers.

Hunt et al. (2006) made several points that merit attention. The first is that being an effective counselor is a necessary precondition. This echoes a basic tenet of D-AT, which is that there are additional skills necessary to work with specific populations, but these skills must be layered on top of basic effectiveness. A related point is that a therapist of the same sexual orientation or with a disability does not necessarily make the person competent to work with similar clients. Nor is it necessary for the therapist to share those characteristics with the client to be effective. A second point is that neither being a lesbian nor a woman with a disability should be overriding (central) characteristics. The women interviewed stressed that they wanted to be viewed and treated multidimensionally.

The third point is that therapists need to learn and do research outside of sessions. Attending conferences, reading journal articles or books, and getting skilled supervision are ways to increase learning about diverse clients. Fourth, practices should be reviewed with an eye toward being both gay- and disability-affirmative. A simple example is to ask about partner status rather than marital status on intake forms. Making note of wheelchair accessibility in public information (e.g., business cards) is a way of signaling awareness of disability issues.

Finally, clients may want to test the waters by waiting to see if a therapist raises issues of sexual orientation or disability, or be more initially confrontational or demanding, to see how the therapist responds. It is helpful if therapists can view these behaviors in light of the daily and ubiquitous stigma and discrimination both lesbians and women with disabilities encounter and be nonjudgmental, accepting, and nondefensive. Hunt et al. (2006) recommend including partners and/or families of choice in therapy, as relevant.

GAY MEN WITH DISABILITIES

We might ask why there is a dearth of literature on gay men with disabilities. As noted in the previous section, there are many overlaps between feminist and disability movements. But gay male culture and disability culture conflict in some ways. Numerous studies suggest that gay males, compared to their heterosexual counterparts, are more body aware and restricted in what is deemed attractive (Nerini, Matera, Baroni, & Stefanile, 2015; Robbins, Wester, & McKean, 2016; Slevin & Linneman, 2010; Swami & Tovée, 2008). This may impact gay men with disabilities adversely.

An early article on gay men with disabilities (Atkins & Marston, 1999) grappled with the theoretical issues among feminism, disability activism, and the queer community. A key point is that there is a norm for bodies which defines both those who are queer and those with disabilities as "others." One way to address this norm has been through autobiographical performances by persons who straddle both gay and disabled identities (see Sandahl, 2003, for a review of four such performances). Another article tackles the heteronormative structure of studies on sexuality and disability (Tremain, 2000). The book *Queer Crips* (Guter & Killacky, 2004), written by men with disabilities, recounts their lived experiences. While none of the works are empirical studies, they lay the theoretical and personal frameworks for research.

A more recent article used a social constructivist view to discuss the dual minority status of being gay and disabled (Hanjorgiris, Rath, & O'Neill, 2004). Although it isn't empirical, it is nonetheless one of the few articles offering suggestions for mental health counselors. Another article, also not empirical, likewise offers suggestions for practitioners (Harley, Hall, & Savage, 2000).

In a small qualitative study of the lived experiences of gay men with disabilities (Olkin, Loewy, Safron, Hall, & Crocket, 2016), we interviewed eight men with disabilities readily visible to others. All of the men had acquired their disabilities prior to age 12 (inclusion criterion) and lived in California or New York. There were several notable themes. The first theme was that the parents' reactions to the disability were paramount in how the disability was thought about, managed, and internalized, just as it is for all children with disabilities. But when gay youths with disabilities come out to parents, there was often the reaction of (a) *not another minority status, are you kidding me?* or (b) *after all we've been through, all I've done for you, now this too?* The message in either case was that the combination of disability and being gay was unacceptable. It also conveyed that being disabled and gay were things the boy was doing *to* someone, his parents.

Another theme was that in gay male interactions a lot of visual cues are used, to signal availability, interest, sexual orientation, so the body and its movements are key communicators. Disability may distort these communications or be visually unappealing (just as was noted many years ago by Asch [1988]).

And third, the disability was a more pronounced part of everyday life, but being gay was a bigger determinant of the men's social circles. Of note to us as researchers was the difficulty of recruitment—most of the gay venues in the northern California area where we did some of the recruitment were not accessible. And transportation to the site of the interviews was problematic (buses not stopping or having broken wheelchair lifts; accessible taxis not arriving). It was discouraging to hear about such pronounced transportation issues in California and New York, two places in the United States with greater diversity. (For a continuation of this study with another group of gay men with disabilities, see Witter, 2016.)

CONCLUSIONS

There are many unknowns about lesbians with disabilities and even more about gay men with disabilities. The issues described in the previous sections have implications for therapy with lesbians or gay men with disabilities. It is incumbent on the therapist to be both gay- and disability-affirmative. The assessment of the personal history has to consider both the awareness of being different in two ways (or more) and the family's responses to both sexual orientation and disability. The internalization of heteronormativity and ableism may lead to depression, anxiety, and lowered self-esteem. Negotiation of being disabled within lesbian and gay culture and being gay in disability culture may leave lesbians and gay men with disabilities feeling like outsiders in all venues. The micro- (and macro-) aggressions experienced from two stigmatized conditions may overwhelm a person's abilities to cope. The way in which two core facets of personhood are negotiated and understood may be an area of needed exploration. And above all, the therapist will have to demonstrably evince both gay- and disability-affirmative stances.

Ethnicity

In thinking about the vast array of ways that ethnicity and disability interact, we must be careful not to conflate ethnicity with SES. Unfortunately, the two are linked often in American culture, with disparities in employment and wealth across ethnic groups (Belgrave & Walker, 1991; James, DeVivo, & Richards, 1993; Oliver & Shapiro, 2006; Pager & Shepherd, 2008; Western & Pettit, 2005). Blacks with disabilities fare worse in many ways compared to White counterparts, in having needs met with activities of daily living (Kennedy, 2001), in mortality rates (Kenneson, Vatave, & Finkel, 2010), and in risk factors such as obesity (Nosek et al., 2008; Rimmer & Wang, 2005) and preterm births (Demissie et al., 2001). Further, there may be overdiagnosis of Black children with putative disabilities (see Sleeter, 2010). Different variables may affect disability and employment for different ethnic groups (see Thorpe, Szanton, Bell, & Whitfield, 2016). Ethnic culture and disability needs to be understood across SES levels. The experiences of Black and Asian children with disabilities is different from that of White counterparts (Ali, Fazil, Bywaters, Wallace, & Singh, 2001). And to complicate things further, education and employment gaps affect political involvement for people with disabilities; unemployed people with disabilities in particular are less likely to view the political system as responsive to their needs (Schur, Shields, & Schriner, 2003). Employment may have increasing benefits for minorities with disabilities, a group which is doubly marginalized (Schur, 2002). People with disabilities are more likely to smoke, be in fair or poor health, not exercise, be overweight, have lower rates of health screenings, and have more difficulty accessing health services (Iezzoni, 2011). Ethnicity compounds some of these factors, as not only do rates of smoking differ across ethnic groups, but the risks associated with smoking likewise differ (Haiman et al., 2006).

Religion is another variable in the mix, and it is a complicated one. Religious observance may afford some protections against disability (Idler & Kasl, 1992, 1997; Johnstone, Glass, & Oliver, 2007; Kaye & Raghavan, 2002), and there are variations across religions in how disability is conceptualized (Schumm & Stoltzfus, 2011). Again, it is easy to confuse ethnicity and religion, since the two often go together. It is useful to think of the three variables together (Miltiades & Pruchno, 2002; Rogers-Dulan & Blacher, 1995). So the interaction of ethnicity and disability is difficult to understand without the variables of SES and religion included.

One key factor in understanding disability for any given client is the definition and role of family. While Euro-American culture focuses mostly on nuclear families, other ethnic groups tend to include more extended family members in their core group (McGoldrick, Giordano, & Garcia-Preto, 2005; Zinn, 1994). These larger numbers included in the family mean that it is more likely that someone within the family has a disability and that there is a greater likelihood of more than one person with a disability in the extended family.

There are many variables that may differ across cultures, including the definition of disability itself. In some cultures, disability may be viewed as just another personal variant, rather than an aberration or abnormality. Other cultures view disability as a manifestation of wrong-doing or sin (i.e., the moral model of disability), which carries a great deal of stigma. The definition of disability is closely allied with the model of disability, but culture puts its own spin on it. For example, an Asian Indian family may hold mostly the moral model of disability, but the specific cultural meaning attached is that the child with a disability will never get married, thus failing to fulfill a key cultural expectation. In contrast, someone from a Mexican American culture may also hold the moral model, but the cultural meaning is that the child should not be expected to work and will continue to live at home and be protected and cared for. In both cases, there may be shame attached to seeking services outside the family, but for very different reasons.

Getting assistance from outside the family is normative in some cultures and anathema in other cultures, so it can be important to ask about the family's beliefs about going outside the family for assistance. In one study of African American families with elder caregivers, there were few differences in the amount of caregiving or likelihood of using outside services between families with employed caregivers and those with caregivers who were not working (Bullock, Crawford, & Tennstedt, 2003). This meant that family members who were employed were doing just as many caregiving tasks as those who were not employed, which can stress the family system. Preferences for care may differ as well. For example, Whites and Hispanics with drug use disorders are more likely to use professional services, and Blacks are more likely to use a 12-step program and clergy (Perron et al., 2009).

Another cultural variable is the relationship of specific cultures to the helping professions, including medicine and mental health. Some cultural groups are quite understandably more wary of the very institutions designed to help families with disabilities (e.g., disability-specific clinics; Social Security Administration), with others being more inclined to avail themselves of services. Even the national organizations that are condition specific (e.g., the National Multiple Sclerosis Society; Polio Health International; Arthritis Association of America) tend to comprise proportionally more White participants, as do the support groups they sponsor. Other ethnic groups are more likely to form groups through community-based agencies or religious organizations than by national associations. These differences should be reflected in the clinician's questions, as well as in recommendations for referrals.

It can be difficult to assess to what degree a given belief or behavior is related to the disability, to the person's culture and community, and/or to the person's family.

Nonetheless, all three levels must be considered when evaluating what is normative in a person's milieu. A behavior might be aberrant in all three domains, or congruent with one or two and incongruent with the others. Of course, the difficulty the therapist has in parsing this out pales in comparison to what it is like for the client to negotiate an identity with myriad and often conflicting social messages and pressures. An example might help elucidate this point.

> Joleen is an African American lesbian woman in a 2-year relationship with a Latina partner. She has lupus, which causes fatigue that waxes and wanes. Sometimes she is on steroids, which causes insomnia and irritability. To the therapist she complains that she "never feels at home anywhere; I'm invisible." She feels rejected by the church for her sexual orientation, by the African American community for her lesbian relationship and the fact that her partner is Latina, by the disability community because it is mostly White, by the lesbian community because they don't seem to understand her disability. She states, "What is normal? Who are my role models? How should I behave? So I stay quiet, then no one sees me."

SPECIFIC ETHNIC GROUPS

As can be seen from the previous discussion, it is exceedingly difficult to delineate even the major ethnic groups and the similarities and differences in the views of disability across cultures. In this section I point readers to some major works and research in this area. There are three books specifically on disability and culture (Bryan, 2007; Instad & Whyte, 1995; Riddell & Watson, 2014).

We know that rates of disability vary across ethnic groups (Steinmetz, 2006), although the compounding factors delineated in the previous section must be kept in mind. The rate of disability is roughly 20% for Blacks, 19% for Whites, and 11.5% for Asians and Pacific Islanders; rates for Hispanics (of any race) range from 3% to 9% (Steinmetz, 2006). Additionally, rates of living in group quarters varies by ethnicity: those who are Black, American Indian, never married, or with less than a high school education are more likely to live in group quarters (Stapleton, Honeycutt, & Schechter, 2012).

One of the early important works on African Americans with disabilities was by Belgrave (1998). Her book is research based, and she has continued to conduct research in this area (c.f., Belgrave & Jarama, 2000). She also has published works regarding Latinos with disabilities (Zea, Belgrave, García, & Quezada, 1997), including a book that is an important work in this area (Garcia & Zea, 1997). Other key works regarding Latinos with disabilities are by Balcazar and Suarez-Balcazar and colleagues (Balcazar, Keys, Kaplan, & Suarez-Balcazar, 1998; Balcazar, Keys, & Suarez-Balcazar, 2001; Fawcett et al., 1994; Hernandez, Keys, & Balcazar, 2000; McDonald, Keys, & Balcazar, 2007). Issues related to immigration and documentation may be particularly acute for Latinos; they are less likely to have medical insurance, presenting a major barrier to rehabilitation and mental health treatment (Alegría et al., 2006).

Asian Americans tend to have the lowest rates of most disabilities (Centers for Disease Control and Prevention, 2008). Having a disability adds to the discrimination Asian Americans and Pacific Islanders experience (Mereish, 2012), and disability is very stigmatized in most Asian cultures (Saetermoe, Scattone, & Kim, 2001). However, Asian American families with disabilities face significant obstacles to accessing services, including language barriers (Smith & Ryan, 1987), finances, transportation, and power relationships (Zhan, 1999); stigma associated with mental health services (Zhang, Snowden, & Sue, 1998); religious beliefs (Chen, Jo, & Donnell, 2004); and underappreciation by clinicians of the differences across Asian cultures (Chan, Lam, Wong, Leung, & Fang, 1988; Chen, Brodwin, Cardoso, & Chan, 2002). There is a significant gap between the number of Asian Americans with disabilities and their utilization of services (Smith & Hancock, 2012).

Approaches to rehabilitation may need to differ across ethnic groups in order to be culturally sensitive and appropriate and to achieve better outcomes (Alston, Bell, & Feist-Price, 1996; Atkins, 1988; Choi & Wynne, 2000; Hampton, 2000; Hasnain & Balcazar, 2009; Hwang, 2006; Moore, 2002; Walker, 1995; Wong-Hernandez & Wong, 2002). Some authors argue that "cultural and ethnic sensitivity alone is no longer adequate; health care professionals must also be *ethnically and culturally competent*, that is, be able to recognize, respect, and engage ethnic diversity in a way that leads to mutually desirable outcomes" (McCubbin, Thompson, Thompson, McCubbin, & Kaston, 1993, p. 1063). However, other authors assert that *cultural sensitivity* has to be the standard, on the grounds that no one person can be culturally competent in more than two or three cultures (Resnicow, Baranowski, Ahluwalia, & Braithwaite, 1998). But culturally adapted interventions are not clear-cut. For example, one study found that cultural adaptations to family interventions for various ethnic groups increased retention by 40% but reduced positive outcomes (Kumpfer, Alvarado, Smith, & Bellamy, 2002).

> Antonio is a Mexican American with an autoimmune disorder that causes stomach pains and cramps, and frequent bowel movements over the course of a day. He has a large extended family of about 100 people that get together most weekends. He has developed a social phobia of being unable to eat in front of others. Stress at work has increased his gastrointestinal problems, which in

turn has reinforced his desire to eat only in private. When the pains and the phobia increased, his work began to suffer, and someone in the employee assistance program at his job suggested that he take a leave of absence to seek treatment. No one in the family knew about the reason for the private eating, which he covered up by taking plates of food when others did but then not actually eating it. Likewise, they did not know he was on leave (he said he was taking comp time off) and that he had sought psychotherapy. The therapist carefully went through the list of relatives with Antonio, to see who might be the easiest to disclose to and most sympathetic. Antonio chose to tell one of his four brothers. The brother responded by suggesting Antonio speak to the brother's wife, who turned out to have some similar gastrointestinal problems, as well as panic attacks. Breaking the secrecy was the beginning of his being more able to discuss his private eating, a symptom which had caused him to feel deep shame and embarrassment. Although there was still a lot of work to be done in treatment, the therapist's work to help Antonio find an ally in the extended family, and its success, increased his trust in the therapy process.

Mental Disorders and Psychiatric Disabilities

Clients with disabilities, like all clients, come to therapy because of a problem. Although the problem they want to address may be directly about the disability (e.g., pain management), it is more likely to be about a mood disorder or anxiety, substance use, relationship problems, parenting issues, or one of the many other issues that generally lead clients to make appointments with therapists. But for clients with both a mental disorder and another disability, the disability can exacerbate and complicate the mental disorder, and vice versa. Mental disorders themselves cause a great deal of disability, as evidenced in a study conducted in 15 different countries, across income levels (Ormel et al., 2008). The authors concluded that mental disorders are undertreated. Additionally, the mental disorder and the disability issues can be so intertwined that they can be difficult to tease apart, such that treatment needs to work on both simultaneously. Untangling the issues might be important for accurate diagnosis and to avoid overshadowing. But it can be difficult to know if such an untangling is important to the broader understanding of the client.

> Amanda is a 26-year old White married female with Crohn's disease, social anxiety, and obsessive-compulsive disorder (OCD). Her primary care physician recommended psychotherapy to reduce stress. Amanda plays competitive volleyball, but sometimes her Crohn's disease means she is late for practice or

has to miss a game. Because of her social anxiety ("I can't make small talk," "I'm uninteresting," "I don't know why anyone would like me") and her OCD, she has trouble telling people about her Crohn's disease and the ramifications (in the bathroom often and for a long time). She fears people will think she is trying to be treated as "special" and fragile and that they may even cut her from the team. When she tries to write an email to say she can't attend a practice at a site without a bathroom she spends about 2 days on the email and has her husband read it before she can finally send it. Her anxiety disorders make dealing with Crohn's harder and exacerbate the inflammation. Having Crohn's disease makes treatment of the anxiety disorders more complex as Amanda struggles with her newer identity as a person with a disorder, evaluating the degree to which the disorder is part of her.

An example of when a temporal relationship between a disability and depression might be important to consider is in a client with multiple sclerosis (MS). A personal and/or family history of depression prior to any diagnosis is the best predictor of depression after a diagnosis (Olkin, 2004). However, MS has a higher rate of depression than many other disabilities and MS is thought to be a direct physiological and biochemical cause of depression (McGuigan & Hutchinson, 2006). More successful treatment of the depression also can increase disease-modifying medication adherence (Mohr et al., 2000) and may alter physiological factors important in MS (Mohr, Goodkin, Islar, Hauser, & Genain, 2001). If the depression occurs only after MS, with no personal or family history of depression, then it's likely that the current depression has a neurochemical basis. Some studies have suggested that the depression associated with MS is a bit more recalcitrant to evidence-based treatments such as cognitive behaviorial therapy (Mohr, Boudewyn, Goodkin, Bostrom, & Epstein, 2001; Mohr & Cox, 2001). Furthermore, it may not be self-limiting without treatment (Mohr & Goodkin, 1999). Even though the depression and MS may have a neurochemical link, it is still important to treat the depression as aggressively as one would in any client. Knowing the depression history and relationship to MS might help the clinician, however, in expecting a longer treatment period, setting realistic expectations, and being more patient when assessing results.

Sometimes the temporal relationship between a disability and depression is conjoined, especially when there is early onset of both the disability and persistent depressive disorder (dysthymia). The developmental history will have elements of each, and disentangling the two might not change the treatment plan at all. For example, in the case example of Sam (see Chapter 3), Sam had polio when he was 2 years old and persistent depressive disorder for about as long. The two are so intertwined that causation is really moot. But as often happens, the depression became attached to early-onset disability issues. For example, Sam was taught that he had to be as good as other children, do all they did, and not complain or cry, despite falling, fatigue, and pain. These lessons became part of his core schemas and, hence, part of his depression, and the depression in turn was linked in his mind to having a disability. The result was that Sam believed that both were immutable, when in fact the depression was treatable, even if the disability was not "curable."

Diagnosis and treatment planning for co-occurring disability and mental disorders can be complicated by the disability. There is the danger of overshadowing (as discussed previously in Chapters 1, 2 and 7), when the presence of the disability overshadows the existence of other mental conditions (Reiss, Levitan, & Szyszko, 1982). This can happen, for example, with substance use disorders. Symptoms may be erroneously attributed to the disability, or medication misuse may be masked because it is being used legally, or people may feel sorry for the person and not want to confront the substance use. If the substance use began as a pain-management technique, relinquishing the substance may be difficult.

Diagnostic overshadowing also occurs when physical symptoms are attributed to mental disorders (Van Nieuwenhuizen et al., 2013). In emergency rooms, the physical health of persons with mental disorders may be adversely affected if the medical issues are viewed as mental conditions. The can be especially pernicious for persons with disabilities, whereby the medical issues are jointly attributed to mental disorders and the disability, both of which overshadow other medical conditions. One study documents the delay in diagnosing a 42-year-old man with schizophrenia with MS (Hayhow, Gaillard, Velakoulis, & Walterfang, 2014). He had complained of a decline in cognitive functioning, paresthesia, falls, and heat sensitivity—all signs of a neurological disorder, but also possibly attributable to schizophrenia (e.g., the paresthesia could be a tactile hallucination). It was several years before he received the diagnosis of MS, as the schizophrenia overshadowed the medical condition.

Diagnosis can be affected by disability when assessment of symptoms is complicated by physical symptoms that overlap with psychological symptoms. Fatigue and concentration are two examples of symptoms common not only to depression but also to a variety of disabilities. It is not clear whether measures of depression should be altered to excise those items regarding symptoms that are possibly due to disability. To give one example, studies originally found that items on the Beck Depression Inventory (BDI) should be omitted when assessing depression in persons with MS (Mohr et al., 1997) but later found the BDI not to be confounded with medical symptoms (Aikens et al., 1999; Benedict, Fishman, McClellan, Bakshi, & Weinstock-Guttman, 2003; Moran & Mohr, 2005). It appears that people with MS self-corrected when answering questions on the BDI, comparing current states to their usual MS-related states (e.g., depression fatigue compared to their typical MS fatigue). (Results were less clear using the Hamilton Rating Scale for Depression, which is a clinician-rated scale; Moran & Mohr, 2005.)

Treatment may be altered by disability. For example, any treatment for mental disorders that utilizes homework would have to account for the disability-related limitations; that is, behavioral activation for depression would need to be realized within the physical and cognitive symptoms of the disability. Cognitive symptoms may require a slower pace, more repetition, built-in reminder systems, phone check-ins, and other compensatory aids. The combination of disability and paranoia is particularly pernicious, as those with visible disabilities do in fact encounter more stares and comments, which can fuel the paranoia. The bottom line is that any mental disorder can attach itself to disability issues, each exacerbating the other, and necessitate careful case formulation and subsequent treatment planning that incorporates both the mental disorder and the realities of the disability.

> Vernon is a 44-year-old African American man with insulin-dependent diabetes and war-related traumatic brain injury (TBI), being seen at a Veterans' Administration medical center, whose main treatment goal was to get a job. He uses alcohol daily, which complicates both diabetes and TBI management. The TBI affects memory and executive functioning. He presented in therapy as cheerful and upbeat, a persona he tried to put on in public. His initial distrust of the White male therapist meant he wouldn't admit to many symptoms or discuss his alcohol use; he hid his occasional homelessness and use of other drugs and denied any symptoms of depression. The therapist chose to disclose his own veteran status as one way to have something in common. He initially focused on Vernon's goal of employment by helping him list his skills and making a resume. In the sessions the therapist worked with Vernon on the computer to conduct job searches and complete applications. Although the therapist had doubts as to whether they would be successful in finding him employment, given the TBI, substance use, and homelessness, his honoring of Vernon's chief complaint helped Vernon feel more respected and worthwhile. When Vernon bungled an interview because he was drunk, it was several weeks before he would admit this to the therapist. But when he finally did, it opened the way for a discussion of his substance use and the effects of use on both his diabetes and TBI. Because this could be framed in terms of the odds of employment, rather than as a judgment of the therapist, it was more palatable as a topic for treatment.

Discussion Questions

1. How might we think about intersectionality? Is it a mosaic that, taken together, makes a whole picture? Is it logarithmic, such that each minority identity compounds the others? What is the effect on the person with multiple minority identities?
2. Why is there more literature on lesbians with disabilities than on gay men with disabilities?
3. Give a clinical example of overshadowing.
4. Why do families with disability have lower household incomes than that of comparable neighbors?

8   D-AT V: Disability Culture and Community

CLIENTS WITH DISABILITIES vary in so many ways that it may seem nonsensical to talk about similarities across such a diverse group. Not only are the disabilities themselves diverse (including physical, such as polio; systemic, such as multiple sclerosis [MS]; learning; intellectual; low vision; blindness; and hearing loss and deafhood), but even within a category of disability, and certainly across categories, disabilities vary along different psychosocial dimensions. Additionally, as discussed in the previous chapter, the disability occurs in a context of gender, age, race/ethnicity, and sexual orientation such that it cannot be considered—or treated—outside of its context.

Nonetheless, people with disabilities share similar experiences socially, politically, and economically and have a shared disability history and common experiences of prejudice, discrimination, stigma, and microaggressions (Hahn, 1993, 1996; Longmore, 1995). The concept of a disability culture is relatively new (Brown, 2002) and not entirely without its detractors, but it has been fairly well established in the literature (Gill, 1997; Gilson, Tusler, & Gill, 1997). A group affiliation may be important, as aligning with one's in-group is one mechanism for coping with discrimination, as evidenced by research on a variety of stigmatized groups (Jetten, Branscombe, & Spears, 2006; Schmitt & Branscombe, 2002; Schmitt, Branscombe, Postmes, & Garcia, 2014). One role of group identity is to protect the psychological well-being of its members (Cronin, Levin, Branscombe, van Laar, & Tropp, 2012). Disability culture is, in part, about identity, self-determination, and community (Gilson et al., 1997), a striving for wholeness and integration (Gill, 1997). Collective experiences of disintegration and segregation, and the rebellion against these, are elements of disability culture (Barnes & Mercer, 2001; Gill, 1997). Culture is in part about sociopolitical, economic, legal, and educational experiences (Peters, 2000), but it is also about music, art, history, humor, media images, food, and social connection. Gill (1997) talks about the different stages of disability identity as (a) coming to feel one belongs (integrating into society), (b) coming home (integrating into the disability community), (c) coming together (internally integrating sameness and differentness), and (d) coming out (integrating the self internally and in presentation. A central question she poses is, "How much do we wish to assimilate into a dominant 'parent' culture that judges our differences as defects? Can we claim citizenship and all the resources of the mainstream without losing the benefits of minority identity?" (p. 41).

Many researchers have struggled to define disability culture (Barnartt, 1996; Brown, 2002; Dupré, 2012; Finkelstein, 1987; Galvin, 2003; Gill, 1995; Longmore, 1995; Scheer, 1994; Swain & French, 2000), including how disability culture might be defined outside of the White mainstream in the United States (Devlieger, Albrecht, & Hertz, 2007; Eddey & Robey, 2005) or in other countries (Ingstad & Whyte, 1995; Reynolds, 2010). In my own version, disability culture has at least a dozen elements that unite people with disabilities, and two elements that are imposed on the group (Olkin, 2005). Herein is a description of some of the elements of disability culture and community. This discussion is followed by some questions that clinicians might use to inquire about a client's degree of knowledge of and affiliation with disability culture and community.

Defining the Group

Defining oneself as part of disability culture is really about identity, as a person with a disability. Think about how a heavy drinker might eschew the label of "alcoholic," because *alcoholic* is a word that contains more in it than a description—it also contains a definition of the self (i.e., one who cannot drink moderately or with control). Similarly, the label of "disabled person" or "person with a disability" carries with it connotations beyond the impairment itself. For example, someone might admit to having insulin-dependent diabetes, or fibromyalgia, or any one of a number of impairments, but not consider themselves a person with a disability. In fact, a review of National Health Survey Data 1998–2000 showed that as a group, Hispanics were less inclined to consider themselves persons with a disability, even if elsewhere on the survey they had indicated a specific impairment and sometimes even hospitalization within the past year for that impairment (Olkin, Abrams, Preston, Kirshbaum, 2006).

A key aspect of any cultural group is defining who belongs within the group (Barnes & Mercer, 2001; Zola, 1993). Disability culture has its in-group (people with disabilities, and often their families and those who have close ties to people with disabilities) and its out-group (everyone else). Within the in-group there is a shared identity (person with a disability or family member of a person with a disability) and affiliation (with the disability community). Having a disability is not a prerequisite for belonging, but having a good grounding in knowledge of disability and an intimate relationship with someone with a disability generally are two core requirements. Thus the disability community could potentially be quite large, as disability affects about 50% of all families. But as discussed earlier, it would not be accurate to say that everyone with a disability in him- or herself or who has a family member with a disability is part of disability culture. To consider oneself part of the disability culture requires believing that one is part of a larger group of people with disabilities, a group which shares some things in common.

Pride and Values

People with disabilities are subjected to daily prejudice, discrimination, stigma, and microaggressions (the hallmarks of the minority experience). In creating a disability culture one goal is to reverse this oppression experienced from without and turn the rejection, ostracization, and isolation into a positive sense of pride and belonging within the group (Hahn, 1988). It may be pride in the disability per se and the wisdom that it has brought with it, as well as the ability to withstand psychological slings and arrows. But the pride may also be in the culture and community. There is pride in the identity as a person with a disability, in the advocacy and activism, and in the common struggles and survival.

The idea of pride in disability can seem odd to outsiders, not a logical conclusion the same way one might be proud of being Russian or Colombian. It is exactly that expectation that makes disability pride so necessary. Being part of a denigrated group requires internal cognitive and emotional mechanisms to cope with that denigration. Finding meaning and pride in disability is one way to cope. The Deaf community was an early adopter of the pride bandwagon (as well as the insistence on being represented and led by Deaf persons). Now the concept of disability pride is more widespread and has reached throughout disparate communities that may never have heard of a disability culture and community. Nonetheless, disability pride is not the norm. Many clients may be confused by any questions about disability pride—"Why would I feel proud of my _____?" This is an area where it is important for the therapist to be completely neutral, to not to make any assumptions, nor convey anything that implies either that disability is a bad thing or that one must take pride in it.

There are specific attributes or goals that are valued within the disability community. Obviously, comfort with disability is one of these, as well as being accepting of others' disabilities. There is also a norm of inclusion, which means making accommodations for impairments that are different from and even more stigmatized than one's own. Within the disability community there is a strong emphasis on good advocacy skills, both on a personal level (getting what you yourself need) and on behalf of the community (e.g., making sure a conference is held in an accessible venue) and society in general (e.g., promoting certain policies and laws). Pride can lead to activism.

> Jenny is a 15-year old Chinese American girl with autism spectrum disorder (ASD) and very high intelligence. She excels in math and language but has trouble with social cues, friendships, and navigation in the daily world. She found an ASD discussion site online and through it the notion of pride in ASD as a condition that is different but not defective. In therapy she questioned this over and over, struggling to understand how something that had marked her as different throughout almost all aspects of her life could be something of which she should be proud. It wasn't until the therapist suggested she read some first-hand accounts of ASD (e.g., Temple Grandin, *Thinking in Pictures*, 2009) that she started to get a glimmer of the idea of ASD community pride. But she did not feel an affinity with people with other types of disabilities, and the therapist did not push this idea at all.

Shared Concept/Model of Disability

Of the three models of disability (moral, medical, and social), the disability community mostly adheres to the social model, in which disability is seen as a social construct and the problems related to disability are mostly from social, economic, political, and interpersonal barriers. Thus advocacy and activism are valued. Within the disability community there are thought leaders who emerge with new ideas that push the boundaries of concepts of disability. Currently, such leaders are arguing that the social model alone does not capture the entirety of disability experience (see discussion in Chapter 6).

It is not uncommon to have a client with a disability who is excellent at advocacy for the greater good of the disability community but not able to be an effective advocate for him- or herself. This seeming paradox may reflect the remnants of the negative aspects of the moral and medical models of disability that individuals have internalized. If the person was raised with stigmatized views of impairment as a defect and otherness, it can be hard to overcome these messages, especially when they are amply reinforced in the media (see discussion of movies in Chapter 6). Then, when starting to embrace a disability identity and learning about the social model, it may be easier to act for the disability community as a whole than for oneself. Possibly acting for a public good is viewed as altruism; acting for oneself is viewed as entitlement.

Shared Social and Personal History

In disability culture familiarity with laws and regulations are important communal ties. Persons with disabilities share membership in a "protected class" (according to both federal and state laws; see Miller, 2008). These protections are defined in federal laws (e.g., Individuals with Disabilities Education Act, the Rehabilitation Act, Americans with Disabilities Act) and in specific state laws governing implementation of these federal laws. States play an enormous role in the interpretation and implementation of laws. For example, someone might assert that a bathroom is "ADA compliant" but this is fairly nonsensical. The ADA specifies that bathrooms should be accessible but does not articulate how this is to be accomplished. It is generally state architectural boards that write prescriptive regulations (e.g., turning radius, slope of ramps).

People with disabilities share a collective history, much as do African Americans, or Jews of Eastern Europe. That history helped shape a world view. The disability civil rights movement, which had a coming of age in the 1970s, affected the collective mind of the disability community, much as Stonewall and ActUP affected the gay community. The independent living movement is newer than other civil rights movements in the United States, and this infancy is reflected still in the group by social ties—knowing someone who knows someone who was at a public protest (at the Capitol steps crawl, for example), or personally having met one of the leaders of the movement (e.g., Ed Roberts). This relative recency also means that disability rights have not taken hold in general society, and thus the disability community is still very much engaged in gaining basic rights, such as access and integration. For example, at many annual meetings of the American Psychological Association (APA) attendees who use scooters or wheelchairs are to use separate transportation to get to the various APA venues. This segregation would be unthinkable for any other minority group, but is allowed as necessary for those with disabilities. This unremarked upon system is legal (the ADA requires accommodations that work, not necessarily the accommodations that the person or persons with disabilities desire) but socially disgraceful.

There is often a chasm between laws and implementation of laws. For example, a federal requires gas stations with more than one attendant on duty to pump gas for customers with handicap placards or license plates, at the self-service rate. However, very few gas stations have more than one attendant on duty, rendering the law fairly useless. But while pumping my own gas one day, I had a 15-minute conversation with a man with a disability (also pumping his own gas) about access, disability laws, gas stations within the greater area, etc. We had a common bond immediately just by virtue of an obvious limp and pumping our own gas. Discussion of rights, laws, and accessibility are frequent ways of bonding with others in the disability community. Such discussions do not rely on the interlocutors identifying themselves as part of the community; virtually everyone with a need for accommodations has experienced the frustration found between laws and implementation.

In addition to the shared sociopolitical history, there are similarities in personal histories—events such as hospitalizations and surgeries, medical traumas, separation from parents, exclusion, always being picked last for teams, being the exception or the misfit, the *one* with the disability. Trading these stories and memories—often macabre, painful, catalytic—is one way that members of the disability community learn about and get close to each other.

The Arts

Culture includes art, music, literature, and humor. These are emerging areas for the disability community. Some artists are little known outside the disability community, such as photographer Pedro Hidalgo, performer David Roche, poet Cheryl Wade, and writers Anne Finger and Kenny Fries. Others are very well known, such as the writer Ved Mehta and violinist Itzhak Perlman. To be included in this group does not mean only that the artist or writer has a disability, but that the disability is embraced in some way, whether it's Perlman's activism to make concert halls of the world accessible, or Cheryl Wades's poetry about bodies with disabilities. Other performers or artists may have disabilities (e.g., Jose Feliciano, Ray Charles, Andrea Bocelli), but this is mostly incidental to their careers and not translated into political or social advocacy.

Ways of eating are also part of disability culture. In a restaurant a patron with a disability might ask the kitchen to cut up the meat before serving it (because of hand limitations), or use a straw whenever drinking to avoid lifting a glass, or use one's fingers to feel food on the plate if blind, or use modified utensils, or have the menu read out loud. Meals out with a group of people with disabilities can be quite an affair, with service dogs under the table, personal assistants feeding someone, various specific requests being made to waiters, chairs removed for wheelchairs, or other wheelchair users transferring to a restaurant chair. All of this might seem quite normal and commonplace within the disability community but unusual and extraordinary to others. Just being seen publicly in a group with other people with disabilities might be a new experience for many.

Drive-through windows are the dream for those who have difficulty getting in and out of cars. Thus fast food may have played all too large a role in the disability community. "Have you ever thought about going to McDonald's as part of your cultural heritage? . . . For people with mobility disabilities fast food restaurants are a cultural icon" (Hahn, as cited in Brown, 2002). The increase in curbside service has opened up more food choices. Drive-through prescription pick-up or ATM access likewise has made things easier. Online shopping and banking and delivery services are a great boon to people with mobility or fatigue issues. And new sites with access features (e.g., all-accessible playgrounds or a paved walkway to a waterfall) become destination outings. These features of disability culture are less readily apparent to outsiders but are often traded information within the community.

Language

All in-groups develop their own language and code, which is one way to identify insiders. In the disability community there is a veritable alphabet soup of initials: pwd—persons with disabilities; TAB—temporarily able-bodied; HI—hearing impairment; ID—intellectual disability; LD—learning disabilities; ADHD, CP (cerebral palsy), MS (multiple sclerosis), SCI (spinal cord injury), TBI (traumatic brain injury), PPS (post-polio syndrome). *Blind* means little to no usable sight, versus *low vision* (VI—visual impairment); lower-case *deaf* indicates hearing loss, whereas upper-case *Deaf* indicates use of sign language and cultural affiliation with the Deaf community. In a *chair* or *chair user* refers to a wheelchair. These designations are convenient shorthand, but also are ways of identifying someone's currency with disability and sociopolitical affiliations as they relate to disability. If someone introduced himself by saying "I'm an MS patient," the listener would learn something by hearing someone refer to himself as a *patient* outside a medical setting. "Polio survivor" is different than "polios." Conversely, if someone said, "I will be coming in a chair" it does not mean they will be bringing a fold-up camping chair, and "I use crutches" is different than "I am on crutches."

There are derogatory words used about disability, and *disability* itself is used to describe problems (*a disabled tanker truck has disabled traffic leading to the bridge*). The most derogatory word is *crippled*. This is an old term for physical disability and is now experienced as denigrating, especially in its shortened version, *crip*. But like many other minority groups, the very word used against a group is embraced by the community and used with pride. Thus some might refer to the disability community as the "crip community." However, it is best not used by outsiders.

There are other words that carry negative connotations, including *the burden* of disability, *patients* to refer to people with disabilities in the community, *caregivers* without differentiating between family members and paid assistants, *the disabled* to refer to collective groups of people with disabilities, *wheelchair bound* instead of wheelchair user, *mental retardation* instead of intellectual disability, *spastics* as opposed to someone experiencing spasticity, and *medical-noncompliance* as opposed to someone make self-determination choices. While language is always evolving, these terms are quite out of favor in the disability community. However, within a specific disability group you might hear terms such as "I'm a polio" or "MSers." Often such terms denote a predominantly medical model of disability and, as such, suggest a primary identity with a specific disability group more than with the disability community at large.

Lest readers despair about language usage with their clients with disabilities, I want to be reassuring. It is better to speak freely than to be tongue-tied for fear of using the wrong words. Over time, clinicians can pick up the language of their clients. And hesitation to talk about disability, or a pause or lowering of the voice before using certain words, will be more noticeable than the wrong word choice.

Disability Norms

Such norms would be different for various disabilities; here I offer just a few examples. Missing chairs at tables or in auditoriums indicate consideration for those arriving in wheelchairs. Someone using crutches might carry something in his or her teeth because the hands are occupied. In disability gatherings people might omit shaking hands upon meeting because some people don't have hands or have no use of their hands or their hands hurt. Asking openly about another person's disability is okay, depending on how it is done. Doors might be left ajar so deaf persons can know to enter without knocking. Verbalizing to an audience or classroom "just speak out" would signal to blind attendees the norms of a group discussion. These are some of the more obvious examples and would be readily apparent to an observer.

But there are other types of norms that are more subtle and important to know when seeing clients, particularly adolescents with disabilities. Here I am using "norms" to mean more typical, not necessarily pathological, but still clinically relevant norms. One example is that teens with disabilities often have a very active imaginary life, owing to social isolation in real life. This fantasy life might include imaginary friends, or false back-stories about the disability, or fantasies of romantic partners. They may stay in relationships with ill-suited friends out of fear of not having other options. Or a teen might talk about doing an activity (e.g., playing on the football team) or being significantly independent in the future (e.g., traveling to Europe), which is completely unrealistic given the physical impairments. These fantasies or plans should not be thought of necessarily as a denial of disability nor as some loss of reality testing. They could mean that, but generally they do not indicate the same underlying cognitive processes as for a teen without a disability. More often I have witnessed my teenage clients outgrow the need for these cognitive aids and become more realistic about their lives. Of course, parsing the line between fantasy and incipient mental disorders can be difficult, but I urge caution here in moving too quickly without understanding the context of the fantasies.

Another clinical observation is that some persons with disabilities are surprised by their own appearance and movements. For example, someone who has limped from birth may not experience him- or herself as limping, because from the inside, walking feels the way it always has. But upon seeing oneself in the mirror, the limp might be jarring. Again, this may not reflect denial or disavowal of the disability. If what you see all around you are people walking without limping, then you might internalize that image for yourself and not experience how you walk differently from others. Or someone with a facial discoloration or scar might not have any internal experience related to the facial feature. For example, a person with a burn mark on her cheek that occurred in an accident 30 years ago might not remember the mark until someone asks about it. Then she might even have to think for a moment to know what the other person is asking about, because in her experience the mark is irrelevant.

> Leticia is a 14-year-old girl with cerebral palsy who uses a push chair and needs help transferring. She has only one friend, a girl who is depressed and who cuts herself. This friend willingly pushes Leticia in the chair around the friend's house and helps her get to the bathroom. Leticia has a fascination with dark, deathlike images and sometimes talks about having momentary impulses to put a scissors down her throat "just to see what it would feel like." She is obsessed with vampire shows and sometimes writes new stories continuing those she sees on TV, making herself a character in them. When strangers ask

about her disability she says she was born at 7 months (not true), or is one of sextuplets (also not true), or that she was in a horrific car accident. Leticia seemed to pride herself on being "weird." The therapist was alarmed at these tales and at Leticia's dark imagination and seemingly self-destructive impulses. But she received consultation from someone more experienced with disability, who suggested that Leticia seemed to be taking her imposed label of "weird" and making it her own. The clinician was advised to accept the outrageous stories and active fantasy life as products of the profound isolation Leticia had experienced since starting school. Nonetheless, active monitoring of suicidal ideation was recommended.

Role Models

Children growing up with a disability are not exposed personally to many role models of adults with disabilities or even peers with disabilities. The idea of mainstreaming—putting children with disabilities into the least restrictive environment—is to have children with disabilities predominantly with children without disabilities. This is a model that applies educationally, and for the most part children with disabilities do better scholastically when they are in classrooms with typically developing children (Zigmond, 2003). (A possible exception is deaf/Deaf children; Geers, 2003; Kluwin, 1993; Lang, 2002). But it may not be the best model socially—if children with disabilities see all around them children without disabilities, they may come to feel as the odd one, the one who is stigmatized, without a group identity or naturally occurring peer group. It is important that at some point children and teens with disabilities have the opportunity to be with other youth with disabilities. Some children are able to go to summer camp for children with the same or similar disabilities, a place in which their disabilities essentially became irrelevant. But not all parents think to do this, or think it is a good idea, or can afford it.

There are public role models of adults with disabilities, but disability often is not proudly displayed. Actors without disabilities usually are the ones who portray characters with disabilities (e.g., Eddie Redmayne in *The Theory of Everything*), even if all portions of the film included the disability (e.g., Daniel Day-Lewis in *My Left Foot*). (And Academy voters love to reward actors who portray disability: e.g., Dustin Hoffman in *Rain Man*, Colin Firth in *The King's Speech*, Geoffrey Rush in *Shine*, Tom Hanks in *Philadelphia* and *Forrest Gump*, Al Pacino in *Scent of a Woman*.) In these cases, imitation may convey that disability is a role, and that actors who really have disabilities are less desirable, even for roles that are about disability.

Some role models are reasonably well known, having started as disability activists but then selected to head government offices either in a state (Ed Roberts, who was head of the Department of Rehabilitation in California) or nationally (Franklin Delano Roosevelt; Judy Heumann, assistant secretary for the Office of Special Education and Rehabilitative Services in the Department of Education, during Bill Clinton's presidency). Others are well known in the disability community but less well known outside it (e.g., sociologists Irving Zola and David Pfeiffer; historian and disability activist Paul Longmore; British sociologist and theorist Michael Oliver). Prominent role models can help make disability a reasonable and expected topic of conversation. And affiliation with others with disabilities is important socially and politically (Dunn, 2015).

Often the role models are selected by outsiders, and the disability community may balk at having their role models chosen for them. Christopher Reeve is an example of a role model selected by outsiders to speak for the disability community. When he appeared on stage at the Academy Awards, in 1996, after his riding accident led to quadriplegia, his mere presence on the stage received a standing ovation. But he was controversial, as he focused on a cure for para- and quadriplegia, and because of his wealth, which allowed him options not available to most people with spinal cord injuries. Marlee Matlin is another example, though her use of voice and ability to lip read is very much outside the norm for the Deaf community (she is postlingually deaf). (The show *Glee* is both a positive example, for including an actress with trisomy 23, and a negative example, by having an able-bodied person portray someone in a wheelchair.) Like most minority groups, the disability community would prefer to pick their own spokespeople and for those persons to have the disability, not to simply portray a person with a disability.

The absence of prominent role models is problematic for children with disabilities, as peer modeling is important. The more the peer is like the child (Schunk, 1987) and the more the model is congruent with the child's style (Lockwood, Jordan, & Kunda, 2002), the more powerful the model. The lack of role models also is a problem for parents raising children with disabilities, as well as for teens with disabilities to learn about their own social group. Given the absence of role models, it can be helpful to suggest films and documentaries for clients to watch and then discuss them with the therapist (or watch them together).

For the teen Leticia described earlier in this chapter, watching the documentary *King Gimp* (1999) over the course of a few sessions was painful but helpful to her. The documentary followed Dan Keplinger, a boy then man with cerebral palsy more severe than Leticia's, from age 13 to about 21. It was important that the therapist had previously seen the film and discussed it with someone knowledgeable about disability, as this helped the therapist understand some of the disability subtleties depicted before she viewed it with the client. This included the role of the mother as a strong advocate (which Leticia also had), the ability to live independently (which Leticia desired but wasn't sure was possible), resilience in the face of attitudinal obstacles, the greater independence a power (versus manual) chair afforded, and the fact that the protagonist is a White male (which opened a conversation about gender and disability).

Therapists may have to help clients connect with disability groups. But as seen in the clinical example at the end of Chapter 6 (Gupta and Lakshmi Singh and their son Devin), some families will not want to connect publicly with disability groups. However, most will want to do so if it can be done privately, out of the public eye. Thus it is helpful if clinicians know about various resources, both those that are readily identifiable (e.g., support groups sponsored by Kaiser or national organizations, local centers for independent living) and those that are less visible. It can be challenging to find the less visible resources, and it may be necessary to make many phone calls to do so (e.g., to resource room teachers, to principals, to local clinics). Some therapists might not feel this is part of their job, but I would argue that it is a part of disability-affirmative therapy. Many families and clients with disabilities would not know how to go about finding resources, or may not want to be identified during the search, or may be overwhelmed with multiple daily life stressors. Having a therapist who does some paving of the path ahead can enhance the therapeutic relationship and be of great service to families. The bottom line is that for children and teens with disabilities, having role models is an important aspect to a positive integration of disability into the self.

Concerns in Common

Communities often are united around issues and concerns, and this is also the case for those with disabilities. Commonalities within the disability community include a focus on physical access, attitudinal barriers to equity, civil rights for persons with disabilities, relevant laws, problems with chronic un- and underemployment, poverty, access to good medical care, and finding and financing appropriate assistive technology. Conversations may focus on these issues often, which to outsiders may seem like an overfocus. But imagine if you were someone whose skin was, say, orange. If you were in a group discussing where to go for dinner, it would be natural for you to ask if the restaurant allowed people with orange skin. You would notice orange people in movies and television, on the street, in the neighborhood.

Similarly, disability can be a lens through which the world is seen, as (lack of) basic access and social (un)acceptance are such key parts of daily life.

The things that other, non-disabled people say and do in the presence of disabled people (i.e., microaggressions, or "death by a thousand cuts"—Nadal, Issa, Leon, Meterko, Wideman, & Wong, 2011) are another common topic. People with disabilities may tell these stories as a way to receive support, to take control of what seems uncontrollable (other people's reactions), to put a humorous spin on them, to bond with disabled peers, and to feel understood.

Others concerns in the disability community relate to sociopolitical issues that are seen as directly relevant to persons with disabilities, such as prenatal testing (focused on testing for conditions that many in the disability community already have) and death-with-dignity laws (will people with disabilities be seen as a drain on resources and pressured to die?). Regardless of one's personal beliefs, the community as a whole might take a political stance that upholds the dignity of the disability community. The political is personal, however, when a client is faced with these difficult situations (a terminally ill family member; a pregnancy), and personal choices may not mirror political choices, creating cognitive dissonance for the client.

Expertise

If you want expertise about, say, Asian American issues, or lesbian agendas, or Muslim belief systems, you generally seek out someone from that community who has such expertise. In contrast, persons with disabilities have been so devalued that they are rarely assumed to be experts on disability. Instead, the field is dominated by able-bodied persons, and such is the invisibility of disability in professional fields that this domination is rarely questioned. But of course people with disabilities have developed expertise. Who better to know whether a bathroom is really accessible, what the legal rights of persons with disabilities are, the latest literature about one's own specific disability, or where to get assistive technology repaired than a disabled person? But persons with disabilities often are not asked for input. (I couldn't help but wonder about this when staying in a hotel recently; the wheelchair-accessible room had a light switch that was foot operated, a problem that would have been obvious to any wheelchair user.)

This expertise does not come with the disability as a package; someone with a new diagnosis will not know automatically about resources, assistive technology, or accessibility. What they do know is how the disability affects them personally. But they may need help finding where to get a car altered, which scooter is good for travel, how to go through airport security in a wheelchair, key words to use to demonstrate "medical necessity" for insurance companies, or who gives discounts on shoes for different sizes on each foot. These are the hidden costs of disability, but they are so hidden from those without disabilities that usually it takes an insider to locate the information. The disability-affirmative therapist will be proactive in locating sources of information for and with the client.

Assistive Technology

Assistive technology (AT) (discussed in Chapter 4) can be simple (a modified fork), unobtrusive (a plastic ankle or foot orthotic), or readily apparent (a wheelchair) and costly (a van with wheelchair lift). Prices vary tremendously, but as soon as an item is labeled as a medical device its costs are considerably higher. An example is the small, 1 by 2 inch piece of foam used as a filter on CPAP machines for treatment of sleep apnea, which costs $25 from a medical supplier; buying foam at a hardware store and cutting it to size costs about $3.

Some AT is classified by insurance companies as *durable medical equipment* and subject to higher copays or exclusion. For example, it is common for insurance to cover a wheelchair but not ramps or lifts or an attached holder for crutches. Furthermore, insurance usually limits the vendors to be used, which in turn limits the options of brands and types of AT. The process of getting AT takes much of the choice away from the consumer, and studies show that this tends to disempower the consumer and make it more likely that the AT will go unused (Philips & Zhao, 1993; Riemer-Reiss & Wacker, 2000; Wessels, Dijcks, Soede, Gelderblom, & De Witte, 2003).

Using AT affects the user's body image. For someone whose onset of disability was in childhood, AT can bring back unpleasant, even traumatic memories. An orthotic might remind the person of a heavy metal full-leg brace; buying shoes might remind the person of ugly corrective shoes; using crutches or a cane can be a reminder of previous surgery. So adopting the use of AT may have many layers of meaning to the person and is rarely a simple transition. Additionally, the use of AT visible to others will immediately change most social interactions in ways both subtle and overt. Different AT has different social connotations and evokes different interpersonal reactions (e.g., a white cane versus a service dog), and these may need to be parsed in therapy before a person can experiment with AT.

Interestingly, those with earlier-onset disabilities are more likely to adopt AT than those with later-onset disabilities (Kaye, Yeager, Reed, 2008; Olkin et al., 2006). This makes sense, in that the person with early-onset disability has to make only one transition in body image (body with disability → body with disability + AT), whereas the person with later-onset disability has to make two transitions (ablebodied → body with disability → body with disability + AT)

Once AT has been selected, actual usage requires not just physical but emotional components (Bates, Spencer, Young, & Rintala, 1993). Once adopted, the AT often becomes integrated into the person's body image and boundaries (Lund & Nygård, 2003). These boundaries must be carefully preserved—the assistive devices become a part of the personal space. Just as you wouldn't go up to someone and start feeling their glasses, scooters, crutches, canes, wheelchairs, and communication devices are defined as parts of the body. The AT functions as an extension of the self, performing tasks with the person. The therapist should treat the AT as part of the person's body and not move or touch it without awareness of what it means to touch a client's body.

Lastly, adoption of AT can change dynamics and roles in the family. Someone who needed assistance with a task may be able to perform it independently with use of an AT. This can have both positive and negative repercussions in the relationship with the former helper. Anticipating such reactions can be helpful, as well as inviting a family member to join a few sessions.

Group Definition

People with disabilities are seen as a group, much the way people of various ethnicities are combined under the term *ethnic minorities*, despite tremendous inter- and intragroup differences. The media may use the term *the disabled* without modification or more explicit explanation and presume shared attributes across disabilities. This is bad enough in the media, but alarming when it occurs in professional literature. Research often conflates many disabilities with important differences, and then reaches conclusions that are overgeneralized to all people with disabilities. Although there is more attention to this in recent times, a search of professional journals in the past 10 years for the term "the disabled" still yields over 11,000 articles.

Conversely and ironically, there is also the reverse problem, wherein each condition is treated separately. Many books on rehabilitation and psychology of disability have chapters titled with names of specific disorders. These discuss each disorder as a separate entity with little attention to the overarching experience of being a person with a disability that cuts across diagnoses. Such attention to individual disorders is necessary at times, but not to the exclusion of the general experiences of stigma, prejudice, discrimination, and microaggressions that cut across disability types. Additionally, the robust hierarchy of acceptability of disabilities also should be acknowledged, wherein some disabilities are more stigmatized than others (Antonak & Livneh, 1995; Deal, 2003; Olkin & Howson, 1994; Schmelkin, 1984; Westbrook, Legge, & Pennay, 1993; Yuker, 1983, 1988).

An analogy may help readers understand the seeming contradiction of people with disabilities being lumped together as one group while commonalities across disabilities are ignored. Imagine a book that examines psychosocial factors in Whites and non-Whites. First, the presumed norm is Whites, against which everyone else is compared. Second, the category of non-White is so ridiculously broad as to be meaningless. Then imagine another book that has chapters labeled with specific Asian cultures: Japanese, Chinese, Vietnamese, etc. In its specificity, this book ignores some commonalities across Asian cultures, commonalities that readers of each chapter might not notice. Both books are helpful, but neither is satisfactory on its own. What we need is to switch between macro- and micro-perspectives, going into details about a specific culture in one area, pointing out commonalities in another area. Similarly, talking about the disabled as a monolithic group shows commonalities but ignores intragroup differences; focusing only on specific disabilities one at a time ignores broader experiences.

As those in rehabilitation are fond of saying, when you know one person with a disability, you know *one* person with a disability. So therapists will have to toggle between their general knowledge about disability experiences and the particulars of each client with a disability they see.

Conclusions

"Cultural competence" is the catch phrase of our times, and disability culture is no exception (Balcazar, Suarez-Balcazar, & Taylor-Ritzler, 2009; Eddey & Robey, 2005; Mackelprang & Salsgiver, 2015; Stone, 2004). Psychologists understand that they best serve clients when they are familiar with the world of the client, including the client's culture. But learning about disability culture is not easy. Disability culture, like disability itself, often is hidden from the mainstream. Disability is not a topic most people are comfortable talking about, and is one in which psychologists receive little training (Olkin, 1999; Olkin & Pledger, 2003). This chapter includes a very brief description of disability culture, albeit from only one person's perspective. It cannot be understood as the final word, or as speaking for all persons with disabilities, or adequately representing the tremendous diversity in the disability community. But that is the most important lesson of all—persons with disabilities share some commonalities, but also myriad differences. As in any therapy, the more you understand the ways your client is like other clients you have seen, but also the specific ways he or she differs from anyone else, the better able you will be to develop a case formulation that fits the individual you have in front of you.

Sources of disability culture can be found at centers for independent living, in magazines geared toward specific disabilities, in disability events (films, comedians, arts)—anyplace where groups of people with disabilities might gather. Many clients have their first encounter with disability culture when attending college, through the office of disability services. Such offices are often run by people with disabilities, hold disability awareness events on campus, have familiarity with varieties of accommodations, and are gathering places for students with disabilities. Of course, not everyone goes to college, or asks for accommodations once in college. And waiting for the client to raise the issue may not be effective, because clients cannot know to ask for something they don't know exists. Thus it may be up to the therapist to introduce clients with disabilities to their own disability culture and community.

Discussion Questions

1. What are five elements of disability culture? What makes them *disability* culture?
2. What are some ways you could help a client discover the disability community?
3. Who are some contemporary role models for children and adolescents with disabilities? What do they model?
4. Go to a medical supply store. Notice prices, types of equipment, customers, location—what do you notice?

9   D-AT VI: Microaggressions—Experiences and Effects

PEOPLE WITHOUT DISABILITIES often believe that the hardest part of having a disability is the physical limitations the disability imposes. But most people with disabilities say that the hardest part has to do with the reactions and behaviors of other people. These might be in the form of the negative attitudes, false assumptions, and interpersonal stigma (Olkin, 1999). The physical aspects might be annoying—a blocked curb cut, a counter that is too high, the difficulty of carrying a cup of tea when using crutches, the lack of audible signals at street light crossings—but these don't usually feel personal. As such, they might not have the same emotional impact as the slings and arrows from others. In this chapter I explore the nature of these slights, and their potential effects on clients with disabilities.

A term for these slights is *microaggressions*, which are unintended slights or social cues by members of a dominant group to members of minority groups about their minority group status, and which make the minority group member uncomfortable (Sue, 2010). Sue defined microaggressions as communications that are brief, commonplace, and verbal, behavioral, or environmental, that contain a hostile message, derogatory meaning, negative slights, invalidation, or insults. These are directed toward a person because of his or her belonging to a marginalized group. Examples might include being overlooked, underrespected, devalued, or being complimented for something counter to stereotype. Sue asserts that when microaggressions occur, they tend to be highly emotionally charged situations, even if neither the aggressor nor the oppressed person is consciously aware of the microaggression. It is important to remember that microaggressions are not generally intended as hurtful—the perpetrator might protest, "But I meant well!" or "It was just a joke." But intent is not the critical variable, as microaggressions are often unconscious manifestations of prejudice, stereotyping, and stigma. They have the effect of offending, wounding, or slighting the recipient. A tell-tale sign of experiencing a microaggression may be heightened emotions.

A few examples can help illustrate this. Suppose Sally, a White woman in her thirties, uses a manual wheelchair since a spinal cord injury when she was 10 years old. If someone says to her, "What happened to you?" she would reply, "I was in a car accident when I was 10." So far this is factual. But if the person then says, "Were you wearing a seatbelt?" there are several implicit messages in this question. First is the need of the questioner to distance him- or herself from the possibility of a similar accident—*if you weren't wearing a seatbelt, but I do wear a seatbelt, then this thing that happened to you won't happen to me.* Inherent in that statement is the idea that being *like you* is a bad thing, something to be avoided. A second message in the question is about blame—*did you do or not do something that caused you to have this injury?* Thus, not only is the person saying that being like you is undesirable, but you are to blame for being like you. If this interchange were a rare occurrence, it might still be bothersome. However, suppose such an interchange happened almost every time you met a new person, or had an encounter with a bagger at the grocery store, the shoe saleswoman, the person next to you on the bus? Then the effect might be even greater, because of its repetition.

This example is a relatively small microaggression with great power, because of the frequency with which it is repeated. The next example is the opposite, a powerful microaggression that happens infrequently but has lasting impact. An Asian man and his pregnant White wife, both of whom are blind, are going to their first appointment with an ob/gyn physician to confirm a positive home pregnancy test. They are excited about this planned pregnancy. The doctor suggests that they might consider terminating the pregnancy because of the difficulty for a child being raised by two blind parents. The doctor does this by asking the couple how they plan to ensure the baby's safety, an unusual question so early in a pregnancy. The doctor then says, "I am happy to go over different options for you about your pregnancy." When the husband says, "What options?" the doctor stammers and hesitates. In this case the message is that these will be unfit parents simply because of their blindness. And this message will reverberate throughout the pregnancy. As new parents, they have their own usual doubts, but now these doubts are compounded by an early outright suggestion that they are not fit to be parents. Imagine the power if the wife's mother, for example, were to ask, "How do you plan to prepare for the baby?" It might be an innocent question, but it might trigger memories of the earlier doctor's question, and the wife may overreact to her mother's question. And if indeed the mother, or anyone else, is conveying doubts about the couple's adequacy as parents, even if infrequently, the net effect of these microaggressions regarding such an important event is great.

You might be thinking to yourself that surely no one in this day and age would be so thoughtless, that these examples are very rare. I assure you, they are not. Even if only 1 person in 100 were to say something that could be construed as a microaggression, think how little time it takes before you have interacted with 100 people: at the gas station, at red lights, in the grocery store, getting the newspaper, chatting with friends, going to work, commuting, shopping for clothes—it takes almost no time. And in my experience, it takes far fewer than 100 people before encountering a microaggression.

Not all microaggressions come from strangers. Perhaps some of the most hurtful ones come from family members. The mother who questions her daughter's ability to have a child, in the previous example, would probably do more harm than a stranger's comment could. If parents never discuss the child's disability it becomes unmentionable. If a brother's house is inaccessible but family events are held there, the person with a mobility disability can become disenfranchised. A long-running family joke may have an undercurrent of negativity. Failure to learn sign language or to take time to repeat things at the family dinner table can exclude a deaf person or one with hearing loss. These can be powerful experiences, and that power can be compounded when the experience is not acknowledged, not spoken about, made light of, or blamed on the victim ("you're too sensitive").

Microaggressions also can be perpetrated by the built environment. Instances might include lack of a curb cut, store aisles that are too narrow, check-out counters that are too high, menus that are not in Braille. Although there are microaggressions from the built environment against other groups, the ubiquity of the difficulties in the built environment means that those with disabilities are likely to encounter multiple such microaggressions in the course of a day. A new type of microaggression is the proliferation of emotional-support animals. It devalues the services that certified and trained service animals provide and can create the impression of such animals as merely pets that are nice to have around. (For a good discussion of the issues see Younggren, Boisvert, & Boness, 2016). Environmental microaggressions, in conjunction with those perpetrated by other people, can add up to considerable stressors for the person with a disability.

Unfortunately, the application of the concept of microaggressions towards those with disabilities is relatively new, and data on the experiences of microaggressions among people with disabilities are scarce. Two studies were reviewed in Chapter 2 (Keller & Galgay, 2010; Timm, 2002); Table 9.1 shows a comparison of the domains found by Timm (2002) and Keller and Galgay (2010). What is interesting is the

TABLE 9.1
EIGHT DOMAINS OF MICROAGGRESSIONS

Domains from Keller and Galgay (2010)	Message	Deeper Meaning	Example	Dimensions from Timm (2002)
Denial of identity or of disability experience	Aspects besides disability are ignored. Disability experiences are minimized.	When I look at you all I see is disability. Your disability experiences are no different from others'.	"I don't think of you as disabled." "Everyone has a cross to bear."	Depersonalization and minimizing
Denial of privacy	Personal information is required.	Your disability makes you open to intrusion.	"What happened to you?"	Violation of personal space and privacy
Helplessness and infantilization	People frantically try to help you, without you asking or needing it. You are treated like a child.	You cannot do anything for yourself; people with disabilities are helpless, just like children. Thus disability is a catastrophe.	"Let me help you reach that." "Let me do that for you." Patting the person on the head.	Helplessness and avoidance
Secondary gain	I am good for helping you; I expect thanks and praise.	You are a charity case just by virtue of your disability.	"We installed an automatic door opener for you!"	
Spread effect	Everything about you is presumed to be due to or about the disability.	You are not normal. You are "special." You are invalidated by your disability.	"You must have better hearing because you cannot see."	

(*Continued*)

Table 9.1 (*Cont.*)

Domains from Keller and Galgay (2010)	Message	Deeper Meaning	Example	Dimensions from Timm (2002)
Patronization	You are praised for almost anything.	Your ability to do ordinary things despite a disability is seen as remarkable.	"You are so brave, or inspiring."	Depersonalization by aggrandizing
Second-class citizen	Your rights are denied as too expensive, too much trouble, not worth it for just you.	You expect too much. Your rights are not important to me. Why waste money on a devalued person?	"Yes, we have a TTY around here somewhere, but no one who's deaf ever calls us."	Violation of civil rights
Desexualization	Attractiveness as a partner is denied.	Disability is unattractive, thus the person with disability is unattractive. Who would date someone like that?	"Was your wife blind when you married her?"	

Note: Compiled from Keller and Galgay (2010) and Timm (2002).

overlap between the two, despite different methodologies. Timm used factor analysis to derive her domains, and Keller and Galgay used consensual qualitative research. Another study found that when students with disabilities were primed for their disability identity, they had lower rates of autonomy-related thoughts, compared to when they were primed for their college student identity (Wang & Dovidio, 2011). Microaggressions prime people for their disability identities and thus may foster more dependent behaviors.

A recent study (Olkin, Hayward, Schaff, & VanHeel, 2016) suggests three more domains of microaggressions in addition to what Keller and Galgay found (2010). The first additional domain is the need for the person with a disability to manage the affect of the other person. That other person might be thinking: *Your disability is making me anxious, but I am not supposed to be anxious around disability, so let me show you how fine I am with disability, by telling you about someone I know who also has a disability.* This *some of my best friends* type of response, in which someone tells you about a remote person in his or her life who had a disability (perhaps the same type as yours, but perhaps of a different type), is an effort to show how comfortable that person is with disability, but in the process is actually showing the opposite. This then calls on the person with the disability to make it more comfortable for the other person—it demands some sort of response from the person with a disability, or the situation gets even more uncomfortable for both parties. But the dilemma for the person with the disability is that acknowledging the story in any positive way is self-denigrating, as if saying, *yes, all of us people with disabilities are alike—if you know one person with a disability, then you must know me as well. Also, I can tell from your story that you are comfortable with disability; thanks for sharing*. Conversely, to react negatively derails whatever was the task at hand, while shifting the focus onto the negative affect of the person with a disability. This can lead to charges of being oversensitive, or unreasonable, or maladjusted to the disability.

The second additional domain is about blaming the person with the disability for his or her disability. For example, a doctor asked a patient with polio how the patient got polio. The real meaning behind the question was not *how is polio transmitted?* but rather *didn't you get the vaccine?* When the patient explained that he got polio before the vaccine came out, the doctor visibly relaxed (*move along people, nothing to see here, just a routine case of pre-vaccine polio*). The ways in which questions are phrased about disability can suggest a causal link: *What did you do to yourself? How did this happen?* By blaming the disability on the person, it serves to distance others, who then judge the person with the disability as faulty in some way.

The third additional domain may be encountered more by women than men with disabilities. It is the denial, usually by professionals, that anything is actually wrong with the person; they attribute symptoms to anxiety or hypervigilance or psychosomatic causes. Telling a woman "but you look fine" or "you're too young to have a disability" or "try to relax more" are examples of this type of microaggression.

All of the microaggressions share a similar impact, in that they highlight the disability, diminish the person him- or herself, and suggest inferiority. We can assume that the accumulation of microaggressions would have a negative impact on people with disabilities. However, although there is documentation of the negative health effects of microaggressions for people of color, women, and people who are gay, lesbian, or bisexual (Sue, 2010), the effects of microaggressions on people with disabilities have not been studied. However, the Olkin, Hayward, et al. (2016) study suggests that women with disabilities encounter a high rate of microaggressions that they find bothersome or very bothersome (see Figure 9.1 for the top four most frequent microaggressions and the top four most bothersome microaggressions). Thus it would seem that there are a few types of microaggressions that get repeated in many ways under different guises, but which have similar underlying messages. As Timm's (2002) earlier work suggests, some of the types of microaggressions will have a greater impact on psychological well-being than others. Further work to replicate her findings is needed.

FREQUENCY	BOTHERSOME
Someone downplays the effects of disability on your life.	Your right to equality is denied.
Someone assumes you need help.	Someone downplays the effects of disability on your life.
You are praised for doing almost anything.	Someone ignores everything about you but your disability.
Your right to equality is denied.	Your sexuality or value as a romantic partner is denied.

FIGURE 9.1 The top four most frequent and top four most bothersome microaggressions experienced by women with disabilities.

Reprinted from Olkin, R., Hayward, H., VanHeel, G., & Schaff, M. (2016). *Women with disabilities: Experiences of multiple identities, microaggressions, and stigma.* Paper presented at the Western Psychological Association, Long Beach, CA.

Clinical Applications

How might a clinician inquire about microaggressions with a client? There is no set way to do this, but if the topic hasn't arisen in its own course, one option would be to use the Disability Hassles Scale (Box 9.1). Or the domains of microaggressions, described earlier, could provide a structure for noticing and reporting on experiences of microaggressions. But one should be cautious—in both the Timm (2002) and Olkin, Hayward, et al. (2016) studies the participants described a heightened awareness of microaggressions during the study. Focusing on them produced more negative affect, as people realized how many daily microaggressions they ignore or shove underground, just to get through the day. And for clients with hidden disabilities who encounter microaggressions, admitting to the microaggression is complicated by the invisibility of the disability. Admitting to the microaggression is disclosing the disability.

It is likely that clients will become more attuned to microaggressions as these are discussed in treatment, and dysphoric or angry affect may result. This doesn't mean that the topic should be avoided, but clinicians might consider warning clients about this heightened awareness and the possible effects on mood. This is likely to be a temporary situation, with mood returning to previous states rather quickly. It is helpful to remind clients that not all battles can or should be fought. Remedies for chosen battles might include assertiveness in confronting others, legal action, complaints to the relevant agency, discussion with sympathetic others, or actively choosing to ignore a microaggression.

So what is the point of holding a magnifying lens on microaggressions? There are several reasons. First, some clients might not realize the connection between these microaggressions and their current dysphoric, anxious, or angry mood. Making the connection can help refute the idea that feelings come out of the blue. This in itself can be a relief. It also gives a pathway to address the mood states.

Second, most clients with disabilities can use some help deciding which microaggressions warrant further responses. It is not possible to tilt at every windmill, so judicious decision-making is called for in sorting through the myriad microaggressions, to take on only those that are worth it—and that one is likely to win. There is no point getting up a full head of steam at, say, the TSA agent who wants you to take off your leg brace and put it through the scanner. You can insist on a body search instead, but telling the agent he is ignorant about disability is not going to prove worthwhile. Nor does it pay to yell at the saleswoman that the immoveable credit card device at the checkout counter is too high—she has no power to change it. But calling over the manager may be worth the time and effort, as the manager could

BOX 9.1
DISABILITY HASSLES SCALE

Hassles are small events that can be irritating or annoying. The following lists a variety of experiences in which people with physical disabilities may feel hassled.

Instructions: Click the "Yes" box if you have experienced any of these events *in the past month*. If you check "Yes," please answer the additional question that asks about your perception of the event or how you experienced it. If you did not encounter a particular event, check the "No" box. Please answer all items.

(*NOTE*: on this version the response choices are only indicated for the first item, but in the version given to participants, response choices would be indicated for the first 40 items.)

In the last 30 days:
  1. I heard a joke about disability.
     No, I have not experienced this in the last 30 days.
     Yes, I experienced this event in the last 30 days. I experienced this event as . . . (*check one of the boxes*)

Positive	Neither Positive nor Negative	Slightly Negative	Moderately Negative	Very Negative	Extremely Negative
☐	☐	☐	☐	☐	☐

  2. I was treated as if I were not there, and my companion provided answers to questions or about my needs.
  3. I was unable to access public transportation.
  4. Family or companions were treated as my caregivers while in my presence.
  5. Others downplayed or minimized my disability (e.g., "I never think of you as disabled").

In the last 30 days:
  6. A stranger asked me about my disability.
  7. I was told where to sit because of my disability or assistive device, when I did not inquire.
  8. I was unacknowledged by strangers (they looked away, failed to address me, did not make eye contact).
  9. I had to wait for a passerby to open a door or assist me in getting something I could not reach or find.
  10. I was asked inappropriate questions about my sex life relative to disability.

In the last 30 days:

11. I needed to repeatedly call or wait for accessible transportation that did not come.
12. I was mistaken for someone else (another person with a disability).
13. Strangers jumped aside or parents pulled their children out of my way in an exaggeration of my need for physical space.
14. Strangers approached me and began describing their medical problems to me in great detail without my asking.
15. I could not participate in a family or social event because the location was not accessible or easy to get to.

In the last 30 days:

16. I waited for or found a handicapped accommodation (e.g., parking space, bathroom stall, dressing room) occupied by a non-disabled person.
17. Others told me that my adaptive equipment (e.g., scooter, wheelchair, crutches, canes, guide dogs) looked like fun.
18. A stranger was unwilling to share a sidewalk or hallway with me.
19. While I was in a public space, a stranger attempted to help by seeking assistance for me, but without my request (e.g., "the disabled person needs help").
20. I was unable to use a ramp, elevator, or bathroom because access was blocked.

In the last 30 days:

21. A store or restaurant clerk told me that there was not enough room for me in their establishment.
22. I was told I was inspirational or courageous because I have a disability.
23. Someone moved my assistive device without my permission (e.g., cane, crutches, wheelchair, scooter) because they believed it was in the way.
24. I was denied my request for reasonable accommodations for my needs related to disability, either at work or school.
25. I left a store or restaurant because there was not adequate accessibility or room for me to get around.

In the last 30 days:

26. I was addressed as "you people" or other labels reflecting on my disability.
27. I was greeted or approached by a stranger whose first comment was about my disability.
28. Another person volunteered to complete my sentence or answer questions for me and was not asked to do so.

29. I was unable to reach or find amenities in public restrooms or items in a store due to inaccessibility.
30. I was unable to obtain or find accessible housing because of my disability.

In the last 30 days:

31. I was told I could be healed by religion.
32. Others downplayed or minimized my experience as a person with a disability (e.g., "everyone has something wrong with them" or "everyone has experienced that; it's not so unusual").
33. Strangers volunteered to provide physical assistance (e.g., grabbing my arm or assistive device, lifting or pushing my wheelchair) without asking me if I needed help.
34. I was unable to use an elevator because it was broken or too small, or the buttons were not labeled or reachable.
35. I was treated differently from my colleagues or friends (e.g., denied equal opportunities or participation in events).

In the last 30 days:

36. When asking for accommodations, I was told, "Gee, no other disabled person has asked for that!" or "It's never been a problem before."
37. I was unable to navigate in a public space because signs were poorly designed, hidden from public view, not set in Braille, or missing.
38. Strangers violated my personal space by touching me without asking (e.g., patting my head or shoulder, touching my leg, patting my guide dog).
39. I was told by someone that if they had my disability they would not be able to handle it as well as I do.
40. An authority figure (e.g., instructor, supervisor, employer) discussed my disability or need for accommodation without my permission in front of peers.

---

41. Think about the above hassles you experienced during the last 30 days. Taken all together, approximately how often did you experience any of these?
    About 1–2 times per month.
    About 3–4 times per month.
    About 5–6 times per month.
    About 1–6 times per week.
    About 1–2 times per day.

About 3–5 times per day.
About 6–12 times per day.
More than 12 times per day.

42. How typical has the past 30 days been for you in regard to the number of hassles you experienced? The number of hassles I experienced in the last 30 days is:

Much *less* than what I usually experience.
Average or fairly typical of what I usually experience.
Much *more* than I usually experience.

Note: Reprinted with permission from Timm, R. (2002). Disability-specific hassles: The effects of oppression on people with disabilities. *Dissertation Abstracts International,* ProQuest Microform UMI #3069626.

make the change. However, it takes emotional energy to do this, so again, is there a rubric for deciding when to fight the good fight?

A third reason to discuss microaggressions is that some clients have trouble containing the rage that these microaggressions can trigger. Especially for those with any history of trauma, a microaggression can evoke feelings of helplessness, which then are countered by rage, which feels more powerful in the moment. But the rage can endanger friendships and intimate relationships, alienate otherwise helpful citizens, and even endanger the person with the disability by engendering a hostile response in return.

Application of Microaggressions to Sam

The first two main presenting problems for Sam were dysphoria and rage. He was having incidents of rage about twice a week. Anger was easily triggered through real and imagined events. The real events were the problems with inaccessibility in his neighborhood, an elevator in his building that broke down frequently, constant upkeep issues with his wheelchair, and general problems in daily living. The imagined events were developed through mind-reading. For example, if the wheelchair repair service did not return his call quickly, he believed that no one would help him, that they didn't care if he couldn't leave the house without his wheelchair. This spiraled into feeling abandoned and helpless, which turned into rage. Then, when the hapless wheelchair repair guy did call, Sam would be foreboding and quickly escalate to yelling. Often he would hang up on someone or trounce out of a store. When he first started treatment he maintained that these outbursts worked; they got other people to do what they should, they got things accomplished. But the price of his outbursts was enormous shame. The shame would cause him to retreat into himself, making it harder to mobilize the energy to get things done, and leave him feeling more depressed and helpless. It took many iterations of this pattern to show Sam that his rage, which felt energizing, powerful, and satisfying in the moment, was self-destructive. One week, a truck was parked halfway on the sidewalk, blocking his path. He got so enraged that he drove his wheelchair full speed ahead anyway, getting jammed between the truck and a fence, the wheels off the ground, completely stuck. This was a great metaphor for the harm his rage did to himself. Then there were two tasks to undertake together. The first was to find alternate ways to respond to microaggressions. The second was to develop a rubric for deciding what battles to fight. Anger was not necessarily the right signal that he should take action. In fact, it might be the very thing mitigating against taking action. Other factors were more important: (a) Is this important to me in my daily life and functioning? (b) Is there a possible solution? (c) What are the consequences to me if nothing changes? (d) Is there anyone who might help me with this issue? (e) How likely am I to be successful?

Discussion Questions

1. Can an able-bodied heterosexual Euro-American male experience microaggressions? Why or why not?
2. How might you affirm the microaggression experiences of a client with a disability?
3. What are some ways to help a client prioritize which microaggressions to respond to?
4. What is an example of someone downplaying the effects of disability?

10 D-AT VII: Friendships and Social Interactions

HOW DOES THIS *person feel about my disability?* This is a core question in most interactions between a person with a disability and any other person. It may not be a conscious question, but it looms there nonetheless. The answer to this question may cause the person with the disability to feel more, or less, comfortable, though he or she may not know the reason for the feelings. Many core concepts related to the social interactions between persons with and without disabilities come from social psychology (Dunn, 2015). One factor is the *fundamental attribution error*, in which observers attribute behaviors to characteristics of the person being observed, rather than to the environment. Thus when a person who is blind bumps into a box on the floor, an observer is most likely to think the person is clumsy or not adjusting well to blindness, rather than to think the box is out of place. Attributes are then assigned to the blind person, who is the problem (rather than the misplaced box). "Person-focused judgments are most likely to occur when a behavior is identified as atypical" (Dunn, 2015, p. 7). Since people with disabilities are generally thought of as atypical, as are their behaviors (e.g., using a cane for guidance), others readily attribute the behaviors to characteristics of the person (e.g., clumsiness). It takes a good deal of contrary evidence to erode this perception (e.g., seeing the blind person successfully navigate many other, even difficult, venues).

We already saw in Chapter 1 that disability often is a defining characteristic, one which is considered more salient than other characteristics of the person. This has been referred to as *essentializing* disability (Dunn, 2015), or the disability becomes the essential and even the sole quality of the person. Interestingly, this seems to erode normal boundaries such that non-disabled people feel free to make personal comments about the disability directly to the person with a disability. In the vignette that follows, the male onlooker made a valuative statement to the woman using a scooter (more in Chapter 11 about why he felt he could do this):

> Rebecca is a woman in her thirties with a mobility limitation who uses a scooter when shopping. She was in the shoe department of a large department store and wanted to reach a shoe on display. She could not quite reach it from her scooter so she stood up and walked two steps to get the shoe. A male customer observed this and said to her "Good for you!" and punched the air in front of him in triumph.

How the person with the disability feels about social interactions changes with the nature of the social interaction and the relationship with the other person(s). Therefore, in this chapter I consider different types of social settings and types of relationships in the context of disability. More intimate partner relationships are discussed in Chapter 12.

Strangers

WITHOUT DISABILITIES

People without disabilities would be surprised at the frequency with which strangers engage with a person with a disability directly about the disability. Often these encounters are infantilizing or demeaning (Dovidio, Pagotto, & Hebl, 2011). As discussed more fully in Chapter 9, many of these engagements are microaggressions. They might take the form of a question ("What happened to you?" or "How long have you used a wheelchair?") or a comment, often intended as a compliment ("You drive that thing really well" to someone who uses a scooter or wheelchair or "You get around really well" to someone who is blind). It could be a comment on the assistive technology ("Bet that thing was expensive" or "That's a great turning radius"). The intent of these questions or comments is often benign, but the effect is to make the interaction *about* disability. The only other place where we see this kind of commenting on a personal attribute is to pregnant women ("When are you due?" "How are you feeling?" "What are you hoping for?"). To see such comments from a different perspective, imagine going up to a person of color and immediately commenting on his or her ethnicity ("Which kind of Asian are you?" or "I couldn't help noticing you are Black"), or saying to a woman you meet on the elevator, "You must be really empathic." Such comments are clearly an invasion of personal space and boundaries.

The social psychology behind such intrusions is discussed briefly in the introduction to this chapter. What is important clinically is not just how often these kinds of events happen to the client, but the client's response to them. Consider the following different potential responses to the question from a clinician: "Do strangers ever make comments to you about your disability?" (a) "I don't mind, I like educating people about disability, it's part of the job"; (b) "I tell them to go to hell"; (c) "It depends on my mood, but mostly I just ignore them and turn away"; (d) "I am so embarrassed; this is why I don't go out in public much." As we can see from these varied responses, what the client thinks and feels and then how the client behaves is an important part of the clinical picture. Handling remarks from strangers is a large part of the experience of disability and can be a source of ongoing stress. It could be helpful for readers to ask any of their friends or acquaintances with visible disabilities about how often these experiences occur, to help understand their ubiquity. Clinicians should not minimize the frequency or the impact of these encounters.

CHILDREN

Younger children are more prone to stare or point, ask impolite questions, be curious, and be ignorant of disability etiquette. This is to be expected, and generally it is not the behavior of the child that is at issue but the response of a parent to the child's behavior. This response might be to yank the child away, to do nothing even when the child is invading personal space or doing something dangerous, explain in a scolding way that what the child asked is impolite, or give factual information in a neutral way. All of these are likely to occur, and as with other encounters with strangers, it is not as important what the children and adults do as it is how a client responds to these events. Generally, I have found clients to be more patient with children and their curiosity than they are with adults, but not always. A client, especially a client without children, may find interactions with children that are about the disability to be more direct and, hence, more unnerving.

STRANGERS WITH DISABILITIES

Interactions with strangers with disabilities or their family members take on a different meaning than interactions with nondisabled strangers. Strangers with disabilities may be signaling solidarity (e.g., a head nod between two people using wheelchairs). Sometimes they might be watching closely to see how something is done (e.g., which line to go through security at the airport). Sometimes they want information about the specific assistive technology (e.g., a van lift) a person uses, how much it costs, where it can be purchased, or whether it works well or not. Even if this kind of encounter happens frequently, I have found most people with disabilities to be very generous with their time and knowledge to others with disabilities. It is difficult to access information about assistive technologies, repair places, best entry points into buildings, handicapped parking accessibility, etc., and the best source of information is other people with similar accessibility needs. Nonetheless, it is important for the therapist to ask about such encounters and how the client responds to them. The answer is part of a picture of the client's comfort with disability and affiliation with disability culture and community.

Not all encounters between strangers with disabilities are positive. Some of the worst offenders can be other people with disabilities. Receiving a negative response from someone else with a disability can hit particularly hard. For example, one blind mother was told by a woman with a similar disability that she had no right to be a parent, that it would harm her child. Hearing this from another blind woman was devastating to the client.

Another type of negative encounter could be when seeing someone with a similar disability but whose symptoms are worse. For example, someone with multiple sclerosis (MS) who is ambulatory may be upset seeing a person with MS walking slowly using a cane, or using a wheelchair and with a colostomy bag. Such encounters can remind the client of what could happen in the future, and how the client responds to this uncertainty is a critical factor in understanding the coping style, the role of the disability in the person's current life, and his or her beliefs about the future. But avoidance of such encounters may keep the client from pursuing support groups, going to disability information or entertainment events, learning about resources, and becoming familiar with disability culture and community.

DOCTORS AND OTHER MEDICAL PROFESSIONALS

Medical professionals see clients for diagnosis and ongoing care, as well as during any injuries or changes in symptoms. For some disabilities there is a protracted period between first noticing symptoms and getting a diagnosis (e.g., Arruda, Petta, Abrao, & Benetti-Pinto, 2003; Chan, Felson, Yood, & Walker, 1994; Hadfield, Mardon, Barlow, & Kennedy, 1996). In many studies the delay was even longer for persons of color (Hadfield et al., 1996; Pachman et al., 1998; Richardson et al., 1992), although a study of autism spectrum disorder diagnosis did not find differences in delay to diagnosis across gender or ethnicity (Wiggins, Baio, & Rice, 2006). There may be delay in diagnosing older persons as well (Burgmann et al., 2006; Webb et al., 2004), possibly because symptoms are attributed to age. At any rate, this time between experiencing symptoms and getting a diagnosis seems to be an extraordinarily stressful period. Often the person undergoes tests to rule out serious and scary disorders. Then, once there is a diagnosis, the client might not know anything about the disorder. So when the diagnosis is finally made, the person is especially vulnerable to any overt and covert messages he or she receives. During such times of heightened emotion the client is more attuned to the comments of the healthcare professional. Often clients remember exactly what a doctor said when they were given the diagnosis. It might have been an off-hand comment, but its impact endured. If it was a positive statement it might be something the client holds onto for hope. If it was a negative statement it can breed resentment and anger toward medical professionals and impact future willingness to engage in collaborative treatment.

Cultural factors are going to be very salient here (Mattingly & Garro, 2000), in terms of illness beliefs, how the client views medicine in general, and ways in which the client interacts with specific medical professionals. Some clients bifurcate care into traditional (western) and nontraditional (complementary and alternative) modalities and feel differently about each. Others might value one over the other or hold each to be helpful. Psychotherapists may be seen as part of the medical field. For example, Sam surprised me by viewing me as a medical professional, as a doctor, and transferred his negative views of medical doctors and low expectations onto me. Thus he expected me to be perfunctory, uncaring, and ignorant about polio and his particular struggles, as this was his (interpreted) experience with prior doctors.

A client's subjective experiences of encounters with strangers will affect his or her initial response to the therapist. This is true of all clients, but with clients with disabilities there may be added layers. That core question is ever present: *How do you see my disability?*

Casual Acquaintances

People who encounter one another daily or weekly are not strangers, but also are not friends. They might be co-workers, or the person who always waits on you at the grocery store, or your mail carrier. The fact that these people will be seen again and again means that the response of the person with the disability has to account for that fact. Yet these casual acquaintances may be even more likely to comment on the disability. This might be to show how much they are okay with it (and thus proving the opposite with comments), or to be able to ask questions about disability from someone they know, or to try to establish a closer relationship, or for many other reasons. What is key here is how the person with the disability reacts to these types of encounters, because the reaction involves juggling myriad social requirements simultaneously. Imagine, for example, a co-worker who seems to comment on the disability or an assistive device frequently, or who touches the assistive device inappropriately, or who parks illegally in the handicapped spot ("I was just running in a for a moment"). The responses to these microaggressions have to be balanced by the nature of the relationship (e.g., gender, ethnicity, power differential, hierarchy) between the person with the disability and the co-worker, as well as what the future relationship might be.

Friendships

Friendships between persons with disabilities and others is a somewhat understudied area but one that is important (Geisthardt, Brotherson, & Cook, 2002). Friendships among children with disabilities have received more research attention than have friendships of adults with disabilities. For children with disabilities, sports is one vehicle of establishing friendships between children with and without disabilities (Martin, 2006; Martin & Smith, 2002), but friendships may not flow readily from proximity (Amado, 1993; Ash, Bellew, Davies, Newman, & Richardson, 1997; Lippold & Burns, 2009) and are not without some conflictual elements (Martin & Smith, 2002). Ethnic and cultural variables obviously also are important in childhood friendships (Turnbull, Blue-Banning, & Pereira, 2000). Severity of disability will be another factor affecting development of friendships (Gordon, Feldman, & Chiriboga, 2005). Friendship patterns may differ for children with and without disabilities. A study on children with and without learning disabilities found that both groups were equally likely to have friends in lower grades, but children with learning disabilities retained fewer friends and were more likely to have friends with learning disabilities (Estell, Jones, Pearl, & Van Acker, 2009). Social media may help foster friendships for children and adolescents with disabilities as it allows some accessibility issues to be bypassed (e.g., transportation, inaccessible housing) and the role of disability is downplayed (Guo, Bricout, & Huang, 2005; Huang & Guo, 2005; Sharabi, 2007).

Adult friendships often involve the disability in many ways, and it becomes a part of the relationship. Young adults with disabilities tend to be less involved in community activities than those without them and are less likely to be employed; these are two characteristics that can limit opportunities for making friends (Newman et al., 2011).

An analysis of friendships between women with and without disabilities cited three elements of friendships: opportunity (to get to know someone with a disability), reciprocity (the ability of each to give to the other and the ways that disability affects this process), and responsibility (how friends relate to each other and to the world; Fisher & Galler, 1988). In relating to the world, there are many social activities that can be affected by a disability. From accessible housing to selecting restaurants (whether for access or food restrictions), to the choice of leisure activities, to management of fatigue, there are multiple avenues of incursion of the disability on the friendship. And if this does not happen in some mutual way, if the friends never consider the needs of the person with the disability, it places a burden on the person with the disability and, perhaps, a limit on the level of friendship.

There are many ways a friend might respond to a disability. The friend might relate to a person's disability as irrelevant (*I don't think of you as a disabled person*). But by negating the disability, the disability is also activated (as in the expression "don't think about the elephant in the room"; Lakoff, 2014). For some people with disabilities this may feel acceptable. I suspect this may be the case for disabled persons who have not incorporated the disability into their self-identity and who prefer the company of non-disabled peers. But for other people with disabilities hearing this may feel like a denial of their reality, much like saying "I don't see skin color" is a denial of the realities of racism.

Another possible response of friends is to feel admiration or awe for the person dealing with a disability. This could become apparent in many subtle or not-so-subtle ways. For example, someone might say, "I can't believe all you do," or "It's amazing how you cope with things," or "I really admire you"—all of which seem like compliments but may contain a meta-message about the disability, that the lowered expectations for the person with a disability have been exceeded. This can be very complex because, in truth, the person with the disability probably is dealing with more barriers, stigma, and discrimination than the non-disabled person. But the idea of people with disabilities being inspirational for others is a common stereotype (more about this in Chapter 11).

Sometimes clients will complain that a friend does not understand their needs (for access, or rest, or pain management). It can be useful then for the therapist to inquire as to if and how the client has explained his or her needs to friends. Sometimes the problem, which seems obvious to the person with the disability, is not so obvious to others. So the client might have to be very explicit about his or her needs. For example, a friend may ask to meet for breakfast, and the client with a spinal cord injury might have to wait for an attendant to help with morning routines before being ready. If the client just responds that lunch would work better, then the problem is likely to resurface. Instead, the client might say that morning meetings are not possible and explain why.

But if there has been adequate explanation (and given more than once), then it might be time to examine the friendship. This can be one of the harder areas for the client with a disability to face. If there has been a history of ostracism or limited opportunities for friendships due to the disability, then the client may feel obligated to keep as friends anyone who is willing to befriend the client. For example, a client with cerebral palsy who had a lot of speech involvement that could make him very difficult to understand was friends with an alcoholic because the alcoholic was willing to befriend him. The alcoholism itself did not mean it was a bad friendship, but other factors related to this did make it so (e.g., chronic lateness, inability to be counted on, not showing up). Willingness to *tolerate* the disability is not a good enough basis on which to build friendships. And, ultimately, being in social circles wherein the disability is not supported is likely to erode the mood and self-esteem of the person with the disability. Exploration of the process of friendship making and keeping may need to be incorporated into the therapy.

My experience and that of my clients with disabilities is that many of the closer friends have had some personal experience with disability, in themselves or in their immediate family members. I have been surprised to learn of some of these experiences; the friendships formed without my knowing about them. What did come across was a basic sense of being comfortable with disability, a willingness to learn more about it and my experiences of it, a ready incorporation of disability needs into any activities and plans, and openness to frank discussion. But many clients find it difficult to talk with friends directly about disability. For example, in our case example of Sam, he would climb the stairs to a second-floor apartment rather than tell his friends they had to meet at a more accessible location, and then he would resent the friends for not anticipating how hard stairs are for him. Another client with paraplegia would cut outings short in order to go to her home bathroom rather than ask for help accessing public restrooms.

As friends age, the previously able-bodied friend may acquire some limitations. This might initially seem to bridge some of the gap in understanding, and it can, but this can bring new problems as well. The client with a disability may feel that those with new impairments complain too much, or think they know what it's been like for the client, or don't have sufficient coping skills, or have such minor impairments that they are overreacting. And two friends with different impairments and limitations can have conflicting disability needs—one needs to walk more, the other to walk less; one needs to eat more calories, the other to be gluten-free; one is trying to stay more active, the other to reduce activities.

There are differences between aging and acquiring a disability, and having a disability and then aging. These differences can be reflected in many ways in the friendship and must be mutually navigated. The therapist should not make any assumptions about disability, friendships, and aging, but rather inquire into these areas and how relationships are affected.

> Ben, a 52-year-old gay male, uses a wheelchair. When he visits a couple he has known for many years their young son always asks to ride on his lap in the wheelchair. Ben readily complied when the child was 2 and 3 years old, but as

the child grew he found it more taxing and irritating. The parents expected Ben to set limits because it was his disability, and Ben expected the parents to do so because it was their child. Therefore, no one said anything, until one day Ben got very irritated and said "no" very harshly to the boy's request. The boy ran off crying and there were hurt feelings all around.

The Therapist

There is not much research on the relationship aspects of psychotherapy between able-bodied therapists and clients with disabilities. (For some work in this area, see Cornish et al., 2008; Frankish, 2009; Grzesiak & Hicok, 1994; Livneh & Antonak, 2005; Wilson, 2003.) Much of what does exist tends to focus more on therapists' skills than on relational aspects (c.f., Artman & Daniels, 2010). The American Psychological Association (APA) offers some suggestions on etiquette with clients with disabilities (APA, 1999), but they are not specific to psychotherapy. APA also has guidelines for assessment of and intervention with persons with disabilities (2012). There is one book of case studies of clients with disabilities, which does contain relational aspects (Blotzer & Ruth, 1995). The question should no longer be equity (of access to services) but effectiveness (Beail & Warden, 1996), although no data exist on accessibility of psychotherapy agencies and practices.

Therapy is fundamentally a relationship. When the client has a disability, the social intricacies of therapy are likely to be interpreted differently by clients with disabilities compared to clients without disabilities (Olkin, 1999). Small behaviors such as opening doors, putting out a footstool, shaking hands, looking someone in the eyes, billing procedures—basically anything that might be affected by the disability—can have different meanings for clients with disabilities than for those without disabilities. And those meanings will vary from person to person, so there are no absolutes to follow, with one exception: the therapist who is uncomfortable with disability will display this in subtle and numerous ways, and be unable to hide the discomfort, and thus must work on him- or herself to get to a place of comfort. Bear in mind that people with disabilities, like those with other types of minority and discriminated status, are experts at figuring out the answer to the central question: *how does this person feel about my disability?*

Conclusions

In this chapter I have raised some issues regarding the social interactions of those with disabilities and other people, parsing it by the level of acquaintance. This yielded many levels of interactions that could be important in assessing and understanding a client with a disability. However, I do not mean to suggest that all of these levels should be part of an intake or asked about in a protocol-like manner. Rather, they are aspects of the client's life that should be elicited and noted as one inquires about other areas. For example, when asking about work, there could be additional questions about relationships with co-workers. For some clients, especially adolescents with disabilities, making a diagram of concentric friendship circles (varying degrees of closeness) could be useful in eliciting how the friendships incorporate the disability. (This idea of intimacy circles comes from interpersonal therapy, e.g., Hill, O'Grady, Elkin, 1992; Strupp & Binder, 1984). One take-home message from this chapter is to obtain the information without prior assumptions.

The second fundamental message is that the relationship with the therapist has to differ from those frequently encountered by people with disabilities. Guidelines that apply for casual encounters may not apply for psychotherapy. For example, generally people with disabilities "should decide how, when, and whether any discussion concerning their disability will occur, how it will proceed, and how much they wish to disclose about the onset, nature, and consequences of their disability" (Dunn, 2015, p. 128). But this may not apply in therapy, a venue in which no topic is necessarily off limits. By asking directly about the disability, the therapist makes it a sanctioned topic and demonstrates comfort with discussion of disability. However, the answer from the client will give vital clues as to when and how to pursue the topic further.

> Isabella, a woman in her forties, was raised in a very poor village in Central America and moved to the United States when she was 19. She had polio as an infant, though her mother denied this, believing Isabella's partial leg paralysis and atrophy were due to poor nutrition. When starting psychotherapy, Isabella could not move into any productive conversation about goals or current problem areas. She needed to spend about five sessions talking about her childhood and the overwhelming fatigue she felt, and her mother's denial of her reality. This moved into discussion of the men in her life, who seemed to share the trait of taking advantage of Isabella and treating her poorly. She spoke about work, and the need to hide her disability to the greatest extent possible. For this therapy to get off the ground, the beginning had to be all about disability and the effect of the disability on virtually every relationship in Isabella's life.

This case of Diego contrasts with the case of Isabella:

> Diego, a man in his late twenties, had cerebral palsy. He had mobility limitations and walked with a limp, mostly to one side. He experienced fatigue

frequently but mostly chose to push through it during the week, catching up on rest on weekends. He was very social and well liked at work. When he began psychotherapy, he wanted to focus on his dissatisfaction with his job and other options for his career. The therapist asked several questions about the effect of the CP on Diego's relationships and kept trying to infuse it into the discussion of career choices. Diego quit therapy, feeling that he wasn't being treated as a person, but rather as a disability.

Discussion Questions

1. What is an example of *essentializing* disability?
2. A client who has a visible disability reports that a friend said, "I don't think of you as disabled." What are your reactions to this? How might you handle it if the reactions of your client are different from your reaction?
3. Go somewhere public and see if you can observe the interactions between a person with a disability and the public. What do you notice?
4. When you first interact with a client with a disability, what are some things you might want to pay particular attention to?

11 D-AT VIII: Affective Prescriptions and Prohibitions Imposed on People with Disabilities

THIS CHAPTER IS divided into three sections. The first section is a discussion of the affective prescriptions often imposed on people with disabilities. These are mourning and depression, gratefulness, and insightful. The next section considers affective prohibitions, namely anger and rage. The last section is a discussion of anxiety and trauma, as these often accompany disability, especially with certain types of disability onset.

Affective Prescriptions

Outsiders (i.e., those without disabilities) hold beliefs about what disability should be like—that it is a tragedy, a loss, a fate full of suffering. They then impose these beliefs on people with disabilities and expect the person with the disability to be in mourning (what has been called, in a classic paper, "the requirement of mourning"; Dembo, Leviton, & Wright, 1956). The disability is equated with loss, and loss must be mourned. This imposition of mourning protects outsiders' belief that disability is an awful condition, even a fate worse than death (as is often portrayed in movies; see Chapter 6). When disability is conceptualized as loss, and therefore must be mourned, then it is a small step to imposing a regimen for the mourning. That regimen was proposed by Dr. Elizabeth Kübler-Ross in her five stages of dying: denial, anger, bargaining, depression, and acceptance (Kübler-Ross, 1975; Kübler-Ross &

Kessler, 2014). These five stages became rapidly ingrained in popular culture. There are several issues here. First, these stages were a discussion about dying, not about loss or grief. Second, Kübler-Ross (1975) herself said that not all people went through these stages, and not necessarily in any order. Third, some have contested the value of thinking of stages of reactions to dying, loss, or grief (Friedman & James, 2008; Konigsberg, 2011). Fourth, for those with congenital or early-onset disabilities there is no loss; the disability is the norm for them. Fifth, the stages of response to dying was a *theory* that was not empirically based and has not stood up to scrutiny (Dunn, 2015). And sixth, believing that the response to disability requires a stage of depression means that the depression, a clinical condition, is normalized, and hence subject to being undertreated.

If disability is conceptualized as loss, it would follow that the greater the loss, the greater the mourning. But this is not the case: a response of depression is not correlated with the severity of the injury or disability (Dwight et al., 2000). (Note that MS may be an exception, since there may be a more direct physiological link between MS and depression; Chwastiak et al., 2002). Depression is more likely predicted by other variables, such as previous history of depression, level of pain (Von Korff, Ormel, Keefe, & Dworkin, 1992), poor sleep quality (Lobentanz et al., 2004), fatigue (Bakshi et al., 2000; Dwight et al., 2000), beliefs about pain (Galli, Ettlin, Palla, Ehlert, & Gaab, 2010), or discrimination (Turner & Noh, 1988).

Some studies do suggest that the lifetime prevalence of depression in people with disabilities is higher than for the general nondisabled population (Neese & Finlayson, 1996; Turner & Beiser, 1990; Turner & Noh, 1988). And presence of depression complicates recovery and rehabilitation, increases length of hospital stay, and reduces independence in activities of daily living (c.f., Lai, Duncan, Keighley, & Johnson, 2002; Silverstone, 1990). However, depression is not the modal response to disability (Elliott & Umlauf, 1991; Olkin 2004). A general estimate is that roughly 30% of persons with acquired disability will experience depression in the year after disability onset (Frank, Elliott, Corcoran, & Wonderlich, 1987; Heinrich & Tate, 1996; Lichtenberg, 1997; Turner & McLean, 1989; Weissman & Myers, 1978). For example, a large study compared community samples of people with and without disabilities and found rates of depression to be 37% and 12%, respectively (Turner & Beiser, 1990). But note that 63% of those with disabilities were not depressed.

The assumption of loss and thus mourning does a great disservice to people with disabilities. So strong is the presumption of mourning that persons with disabilities who are not depressed are often labeled as being in denial. And defining depression as normative in response to disability results in accepting a condition that can and should be treated as aggressively as it would be for persons without disabilities. Clinicians should, as always, assess for depression. And should they find it in a client with a disability, it should be one focus of treatment. But the absence of depression should not be taken as failure to properly "mourn" the disability, nor as denial of the disability.

Suppose the person with the disability is not depressed—how then are outsiders to reconcile the belief in disability as misfortune and tragedy, with the apparent evidence to the contrary? The disabled person is then elevated to a superhuman status, someone who is exceptionally brave, courageous, inspirational, plucky, miraculously able to get up each morning and go about the day, ever with a smile, despite the disability. This elevation in status results in a paradox: the affective prescription is to both be in mourning and yet eternally brave and plucky. For example, a study of pain and disability in osteoarthritis measured three mood states: anxiety and depression, or cheerfulness (van Baar, Dekker, Lemmens, Oostendorp, & Bijlsma, 1998).

This affective prescription is often seen in newspaper accounts of a person with a disability who has achieved something newsworthy. The disability is paramount in the story lead-in, and the person is described as having good humor, a ready smile, cheerfulness, and always a kind word. In these stories the person with the disability has done something positive, such as winning an award, or donating time, or achieving something. For example, in a story describing a winery start-up by a woman with MS and her husband, the new enterprise is seen as an outgrowth of her need to find a different kind of work from her previous employment, rather than as a change in direction that other adults choose. The woman is described as never succumbing to the MS, and her mood as upbeat and positive.

Conversely, when the person with the disability has done something negative, the disability is seen as a tragedy. This is more often the case when the disability is a psychiatric disorder. The disability is not only the defining characteristic of the person in the story, but the thing that made that person do what he or she did that was newsworthy. The message is that the particular disability leads to this kind of behavior. So if the winery started by the woman with MS and her husband failed, it might be ascribed to the difficulties of running a business by a person with MS (as opposed to the high rate of failures of new businesses, or increased competition in the field).

A different way to think about responses to disability, first suggested by Wright (1960), involves changes. These are enlargement of the scope of values, subordination of physique relative to other values, containment of disability effects, and transformation of comparative-status values to asset values. This model has been incorporated into a positive psychology of rehabilitation (Chou, Chan, Phillips, & Chan, 2013) and studied with various disabilities (Keany & Glueckauf, 1993; Melamed, Groswasser, & Stern, 1992; Soundy et al., 2012). Enlargement of the scope of values can mean learning to value things that were previously underappreciated. Subordination of physique means that the single value of the body is not decisive in determining one's value (Frick, 1985). Containment of disability effects is about the spread effect (see Chapter 4)—not allowing others to see disability as the sole or even defining characteristic. And transformation of comparative-status values to asset values means that things are no longer judged in relation to non-disabled norms. New ways of accomplishing tasks are not compared to able-bodied or previous norms, but intrinsically valued for their effectiveness. For example, using a wheelchair is not compared to walking, but is valued in its own right as an effective means of mobility and fall prevention.

There is yet another imposition on the characters of people with disabilities: this is to benefit from the disability by newfound learning, insight, and meaning. In fact, onset of disability may lead to introspection, re-examination, new appreciations, and deeper meanings. But assumptions that this has or should occur puts enormous pressure on people with disabilities. Furthermore, some clients with disabilities put this pressure on themselves, searching for meaning in random acts (e.g., a car accident that led to injuries). Wright (1983) differentiates between soul-searching (e.g., deriving deeper meanings from disability) to soul-torturing (e.g., fruitless efforts to answer the question of *why me?*). Other positive side effects, in addition to deeper meanings and truths, are the so-called perks attached to disability, such as designated parking spaces, or getting to be first in line, or not having to pay for parking. These "perks" are seen in isolation, without the contextual factors that make it necessary for someone to have a better parking spot, or without seeing the frequent misuse of such spots by non-disabled drivers. Seeing the perk without context makes it seem more special, and less deserved. Hence the ongoing debate in my hometown over why people with disabilities do not have to feed the meter when parking (in the crowded) downtown. Invisible are the statistics about un- and underemployment of people with disabilities, lower incomes and higher costs; the impossibility of going certain places if parking is too far; the need for van accessibility; the sequelae of many disabilities, such as pain and fatigue. Others might think, "It must be nice to get that [perk], I wish I could have that." But if shown the whole package of what comes with that perk, they would likely feel very differently.

Before leaving this section on affective prescriptions, there is one more that needs mentioning, which is the idea that the person with the disability is *lucky*. Someone who has a spinal cord injury from being hit by a drunk driver might be told he or she is lucky not to have died. Or someone who survived polio is said to be lucky to have survived. Or someone with one blind eye is told she is lucky she still has one eye. The irony is that this is said by people with two good eyes, who were not hit by drunk drivers, who didn't have polio. The message is that the person with the disability should be *grateful* for his or her "luck."

In sum, thus far, we see many affective pressures on people with disabilities, that is, what they *should* feel. They should go through depression, as an appropriate response to the loss of disability. If not depressed, this may indicate denial, or it may be due to superhuman qualities of the person. Those qualities require the person to be always cheerful, brave, courageous. They should feel lucky the disability is not worse, and grateful for the advantages accrued from disability.

> A therapist was seeing a 10-year old girl, Sarah, with muscular dystrophy, for some obsessive-compulsive behaviors. She had a loving family and was very close to her older sister, age 16. Toward the end of the school year the sister decided she would spend the summer at a pre-college art program. Sarah became occasionally teary when she thought about her sister being gone for several months, though she was not depressed or withdrawn. Nonetheless, her teacher called the therapist and reported how concerned she was about Sarah. She reported that Sarah was just not her "usual sunny self," and wondered if approaching puberty and boy-girl interest was making it hard for Sarah socially, as she would undoubtedly feel more rejected as a romantic partner. Thus a normative child response to an upcoming stressor was seen as an unacceptable alteration of Sarah's usual disposition. Even the slight dip in mood that she was experiencing was labeled as very problematic and related solely to her disability, not to the contextual familial factors.

Affective Prohibitions

The previous section discussed the emotions persons with disabilities are supposed to have. There is a reverse pressure as well: emotions they are not supposed to have. Chief among these is the prohibition against anger. Anger might be interpreted as denoting maladjustment to the disability, or not being grateful enough, or not appreciating how lucky the person is. In spite of the pervasive stigma, discrimination, and oppression that people with disabilities experience, anger is seen out of context from its social roots and attributed to personal characteristics (the primary attribution error).

A corollary of anger is rage. Rage might be defined as a more primitive and powerful emotion than anger. It has an intensity that denotes feelings of violence and loss of control. Clients with disabilities may experience rage at some of the injustices they have experienced. To use Sam as an example, he often experienced rage in which he would lash out at someone. It was not uncommon for him to get thrown out of stores or to make another person cry. For example, when he wedged himself in his wheelchair between a fence and a truck when enraged that the truck was partly on the sidewalk, he had to be rescued by a stranger, who must have wondered how it happened. Such seemingly self-destructive behaviors can seem inexplicable to others. However, they result from a combination of myriad daily reminders of being invisible or second class or unacceptable, plus difficulties with managing emotions. Some clients, like Sam, may be aware of their own rage ("I had another incident") and some may behave as if enraged without acknowledging the emotion.

Interestingly, most books on disability have the words *anxiety* and *depression* in the index, but few have *anger* or *rage*. What does exist regarding disability and anger seems to focus on the relationship between anger (expressed or suppressed) and pain (Duckro, Chibnall, & Tomazic, 1995; Greenwood, Thurston, Rumble, Waters, & Keefe, 2003; Kerns, Rosenberg, & Jacob, 1994; Moix, Kovacs, Martín, Plana, & Royuela, 2011; Sayar, Gulec, & Topbas, 2004; Tschannen, Duckro, Margolis, & Tomazic, 1992), teaching anger management techniques to persons with specific types of disabilities, such as intellectual disability (King, Lancaster, Wynne, Nettleton, & Davis, 1999; Rose & Gerson, 2009; Taylor, 2002), or as an effect from traumatic brain injury (Khan, Baguley, & Cameron, 2003; Prigatano, 1992) or dementia (Alexopoulos et al., 2005).

One of the few rehabilitation books that does discuss anger (Falvo, 2014) suggests that anger might be a result of perceived injustice at the injury, blame (at self or others), frustration, and/or "realization of the seriousness of the situation and the associated feelings of helplessness" (p. 15). The author suggests that rehabilitation could help people appropriately express anger and gain more of a sense of control over their situation and environment.

Discussion of rage appears in books in disability studies or by disability scholars who have disabilities themselves (c.f., Asch, 2002; Linton, 1998; Longmore, 2003; Morris, 1999), where rage is seen primarily as a result of social injustice (Barnes, Mercer, & Shakespeare, 1999; Gilson & Depoy, 2000). This is very different from the idea of anger as a stage of adjustment or acceptance, as discussed in the previous section. Rather, it is seen as a normative response to stigma, discrimination, prejudice, and exclusion. Nonetheless, clients often need help in understanding, titrating, and expressing anger and rage.

Anxiety and Trauma

Anxiety is a somewhat frequent concomitant of disability. It can be due to changes in body image, pain, side effects of medications, early experiences related to being a child with a disability, or trauma related to the disability onset (see Kennedy, 2012).

Anxiety is a natural reaction to threat, and disability can pose a threat to health, housing, finances, employment, socialization, and general well-being (Falvo, 2014). Many disabilities have uncertain courses, both for the future and from day to day, and that can engender anxiety as well.

Experiences directly related to the disability can be anxiety-provoking. Those with early onset might have experienced separation from parents during hospitalizations, baffling events without explanations, pain, messages about unacceptance of certain emotions ("just be a brave boy or girl"), scary medical procedures, medical stripping, even sexual abuse from staff or caregiving personnel (e.g., orderlies, paratransit bus drivers, sanitation staff). A later onset of a disability might be associated with a traumatic event (e.g., wartime, car accident). Additionally, as discussed previously, the period between noticing symptoms and getting a diagnosis can be extraordinarily anxiety-provoking for many people.

There are other sources of anxiety as well. There may be fears about personal safety, getting stuck somewhere, not being picked up by public transportation, cars breaking down, dropping the baby, dying, or increases in pain or fatigue. Assessment of anxiety can be complicated by its association with depression, pain, fatigue, and other disability symptoms (Smart, Blake, Staines, & Doody, 2012; Stebbings, Herbison, Doyle, Treharne, & Highton, 2010). Anxiety is often overlooked in primary care settings (Memel, Kirwan, Sharp, & Hehir, 2000; Weiller, Bisserbe, Maier, & Lecrubier, 1997). Just as depression seems to be both a result of and a risk factor for disability, it appears that anxiety carries a similar two-way relationship (Brenes et al., 2005; Gulseren et al., 2006; Lenze et al., 2001).

Many interventions are available for the anxiety associated with disability; it can be important for the therapist to address the anxiety directly (Lantéri-Minet, Radat, Chautard, & Lucas, 2005), as anxiety is associated with greater disability and poorer quality of life (Sareen et al., 2006). In some cases, education about the disability or its symptoms may alleviate the anxiety (Louw, Diener, Butler, & Puentedura, 2011). Improving pain self-efficacy (the belief that one is adequately equipped to manage pain) can be one way to reduce pain intensity, thereby affecting anxiety levels (Meredith, Strong, & Feeney, 2006). It should be noted that, whereas depression is associated with reduced compliance with medical treatment, the results regarding anxiety are more equivocal (DiMatteo, Lepper, & Croghan, 2000).

> Renee, a 14-year-old girl with spina bifida, uses a wheelchair. She does not like going to malls with friends because, if she had to go to the restroom, she needs assistance and does not feel her peers are trustworthy to help her with this. The therapist helped her plan very small steps toward increased independence. In sessions they behaviorally rehearsed certain activities that were potential

impediments, such as Renee getting herself over a 1-inch bump in a doorway. They discussed what to do in different problematic scenarios. A main focus was on Renee's ability to cope if there was a problem. The first attempt at going to the mall was made with Renee's mom sitting in the car in the parking lot reading, and available should Renee text her. This process of learning to predict, prepare, and practice had to be repeated for additional small steps in her life, often with many iterations.

In another example, an adult female client was anxious about airline travel, having never done before it with her scooter. She wanted to make this trip to her son's college graduation but but didn't know it could work with her scooter. Thinking about it caused her a great deal of anxiety, and she put off making reservations to attend this important family event. The therapeutic approach was similar to that with Renee: predict, prepare, practice. The therapist used cognitive rehearsal, walking through each step of the way—where to park, where to go if all the handicapped spots were taken, using the lift on the bus to the airport, getting through airport security without getting out of the wheelchair, ensuring early boarding, getting to the seat on the plane, getting the wheelchair once the plane landed, finding accessible transportation to the hotel. This rehearsal alleviated the anxiety sufficiently for her to make the trip.

Of course, not all therapists will know how to navigate travel with a scooter. Some homework and sleuthing may be involved, either by talking with someone with a disability who has traveled with a wheelchair or scooter, or by visiting the airport and observing, or by learning from other clients with disabilities their travel tips and techniques.

Conclusions

People with disabilities commonly experience pressure to conform, "accept" the disability, and deny the realities of oppression. As such, attention to these emotional constraints is a vital part of disability-affirmative therapy. People with disabilities are subjected to emotions that are imposed, the paradox of being either in mourning or superhuman and inspirational, being told one is lucky, the expectation of gratefulness, coping with depression or anxiety, and experiencing others' negative reactions to anger and rage. The therapist will need considerable skills and agility in helping clients to recognize, acknowledge, and manage (which is not the same as suppress) emotions.

Discussion Questions

1. Why is it so unacceptable for people with disabilities to be angry?
2. You have a client who seems depressed since a recent exacerbation of her multiple sclerosis symptoms. How might the MS affect your assessment of this client?
3. How might the MS in the client who started a winery affect the treatment plan?
4. Look at your local newspaper, in the "Living" or "Leisure" (or equivalent) section, and find a story about a person with a disability. How is the affect of that person described? What is the main point of the story? What is the perspective of the writer?

12 D-AT IX: Families and Intimate Relationships

IN CHAPTER 10 I discussed how disability affects the client's social interactions. This chapter continues that discussion but for more intimate relationships, starting with children with disabilities in families, then partners with disabilities, and finally parents with disabilities. Regarding parents with disabilities, issues such as sexuality, pregnancy, and childbirth will be addressed.

Children with Disabilities and their Parents

The literature on children with disabilities is vast and cannot be adequately summarized here. Rather, in this section I will examine the kinds of questions that are addressed in the research and the progression of ideas over the past few decades. Up until about 1995, much of the literature on babies born with disabilities presumed a tragedy (Risdal & Singer, 2004), hence the requirement of mourning (as discussed in Chapter 11) on the part of the parents. Olkin (1999) quotes several examples of articles exhorting parents to grieve the loss of the hypothetical healthy, non-disabled, whole child they did not have before they could bond with the defective child they did have. In this literature children with disabilities are thought to be burdens on the family's resources—financial, daily hassles, emotional, and psychological (Quittner, Opipari, Regoli, Jacobsen, & Eigen, 1992). However, it seems that many of the factors that cause all parents stress are the same for families with children with disabilities (Warfield, 2005). These include the number of children they have (the greater the number the more stress and the less financial stability reported), adequate childcare, spouse support, and work–home balance. Job satisfaction may serve as a buffer against the experiences of home stressors (Warfield, 2005). The pervasiveness of this perspective of children with disabilities as a loss and burdens led Yuker (1994) to urge researchers to "stop studying the presumably horrible negative effects of a child with a disability on parents and siblings" (p. 12).

Another common research question has been about the effects of having a child with a disability on the marital relationship. Inherent in this question is an assumption that children with disabilities will have a differential impact on parents than will children without disabilities. But this negative assumption is not well supported (Gavidia-Payne & Stoneman, 2006; Sobsey, 2004). In a meta-analysis of the marital adjustment of parents of children with disabilities, the disability of children had a smaller impact on the marital relationship than would be expected (Risdal & Singer, 2004). However, there was a small effect size of having a child with a disability on the marital relationship. And the rate of divorce in such families increased by 5.9% compared to families of typically developing children. Further, economic studies suggest that the long-term health effects on mothers caring for children with disabilities are more deleterious than the effects on the breadwinning father (Burton, Lethbridge, & Phipps, 2008). Whether any of these effects (health, divorce, marital strain) could be attenuated by more community supports, employment leave policies, and less isolation for families of children with disabilities is a question that only recently has begun to be addressed (see later discussion in this chapter).

Slowly, the focus in research on children with disabilities shifted to resilience and bonding in families (c.f., Bogdan & Taylor, 1989; Gill, 1994), including ideas about variability, adaptation, resilience (Risdal & Singer, 2004), and even positive aspects of having a child with disabilities. For example, studies began to ask about the positive aspects of parenting a child with a disability (see Ferguson & Asch, 1989, for a review; see also Hastings & Taunt, 2002; Poston et al., 2003). Parents reported a range of positive effects and generally held a positive outlook on the future for their children. Parents who themselves have disabilities have also become researchers, which has brought very different perspectives and questions to research (Risdal & Singer, 2004). For example, four assumptions were criticized and refuted with empirical data (Risdal & Singer, 2004): 1) examining families only for negative impacts and signs of distress; 2) viewing any distress in the family as a direct outcome of the children's disabilities, without any mediating or moderating variables; 3) an assumption of great similarity in the responses of families with children with developmental disabilities; and 4) assuming family stress to be unremediable and that interventions that worked with other families (e.g., social support, coping skills training) would not be effective.

It has only been in the past 15 years or so that the research has really shifted paradigmatically to policy implications to support children with disabilities and their families. For example, Warfield (2005) has called for more childcare that specializes in children with disabilities. She specifically has advocated for incentives for workers, more training, and vouchers for families to have paid childcare in the home for some children with certain types of disabilities. Others have identified 18 core concepts of policies affecting the lives of children with disabilities and their families, as distinct from general family policies, although families with children with disabilities are affected by those as well (Turnbull, Beegle, Stowe, 2001). Also noteworthy is that before passage of the Affordable Care Act, about 9% of children in the United States did not have health insurance coverage (Bloom, Cohen, & Freeman, 2009). This is critical, in that higher rates of developmental disabilities are associated with low income and public (or no) health insurance (Boyle et al., 2011).

Economics is a tremendous factor in the lives of children with disabilities, and that has been the focus of several articles (Parish, Rose, Grinstein-Weiss, Richman, & Andrews, 2008; Park, Turnbull, & Turnbull, 2002). Children with disabilities are much more likely than typically developing children to live in poverty (Parish & Cloud, 2006; Park et al., 2002), and with single mothers. Single mothers often have little leeway in choosing to work on not. One study found that the rate of working was the same for single mothers of children with or without disabilities and that married mothers of children with disabilities were more likely not to enter the job market (Porterfield, 2002). However, any state or federal benefits that mothers of children with disabilities receive is not adjusted for the severity of the disability and the resultant care needs (Curran, Sharples, White, & Knapp, 2001). Yet the care of children with severe disabilities may prevent a parent from working, putting the family in danger of reduced income and of living in poverty. Parish and Cloud (2006) cite the following factors that make poverty more likely in families of children with disabilities: elevated costs associated with disability, low levels of public income benefits, difficulty balancing employment and caregiving tasks, unavailable or high-cost (or inappropriate) childcare, and inadequate leave time policies.

Just as all parents shape the lives of their children, so, too, do the parents of children with disabilities, but in some ways to an even greater degree. Parents are the ones to find doctors, procure funding, monitor physical and emotional progress related to the disability, assist with activities of daily living, insist on educational accommodations, and help the child navigate the labyrinth of childhood with a disability. Some parents are very good at this, others not as good. In either case, parents have few if any role models or guides for how to best help a child with a disability. They may not even know other such parents, just as the child may not know peers with disabilities. They may seek therapy for themselves to get input on raising their child, or they may request help for the child who is socially isolated, depressed, or struggling with disability issues. They may want to know if their child can have what they deem to be a "normal" life (marriage or partner, children, employment, friends). They may struggle with how much to push and when to accept limitations. They may need help knowing how to approach teachers and principals, what laws mean, and how to make sure the individual education plan is appropriate.

Culture, ethnicity, and socioeconomic status (SES) are huge areas to be understood when working with children with disabilities and their parents. Since these are areas relevant to all clients with disabilities, why the need to emphasize them here? Because the parents' beliefs about the causes of the disability, their degree of comfort or shame about the disability, their willingness and ability to procure services for their children, and their interface with the educational system are going to affect the lives of their children enormously, and these beliefs are greatly affected by culture. For example, in the documentary *King Gimp*, the role of the mother as a strong advocate is clear. She fights to have her son mainstreamed, and she encourages him to do all he can, including painting with a head stick. Ultimately, he is able to go to college. But suppose the mother (whose husband left shortly after their son was born) believed that her son's disability was a punishment for her own misdeeds, that he was an embarrassment who had to be hidden from her community? She would not have fought the school system to get him an appropriate education, nor encouraged his belief in himself. This is not a farfetched response, nor is it a scenario only associated with parents with lower levels of education. It is a reality for large segments of the population and is especially prominent in certain immigrant groups. Beliefs from the country of origin often follow parents to the new country. The implication for therapists generally is that requiring families with children with disabilities to attend therapy in an office or agency may be counter to the families' culture. Meeting in parks or coffee shops or in the home may be required in many instances. Not every therapist will undertake this kind of work. Nonetheless, therapists need to know that the families seen in private practice are going to be different from the families described here, as these latter families would not come to a therapist's office.

Many children with disabilities receive federal funding (e.g., Medicare), which has rules and regulations that are so arcane that they can be difficult to navigate. Furthermore, the rules often make no sense. For example, as previously discussed, parents of a teen who uses a manual wheelchair felt the teen would be more independent with a motorized wheelchair. Medicare will not approve a motorized wheelchair unless the family has a way to transport it, but the family cannot afford to buy a modified van, a cost Medicare doesn't cover. To cite a different example, a single mother of an 18-year-old with autism spectrum disorder was worried her son would not have access to money if something happened to her, so she put his name on all of her bank accounts. This made him ineligible for Social Security Disability Insurance, which then demanded the family pay back the money the son had been receiving. These kinds of catch 22 are common.

Although children with disabilities are more like than unlike their non-disabled peers, there are some issues I've seen regularly in clinical practice that seem more common for children with disabilities. Some children with disabilities become more socially isolated around middle school, and this may persist through high school. As mentioned in Chapter 8, I have seen several teens who have had rich fantasy lives, including fantasy boyfriends and girlfriends. These fantasies can be quite elaborate and ongoing, seeming to occupy a great deal of the teens' lives. Often the teens are not disabled in their fantasies. Many go through a phase (middle or high school) when they lie about the causes of the disability (often with fantastical stories). If neuropsychological testing is done, they may be high on what looks like incipient schizophrenia, but this would be a false positive. Additionally, some teens make themselves "weird" so as to control the message they send to others. For example, rather than being ostracized for the disability, the teen might dress peculiarly or have offbeat taste in music and then ascribe the rejection to these controllable factors. And lastly, the quest for independence can be greatly complicated by any need for assistance with activities of daily living and the limited accessibility of other people's houses and cars.

It might seem helpful if the therapist has a disability. The therapist could be a role model and show that "normal" adult life is possible. In my experience, my disability has been helpful for the parents. But sometimes it is not helpful for the adolescent. If the therapist has a disability, teens might see the therapist as so far ahead of them psychoemotionally as to be unreachable (providing mastery modeling, when they need coping modeling). Furthermore, the therapist may understand issues at too deep a level for the teen to tolerate. And teens may not be comfortable with disability being mirrored back in such a salient way, preferring to believe the disability is not as prominent in themselves.

Conversely, the therapist without a disability may not be viewed as credible. Trying to show credibility by asserting you know people with disabilities will not go over well. Instead, the comfort and knowledge have to be demonstrated from the start—how accessible the office is, whether paperwork is in alternate formats, not shying away from touch, bringing up topics requiring insider knowledge, talking about disability without stumbling over specific words, and having expectations of positive quality of life.

Partners

Marriage and partnerships are important areas of study for people with disabilities. Marriage confers benefits across a variety of fatal and nonfatal chronic diseases, functional impairments, and disabilities; these benefits accrue across demographic groups (Pienta, Hayward, & Jenkins, 2000; Waite & Gallagher, 2002). Attitudes toward marriage and the values of family are the same between persons with and without disabilities (Błeszyńska, 1995). Marriage may promote acceptance of disability (specifically MS), at least for men (Harrison, Stuifbergen, Adachi, & Becker, 2004). So marriage and partnering can be especially important for people with disabilities.

A comparison of young adults with and without disabilities 4 years post–high school showed some interesting differences in sexual experiences and marriage (Newman, Wagner, Cameto, & Knokey, 2009). At the time of leaving high school, fewer youths with disabilities than those without had had sexual intercourse (73% versus 83%), but they were more likely to have used contraception (87% versus 75%) and, specifically, condoms (70% versus 46%). Despite higher use of contraception, they were only slightly less likely to have had a child by 4 years post–high school (11% versus 14%), although rates varied by ethnicity (African Americans were more likely to have had a child than Whites or Hispanics). The rate of marriage within 4 years of leaving high school was 10% for those with disabilities (15% for those without disabilities); this rate was not significantly different across disability categories, but it varied by ethnicity, with Whites and Hispanics more likely to be married than African Americans.

A follow-up comparison was done for youths with and without disabilities 8 years post–high school (Newman et al., 2011). At this point the rate of marriage was 13% for those with disabilities versus 19% for those without disabilities. The rate of having children was the same for those with and without disabilities (29% and 28%) but over twice as high for those with disabilities who had not finished high school than for those with disabilities with at least a post-secondary education. And women with disabilities were much more likely to have had a child than men with disabilities (42% versus 22%), as were more African Americans than Whites (45% versus 26%). Intriguingly, 83% of the adults with disabilities who were parents had the child living with them; it begs the question of what happened in the cases of the other 17%.

There is not much professional literature on partners with and without disabilities, compared with other topic areas. Given the overall paucity, it is surprising that there are at least 15 articles just on partners of a person with profound intellectual and multiple disabilities (Hostyn & Maes, 2009). Another common focus has been on women with disabilities who experience violence in their relationships (c.f., Brownridge, 2006; Hassouneh-Phillips & McNeff, 2005; Milberger et al., 2003). And some articles focus on the "burden" on the "caregiving" partner (c.f., Post, Bloemen, & De Witte, 2005), which is about only one aspect of the relationship. Such articles on caregiving tend to assume that caregiving is one-way, from non-disabled to disabled partner, and express concern about caregiver burnout. There are several aspects missing from such caregiver literature. One is the mutuality of relationships, and the reciprocity of emotional and supportive tasks is not examined. Additionally, the sociopolitical and economic structures in society that help or hinder such relationships often are ignored. A more positive approach is a small qualitative study of collaboration in the marriage of four people with disabilities (Schulz, 2008). The author found that there was a context of love and respect in the marriages, but also unique challenges, including imbalances in contributions related to physical tasks and either needing—or fearing—time alone. Being alone presents some unique challenges for women with disabilities (Olkin, 2003) and, presumably, men with disabilities as well.

The dating and courting aspects for people with disabilities have received little empirical attention, but there are a few studies on this area. One study in Sweden found that there was non-random matching between couples with disabilities; disabled people tended to match up in the dating process (Nakosteen, Westerlund, & Zimmer, 2005). This finding would need to be investigated in other countries, especially those with less of a socioeconomic safety net than Sweden. Regarding professed attitudes toward dating people with disabilities, one study compared attitudes of college students toward dating people with disabilities across three cultures: American, Taiwanese, and Singaporean. The American women indicated the most favorable attitudes. (Women in general show more favorable attitudes toward disability than do men; Dunn, 2015; Hergenrather & Rhodes, 2007). In a second study on willingness to engage with people with disabilities, Hispanic students who were preparing to work in the helping professions were least willing to marry or form a romantic partnership with people with disabilities, compared to more distant relationships (friendships, acquaintanceships). The results showed the same robust hierarchy of acceptability found in many previous studies, with cognitive and psychiatric disabilities at lower levels, compared to sensory, physical, and health impairments (Miller, Chen, Glover-Graf, & Kranz, 2009). A third study on romantic attraction to people with disabilities was done using both stated attraction and implicit bias (Rojahn, Komelasky, & Man, 2008). Participants were college students, and results showed that their stated self-reported romantic attractiveness was equal to those with and without disabilities. However, the implicit association test showed a clear preference for non-disabled over disabled potential partners.

An early writer on dating issues for people with disabilities is Carol Gill (1996). She states that fewer people with disabilities marry and that they do so later in life than those without disabilities. Overall, the results are less clear-cut, with some studies finding what Gill cited (e.g., Asch & Fine, 1992; Olkin, Abrams, Preston, & Kirshbaum, 2006) and others not (as seen in the studies just cited). Women with disabilities are less likely to find male partners than are men with disabilities to find female partners (Gill, 1996). And women with disabilities are more likely to be separated from a spouse or partner than women without disabilities and men with disabilities (Hanna & Rogovsky, 1991). Information on lesbian and gay couples was discussed in Chapter 7, but generally, difficulties in partnering for people with disabilities occur in same-sex relationships as well. Gill cites several barriers to partnerships for people with disabilities, namely general devaluation of people with disabilities, greater likelihood of histories of physical (and sexual) abuse, family disapproval of partners with disabilities, and practical and financial burdens due to inaccessibility and unhelpful policies.

One study compared dating issues for women with disabilities and a female friend without disabilities (Rintala et al., 1997). The women with disabilities were disadvantaged in dating frequency, perceived constraints on attracting partners, and cited personal and societal barriers to dating. The two groups were similar in perceived communication problems. Another article by this research group reported that 52% of the women were in a serious relationship at the time of the study, compared with 64% of the women without disabilities (Nosek, Howland, Rintala, Young, & Chanpong, 2001).

One key variable in relationships in which one person has a disability is whether the relationship formed pre- or post-disability. In pre-disability relationships the partnership formed on the basis of one set of parameters, and those parameters shifted when one partner incurred a disability. These relationships are called pre-injury marriages or partnerships (Olkin, 1999). Alternately, a partnership may form between one person with and one without a pre-existing disability (post-injury partnerships). And, of course, there may be partnerships in which both parties have a disability. The issues are going to be slightly different for each of these three groups. In general, pre-injury marriages fair somewhat worse than post-injury marriages (Olkin, 1999). This makes sense, as the onset of a disability causes disequilibrium, exacerbates pre-existing conflicts, challenges roles, adds financial concerns, and incurs stigma. In the face of these stressors, "couples may cling together or push apart" (Olkin, 1999, p. 117). In post-injury marriages, the disability is already a part of the forming partnership. Such partnerships may have attributes that make them different from other couples (Crewe & Krause, 1988, 1990, 1992). But whether the disability is pre- or post-partnership, such partnerships are more flexible in gender roles than partnerships without disabilities.

Whether the partnership formed pre- or post-injury, the clinician cannot safely make any assumptions about the union—how it started, what attracted the partners to each other, how the disability is thought about and managed, the degree to which the disability is relevant in the daily lives of the couple, and how the partners react to the comments and prejudices of other people. For example, the disability onset story is often told from the perspective of the person with the disability, but it can be equally important to hear the story from the partner's perspective and to move from "this happened to *me*" to "this happened to *us*" (McNeff, 1997; Rolland, 1994). Many aspects of the story can be traumatic for the partner as well as the person with the disability. Gay partners who are not legally married may be excluded from discussions by medical professionals, or a gay relationship may be outed to family and others during the process of medical interventions. Thus an open-ended question in therapy about the process for the partner can reveal important clinical information. Just as for any story about a couple or family, there are specific aspects to listen for: points of agreement and differences, ability to cope with previous stressors, ability to adapt to new information or conditions, how and where the couple got stuck. Able-bodied partners often experience discrimination and stigma by association. They may be assumed by others to be "caregivers," they might be asked overly personal questions, or they might be assumed to be especially saintly or charitable to be with a partner with a disability or to have low self-esteem and thus to have settled for a disabled partner (Olkin, 1999). In one study (Goldstein, & Johnson, 1997), students did an adjective checklist for partners of a male or female with and without a disability. The partners of people with disabilities were perceived as more trustworthy and nurturant, but they were less likely to be perceived as intelligent, sociable, or athletic. The implication is that a person must have special nurturing qualities to be with a partner with a disability and subordinate other social interactions and athletic activities.

Although some researchers (e.g., Rolland, 1994) have suggested that the disability be externalized (e.g., thought of as a third partner, rather than something inherent in the partnership), I disagree with this position. My experience is that couples need to incorporate the disability into their mutual identity. For example, the partner without a disability should be alert to disability access issues, just as is the partner with the disability. The perspective is not, "this is something I do *for you*," but "this is something *we* do."

Combined effects of aging and disability also need to acknowledged. Thus even partnerships that began with a disability are going to experience new changes and stressors. And the partner without a disability may acquire new limitations with aging, shifting the balance between the partners. Given all the permutations and combinations of disability, aging, and partnerships, a good intake should attempt to gain a temporal history of these aspects of the relationship.

The titration all couples go through to regulate their optimal closeness and distance can be challenged by a disability. One partner may perform more intimate tasks than is typical for partners (e.g., helping change a catheter). This can stress a partnership that had been comfortable with a more distant balance. Or the intimacy can bring close partners even closer. As with couples without disabilities, problems arise when the two partners have differing optimal closeness set points.

Sometimes both partners have a disability. The disability may have been an attracting factor (thinking another person with a disability will understand more), or circumstances may have put the two in proximity (such as an educational or support group about the disability). And there may indeed be a deeper level of understanding about disability issues on both parts. However, there can be complications as well. The needs of each partner may be opposite (one with MS cannot tolerate heat, the other with spinal cord injury cannot tolerate cold). And they may each be in different places psychoemotionally with regard to their acceptance of and response to disability. One person may say that the disability has to be embraced, and the other might say that is it important to fight the disability. One may meditate as a way to reduce stress, and the other may drink for the same reason. One may feel learned helplessness in life, and the other may believe everything happens for a reason. As these examples show, there cannot be an assumption that mutual disability means the partners have similar world views.

I don't want to minimize the real and often difficult aspects that can occur in a partnership with a disability. Disabilities in general are time consuming and can be costly (e.g., in lost wages, or out-of-pocket expenses for equipment or making something accessible, or hiring help). There can be pronounced fatigue and pain to contend with on a daily basis or unpredictable exacerbation of symptoms. Assistance with activities of daily living may require more time and/or effort than there is to go around. Uncertainty over the future course can be stressful to both partners. How partners face and cope with these factors may be a large part of the therapy. But there is also the possibility that the couple is coping well with these factors and instead has concerns unrelated to disability. Inquiring about this area has to be done compassionately. Some couples will be insulted by a therapist asking about routine matters ("Who takes out the garbage?" "Do you have to have help with self-care?"); if they feel these are being well handled, the questions can seem intrusive or ignorant. Thus it might be better to start with a more basic question: "Do you think the disability is part of this [presenting problem]?" If yes, then "How so?"

SEXUALITY

The study of sexuality in persons with disabilities is relatively new, with little written prior to the 1970s (Milligan & Neufeldt, 2001). Barbara Waxman (1989; Waxman & Finger, 1994) was one of the early writers to make sexuality an issue of accessibility. Yet even now the view of people with disabilities as "sick and sexless" is pervasive (Anderson & Kitchin, 2000, p. 1164). Sexual attractiveness and desirability are particularly rooted in cultural values and norms (Shuttleworth & Mona, 2002), and there are many negative assumptions about the sexuality (or lack thereof) of people with disabilities. Persons with disabilities are often misjudged as asexual or limited in sexual feelings or abilities (Lund & Johnson, 2015), and they may have internalized the pervasive negative messages about disability (Chance, 2002; DiGiulio, 2003). Families may inadvertently reinforce the idea of the child or adolescent with a disability as asexual. For example, one of the most frequent questions I am asked by the parents of my teen clients with disabilities is whether I am married and if I have children. They seem to be saying that if this is possible for me as a woman with an apparent disability, then perhaps it might be possible for their children; surely this insecurity was communicated to the children. In fact, there is very little known about the dating and partnering between people with and without disabilities (Chance, 2002). Those with early-onset disabilities do tend to start dating and having sexual relationships at a later age than peers without disabilities (Gill, 1996).

There are many systemic barriers to sexuality for people with disabilities. Vulnerability to exploitation carries with it the possibility of exposure to HIV and other sexually transmitted diseases (DiGiulio, 2003; see Andrews & Veronen, 1993, for a list of eight reasons why people with disabilities are more vulnerable to sexual exploitation and abuse). Health behaviors such as pap smears are less commonly performed for women with disabilities than those without (Tilley, 1996), owing to inaccessibility of examining rooms and to preconceived notions of asexuality (Welner, 1999). They are also less likely to have access to family planning services (Anderson & Kitchin, 2000). People with disabilities are rarely the targeted audience for sexual education campaigns. Reduced employment leads to reduced socialization and fewer opportunities to meet potential partners. The general economic, educational, and social disadvantages common to people with disabilities (Ballan, 2008) carry high risks in themselves, in addition to the disadvantages due to disability itself.

Both sexuality and disability are value-laden topics. Clinicians are not immune to many of the negative and stigmatizing views of sexuality of people with disabilities (DiGiulio, 2003; Esmail, Darry, Walter, & Knupp, 2010; Hyland & McGrath, 2013); these views are especially profound regarding people with intellectual disabilities (Parchomiuk, 2012; Young, Gore, & McCarthy, 2012). Sexuality as a source of pleasure is mostly missing from the discourse on sexuality and disability (Tepper, 2000). In contrast, Shakespeare (2000) argues that "there is a danger in overstating the importance of sex, as opposed to friendship and intimacy" (p. 159). And other authors have discussed asexuality as a legitimate sexual orientation (Lund & Johnson, 2015). These opposing opinions speak to the need to approach sexuality and disability without preconceived notions.

It is important to note that diversity within studies on sexuality and disability has been somewhat lacking, including on women with physical disabilities (Yoshida, Li, & Odette, 1999). A review of 54 studies from 2002 to 2006, including over 11,000 participants, found inconsistency in reporting of cultural information and an underrepresentation of ethnic minorities (Greenwell & Hough, 2008). (See Box 12.1 for a list of references specific to sexual minorities with disabilities.)

Surveys of various professionals suggest a lack of adequate training in sexuality and disability (Caruso et al., 1997; Kazukauskas & Lam, 2009). In a survey of sexual health education in different disciplines, students in psychology reported the lowest quantity and quality of education compared to students in other disciplines (Valvano et al., 2014). Only 11% of APA-accredited programs in clinical and counseling psychology have any courses on disability, and these are most likely to be on one of three disabilities (intellectual disabilities, learning disabilities, or autism spectrum disorders; Olkin & Pledger, 2003). Similarly, only 12% of 192 programs in social work had core courses related to people with disabilities (which may or may not have included material on disability and sexuality; Ballan, 2008). A small study of the experiences of sexual and marital therapists working with clients with physical disabilities found that such clients evoked stronger emotional responses than other clients, and participants reported feeling anxious raising issues of sexuality and disability (Parritt & O'Callaghan, 2000). These findings all point to a need for more training for clinicians in sexuality and disability. Such training seems to have lasting effects on knowledge, comfort, and attitudes of rehabilitation practitioners (Fronek, Kendall, Booth, Eugarde, & Geraghty, 2011), even if the training is brief (Higgins et al., 2012). Regarding training, Ballan (2008) offers six specific lecture points on disability and sexuality, along with a field placement exercise and three classroom exercises.

In addressing sexuality of people with disabilities, there can easily be a too-rigid adoption of the model of "normal" sexuality (with four stages of excitement, plateau, orgasm, and resolution as per Masters and Johnson, 1986) and a male-centric perspective in which sexual behaviors are meant to lead to intercourse and orgasm. However, sexual expression and responses may be more varied for people with than without disabilities, and such variation should not necessarily be thought of as a sexual dysfunction (Dune, 2012). The *DSM-5* (American Psychiatric Association, 2013) notes

BOX 12.1
REFERENCES ON DISABILITIES AND SEXUAL MINORITIES

Gay Males with Disabilities

Bennet, C., & Coyle, A. (2007). A minority within a minority: Experiences of gay men with intellectual disabilities. In V. Clarke & E. Peel (Eds.), *Out in psychology: Lesbian, gay, bisexual, trans, and queer perspectives* (pp. 125–143). West Sussex, England: John Wiley and Sons, Ltd.

Blanchett, W. J. (2002). Voices from a TASH forum on meeting the needs of gay, lesbian, and bisexual adolescents and adults with severe disabilities. *Research and Practice for Persons with Severe Disabilities, 27*(1), 82–86.

Blythe, C., & Carson, (2007). Sexual uncertainties and disabled young men: Silencing difference within the classroom. *Pastoral Care in Education, 25*(3).

Cain, R. (1991). Stigma management and gay identity development. *Social Work, 36*(1), 67–73.

Davidson-Paine, C. D., & Corbett, J. H. (1995). A double coming out: Gay men with learning disabilities. *British Journal of Learning Disabilities, 23*, 147–151.

Genke, J. (2004). Resistance and resilience: The untold story of gay men aging with chronic illnesses. *Journal of Gay and Lesbian Social Services, 17*(2), 81–95.

Hanjorgiris, W. F., Rath, J. R., & O'Neill, J. H. (2004). Gay men living with chronic illness or disability: A sociocultural, minority group perspective on mental health. *Journal of Gay and Lesbian Social Services, 17*(2), 25–41.

Henry, W. J., Fuerth, K., & Figliozzi, J. H. (2010). Gay with a disability: A college student's multiple cultural journey. *College Student Journal, 44*(2), 377–388.

O'Neill, T., & Hird, M. J. (2001). Double damnation: Gay disabled men and the negotiation of masculinity. In K. Backett-Milburn & L. Mckie (Eds.), *Constructing gendered bodies* (pp. 204–222). New York: British Sociological Association.

Sinecka, J. (2008, August). 'I am bodied'. 'I am sexual'. 'I am human'. Experiencing deafness and gayness: A story of a young man. *Disability & Society, 23*(5), 475–484.

Stauffer-Kruse, S. (2007). Gay men with learning disabilities: UK service provision. *Journal of Gay and Lesbian Psychotherapy, 11*(1), 145–152.

Lesbians with Disabilities

Asch, A., & Fine, M. (1997). Nurturance, sexuality, and women with disabilities. In L. J. Davis (Ed.), *The disability studies reader* (pp. 241-258). New York: Routledge.

Drummond, J. D., & Brotman, S. (2014). Intersecting and embodied identities: A queer woman's experience of disability and sexuality. *Sexuality and Disability, 32*, 533–549.

Gill, C. J. (1993). Dating and relationship issues. *Sexuality and Disability, 14*(3), 183–190.

Hunt, B., Matthews, C., Milsom, A., & Lammel, J. A. (2006). Lesbians with physical disabilities: A qualitative study of their experiences with counseling. *Journal of Counseling and Development, 84*(2), 163–173.

Hunt, B., Milsom, A., & Matthews, C. R. (2009). Partner-related rehabilitation experiences of lesbians with physical disabilities: A qualitative study. *Rehabilitation Counseling Bulletin, 52*(3), 167–178.

O'Toole, C. J., & Bregante, J. L. (1993). Disabled lesbians: Multicultural realities. In M. Nagler, (Ed.), *Perspectives on disability* (2nd ed., pp. 261–271). Palo Alto, CA: Health Markets Research.

O'Toole, C. J., & Brown, A. A. (2002). No reflection in the mirror: Challenges for disabled lesbians accessing mental health services. *Journal of Lesbian Studies, 7*(1), 35–49.

Shakespeare, T. (1999). Coming out and coming home. *International Journal of Sexuality and Gender Studies, 4*(1), 39–51.

Tilley, C. M. (1996). Sexuality in women with physical disabilities: A social justice or health issue? *Sexuality and Disability, 14*(2), 139–151.

Vaughn, M., Silver, K., Murphy, S., Ashbaugh, R., & Hoffman, A. (2015). Women with disabilities discuss sexuality in San Francisco focus groups. *Sexuality and Disability, 33*, 19–46.

Wadle, D., & O'Toole, C. J. (2010). "I feel so vulnerable": Lesbians with disabilities. *Lesbian Health, 101*, 347–362.

Gay Males, Lesbians, Bisexuals, and Transgender Persons

Brothers, M. (2003). It's not just about ramps and Braille: Disability and sexual orientation. In K. Zappone (Ed.), *Re-thinking identity: The challenge of diversity* (pp. 49–68). Belfast: Joint Equality and Human Rights Forum.

Cochran, S. D., & Mays, V. M. (2007). Physical health complaints among lesbians and gay men. *American Journal of Public Health, 97*, 2048–2057.

Dispenza, F., Harper, L. S., & Harrigan, M. A. (2016). Subjective health among LGBT persons living with disabilities: A qualitative content analysis. *Rehabilitation Psychology, 61*(3), 251–259.

Fredrickson-Goldsen, K. I., Kim, H. J., & Barkan, S. E. (2012). Disability among lesbian, gay, and bisexual adults: Disparities in prevalence and risk. *American Journal of Public Health, 202*(1), 16–21.

Harley, D. A., Hall, M., & Savage, T. A. (2000). Working with gay and lesbian consumers with disabilities: Helping practitioners understand another frontier of diversity. *Journal of Applied Rehabilitation Counseling, 31*(1), 4–11.

Harley, D. A., Nowak, T. M., & Gassaway, L. J. (2002). Lesbian, gay, bisexual, and transgender college students with disabilities: A look at multiple cultural minorities. *Psychology in the Schools, 39*(5), 525–238.

Kattari, S. K. (2015). "Getting it": Identity and sexual communication for sexual and gender minorities with physical disabilities. *Sexuality & Culture, 19*, 882–899.

LeBlanc, J. M., & Tully, C. T. (2001). Deaf and hearing-impaired lesbians and gay males: Perceptions of social support. *Journal of Gay and Lesbian Social Services, 13*(3), 57–84.

---

that "a sexual dysfunction diagnosis requires ruling out problems that are better explained by a ... medical condition" (p. 423). Further, "if the sexual dysfunction is attributable to another medical condition ... the individual would not receive a psychiatric diagnosis" (p. 424). Criterion D in most of the diagnoses in the chapter on sexual dysfunctions include a rule-out for dysfunction caused by a medical condition. Therefore, clinicians are urged to be cautious in diagnosing difference in sexual expression as a dysfunction.

Much of the literature on sexuality and people with disabilities has focused on abuse, victimization, and asexuality (Chance, 2002; Guldin, 2000; Lund & Johnson, 2015) or relegated sexuality to the background in deference to more practical issues of accessibility and healthcare (Higgins, 2010). A number of studies of youth and young adults with disabilities suggest that these youths lack information about sexuality and the effects of their particular disability on sexuality (Berman, Harris, Enright, Gilpin, & Cathers, 1999; East & Orchard, 2014) or lack education about contraception and sexual expression (Porat, Heruti, Navon-Porat, & Hardoff, 2012; Wiwanitkit, 2008). Youths with disabilities may well have reduced opportunities for sexual partners (Gordon, Tschopp, & Feldman, 2004; Mckenzie & Swartz, 2011; Wiegerink, Roebroeck, Bender, Stam, & Cohen-Kettenis, 2011). For example, in one study (in multiple, mostly English-speaking countries) results indicated that the presence and severity of physical disability were related to increased likelihood of being single (Taleporos & McCabe, 2003).

Sexual expression between partners with disabilities (whether one or both partners have a disability) is as much a part of couple's therapy as it is for any couple. Not every couple's therapist is proficient in sex therapy per se, much less with people with disabilities. But this is an important area for exploration, and some specialized knowledge on the part of the therapist may be warranted. Topics such as management of fatigue, alternate erogenous areas, placement of catheters, and a variety of positions are going to be relevant.

Given the pervasiveness of negative messages encountered, some clients with disabilities may need affirmation of their right to sexual lives and assistance to feel romantically and sexually attractive to others (Sandowski, 1993). The relationship between sexuality and quality of life in people with disabilities has not been well studied. An exception is a study in Canada on 60 people with congenital physical disabilities and 60 non-disabled persons matched for age and gender (McCabe, Cummins, & Deeks, 2000). Notable was the low rate of sexual interactions for the participants with disabilities. Quality of life scores were below normative standards. However, there was a low level of association between sexuality and quality of life. This should not be taken to mean that sexuality is less important to people with disabilities, as respondents expressed a high desire to know more about sexuality. And another study did find an association between sexual intimacy and importance and quality of life (McCabe et al., 2000).

The Sexuality Information and Education Council of the U.S. (www.SIECUS.org, 2002) notes that all persons with disabilities have a right to sexuality education, healthcare, and sexual expression and urges training for those who work with disability populations. In their compilation they note that there are not many recent resources. However, since that publication, over three dozen articles have been published on sexuality and disability in general, not including articles specific to different disabilities (e.g., Blackmore, Hart, Albiani & Mohr, 2011, and Gumus, Akpinar, & Yilmaz, 2014, regarding multiple sclerosis; Bernert, 2011, and Löfgren-Mårtenson, 2013, regarding intellectual disabilities; Buzzelli, di Francesco, Giaquinto, & Nolfe, 1997, regarding stroke; Ide, 2004, regarding limb amputation; Ozcan, Sahin, Bilgic, & Yilmaz, 2011, regarding women with diabetes; Parker & Yau, 2012, regarding women with spinal cord injury; Wiwanitkit, 2009, regarding women with lower paraplegia).

Inclusion of sexual issues in therapy with clients with disabilities will rest on the same basic principles as sex therapy in general, with the addition of some specialized knowledge and skills related to disability. Since people with disabilities are so often thought of as desexualized, if the therapist doesn't ask about this area it can be especially disturbing to the client(s). The PLISSIT model (Permission, Limited Information, Specific Suggestions, Intensive Therapy; Annon, 1976) is one approach. Permission may be needed if the client with a disability feels undesirable or a partner has lost some interest post–disability onset. Information and suggestions may need to be tailored to the specifics of the disability. The ALLOW model (Ask about sexual activity and function, Legitimize the client's concerns, address Limitations due to lack of comfort or knowledge, have Open discussions of sexual issues to allow for assessment and possible referrals, and Work collaboratively to develop a treatment plan) was designed for healthcare professionals (Hatzichristou et al., 2004). It places greater emphasis than does PLISSIT on the collaborative process in designing a treatment plan. (See Dune, 2012, for a comparison of the PLISSIT, ALLOW, and Kaplan models, as well as specific questions that can be asked about pre-existing, disability-specific, and partner factors.)

For some people with disabilities sexuality is limited by social exclusion, that is, by the problem of attracting partners (Chance, 2002). And for some, sexual expression itself is altered by the disability. Sexual activity might need to be redefined as mutual pleasure or intimacy rather than intercourse as the goal (Chance, 2002). Other areas of the body besides the typical erogenous zones may prove to be pleasurable when stimulated. The need to broaden the repertoire may involve increased sexual communication and intimacy. But the de-emphasis on intercourse as the goal of sexuality may be more difficult for men with disabilities than for women with disabilities (Chance, 2002).

Many people erroneously assume that paralysis is always accompanied by loss of sensation. This often is not the case. To use myself as an example, my right leg is paralyzed from the thigh down but is acutely sensitive to heat, cold, injury, and pain. Men and women with spinal cord injuries often are able to achieve orgasm (Sipsky & Alexander, 1997). Erection, orgasm, and ejaculation are separate functions, and one may be impaired without the others.

Many practical suggestions are available for aiding sexual activity. Decrease in vaginal lubrication can be aided by vaginal lubricants. A water bed may help with weight distribution, and the rocking motion can be stimulating. Men with spinal cord injuries can sometimes have reflex erections through direct manual stimulation. Various positions can relieve pressure. There are many vibrators on the market, and some have special adaptive mitts or handles for those with limited hand use (independent living catalogues are the best source). Colostomy bags can be emptied, the seal secured, and the bag covered by clothing to reduce its impact. (For other practical ideas, see also suggestions from the American Cancer Society, 2002, which has separate booklets for the man or woman with cancer, and Chance, 2002.)

Some good resources related to sexuality and disabilities that could be useful to clinicians and to their clients are several films. These include *SexAbility*, a documentary film on sexuality and disability (https://www.youtube.com/watch?v=izZPJPZTlcI); *The Sessions* (Fox Searchlight Pictures, 2012), a fictionalized account of sexual encounters with a surrogate, based on a memoir by Mark O'Brien; and *Wheelchair Sex & Disability Love* (https://www.youtube.com/watch?v=RXCBMuRpJI4). Two other films are considered disability and sex positive: *Hyde Park on Hudson* (2012), about FDR, and *Rust and Bone* (2012), a French drama about a double-arm amputee. Additionally, there are two critiques of films depicting sexuality and disability (Byrd & Elliot, 1985; Harris, 2002). Some useful websites include www.facingdisability.com, www.teachingdisabilitystudies.com, www.sexualhealth.com (which is about sexuality for all persons, not just those with disabilities), and the website for the Center for Women with Disabilities (crowd@bcm.edu) at Baylor College of Medicine.

A good but slightly old book on the topic is *Sexual Function in People with Disability and Chronic Illness: A Health Professional's Guide* (Sipski & Alexander, 1997). A journal devoted to the topic is *Sexuality and Disability*. Also recommended is *The New Our Bodies Ourselves* (Phillips & Rakusen, 1989), which has a section on women with disabilities. National organizations often publish pamphlets or manuals specific to the disability they serve, such as *Sexual function for men after spinal cord injury* (Craig Hospital, 2015) and *Sexuality for women with spinal cord injury* (United Spinal Association and University of Alabama Model SCI System, 2007; available for download, along with useful resources).

In the following clinical example, the therapist actively makes suggestions to the male client of things to try in order to encourage sexual activity, as the client's relationship with his girlfriend seems to be sufficiently solid and able to tolerate some trial and error:

> Robert is an attractive Greek-American male in his mid-thirties. He has been experiencing pain of unknown origin in his testicles and lower abdomen. The problem is possibly vascular, as eating and sexual activity both activate the pain. A previous sexual relationship with a woman ended because pain during and after coitus had reduced sexual activities to zero. His current relationship with a woman is less based on sex and more on compatibility, but the lack of sex has become an issue. The girlfriend feels rejected and unattractive to Robert, even though she knows the issues are not about her. In session, the therapist asked about sexual activity that did not include intercourse, with more focus on the girlfriend's sexual needs. Robert replied that he lived with his parents and his girlfriend lived with her parents, making it difficult to find privacy. The therapist asked what Robert would do if he were able to have intercourse, how he would ensure privacy. Robert laughed and said he'd find places—in the back of a car, out in the field, in the woods. It then became clear to him that if he were more motivated he'd find a way, so he should find a way to engage in sex play with his girlfriend. Additionally, the therapist suggested trying an ice pack on the painful areas post-ejaculation, to see if it reduced the pain.

Parents with Disabilities

In the United States, there are approximately 15 to 20 million children under age 18 being raised by parents with disabilities (Olkin et al., 2006; Preston, 2012). Although data are inexact, extrapolations from smaller data sets indicate that about 15% of all children under age 18 live in families with a parent with a disability (Preston, 2012). About 13% of children without disabilities grow up in families with a parent with a disability (Preston, 2012), and this number is higher for children with disabilities (33%; Avery & Hogan, 2007). Rates of parenting differ by disability type; those with sensory disabilities are most likely to be parents (although data are not separable by visual or hearing impairments; Preston, 2012).

Parents with disabilities are overrepresented among those receiving Temporary Assistance for Needy Families (TANF; Sweeney, 2000). The greatest number is parents with psychiatric disabilities (major depression, PTSD, or generalized anxiety disorder), but at least one fifth are parents with physical impairments. Economics may be the most important difference between parents with and without disabilities, as parents with disabilities are over twice as likely to be unemployed (Preston, 2012), and when employed they have household incomes about $15,000 lower than that of comparable neighbors (Olkin et al., 2006). The largest survey of parents with disabilities (Toms Barker & Maralani, 1997) noted that the practical areas in which the parents needed assistance were recreation, lifting and carrying babies and small children, and transportation. However, social barriers were also very pronounced: 32% reported discrimination, 14% received pressure to be sterilized, 13% felt pressure to have an abortion, and 15% experienced efforts to have their children removed. These data are noteworthy, as the sample comprised more parents with physical disabilities than those with other types of disabilities and were mostly well educated. Those with other types of disabilities and of lower SES are probably even more disadvantaged in these areas.

In most cases, the woman with a disability is able to conceive and carry to term a pregnancy, and a man with a disability to produce sperm. In general, it is safe to assume that people with disabilities can bear children. The issue generally is not how the disability will affect procreation, but how pregnancy and childbirth might affect the woman's disability. Some disabilities actually improve during pregnancy (e.g., MS). But the additional weight can be difficult for someone with mobility limitations. And in some disabilities pregnancy can be risky (e.g., insulin-dependent diabetes). Data indicate that women with disabilities tend to delay childbearing a bit longer than non-disabled women (Olkin et al., 2006; Preston, 2012). For example, a study of women with disabilities using their friends as the control group (Nosek et al., 2001) found that 38% of the women with disabilities had borne children, compared to 51% of the women without disabilities. Another report (Preston, 2012) stated that women with disabilities are older at first childbearing (39 years) than women without disabilities (36 years). The delay in childbearing has consequences, as age itself is a risk factor in pregnancy.

Parents with disabilities are often portrayed in the professional literature as subpar, even damaging to their offspring, mostly because many studies have gone in looking for pathology (Kirshbaum, 2000; Kirshbaum & Olkin, 2002). Often there is a conflation of disability and illness, acute episodes and chronic disability, and cognitive and physical disabilities. There is vast overgeneralization from one type of disability to another, without consideration of important distinctions. For example, an article titled "Persons with Disabilities as Parents: What is the Problem?" is actually about parents with intellectual disabilities (Reinders, 2008). We see this overgeneralization in articles repeatedly (Kirshbaum, 2000, cites other examples). Nonetheless, there are differences in families with disabled parents compared to those families in which parents do not have a disability (Hogan, Shandra, & Msall, 2007). However, this difference is attenuated by lower income and a higher probability of children being in a single-parent home when the parent is disabled.

There are many problems with the literature on parents with disabilities (c.f., Kirshbaum & Olkin, 2002) that I will summarize briefly here. First, disability is assumed to be the independent variable, without screening or matching for other important variables (such as the higher incidence of abuse of children with disabilities, or the greater rates of unemployment and poverty for adults with disabilities). Second, the heterogeneity across disabilities is ignored, as is the wide variability in functional levels within one type of disability. Findings from one type of disability (e.g., intellectual disabilities) is erroneously generalized to other types of disabilities. Third, disability barriers (e.g., written materials from the school for parents who are blind) are ignored. Fourth, there has been confusion over correlation versus causation. Some factors may be associated with parents with disabilities but not be caused by the disability. Fifth, the circumstances of the onset of the disability are not delineated, when the onset may have been traumatic (e.g., accident, parent in the hospital). And sixth, there is often an assumption of parentification, that the children will take on responsibilities beyond their developmental level and years (see later discussion).

As I wrote with a colleague earlier (Kirshbaum & Olkin, 2002):

> Parenting has been the last frontier for people with disabilities and an arena in which parents are likely to encounter prejudice. Researchers have found that parents with disabilities experience prejudice about their rights or abilities to parent. In a national survey of almost 1,200 parents with disabilities, about 15% of the parents reported attempts to remove their children. Indeed, about 7% of over 300 undergraduate psychology majors did not think people with disabilities should be parents at all. It seems that the stigma attached to disability encompasses a threat to the right to parent for persons with disabilities. Thus the legal rights of parents with disabilities, especially in custody decisions, is a fundamental issue for all parents with disabilities. This threat underscores

the importance of appropriate and culturally sensitive research on parents with disabilities, and of being mindful of how research on parents with disabilities can be misused against this politically vulnerable population. (p. 67)

Children of parents with disabilities often are referred to as *carers* (British) or *caregivers* (American) (Prilleltensky, 2004), with the assumption of role-reversal and parentification of the offspring of parents with disabilities. If there are concerns about parentification, two factors need to be considered. First are the findings of a study that compared responses of parents with and without disabilities and the responses of their teens (Olkin et al., 2006). They found that although teens of parents with disabilities do tasks that other teens do not do, even ones that may be necessitated by the parent's disability, the parents compensated by reducing tasks elsewhere. Thus the overall number of chores was the same for teens of parents with and without disabilities. Second, clinicians can use a series of questions I developed to ask about tasks that children of parents with disabilities might be asked to perform. This series of questions provides a systematic way to assess the appropriateness of any specific task, through inquiry of 13 factors (Olkin, 1999; see Box 12.2).

Not only is the literature on parents with disabilities pathology oriented, but there is documentation that parents with disabilities are more likely to lose custody of their children. In a study of the practices of psychologists doing custody evaluations on divorcing parents with disabilities, 70% of the respondents had performed such evaluations, even though 85% reported having received no training for evaluations of parents with disabilities (Breeden, Olkin, & Taube, 2008). The tests used, procedures, and norms were not changed when evaluating parents with disabilities—that is, there were no accommodations based on disability. Therefore, some of what was being evaluated was directly affected by the disability and was not about parenting per se. In a review of court custody cases in Australia, parents with disabilities featured in 29.5% of cases (Llewellyn, McConnell, & Ferronato, 2003). The primary disabilities were psychiatric disorders (21.8%) and intellectual disability (8.8%). The authors concluded that there was a significant relationship between parental disability and outcome, with a disproportionately larger number of children of parents with intellectual disabilities being made wards of the court. Results were more pronounced in a comparison of court custody cases in Australia and England, with more children being placed outside the home and family network in England (Booth, Booth, & McConnell, 2005). In the United States the rate of out-of-home placement for children of parents with intellectual disabilities is estimated to be 40–60% (Preston, 2012). Regarding parents with intellectual disabilities, a study in Quebec found that losing custody was not related to the mothers' health, their adaptive behaviors, the behaviors of the children, or the number of

> BOX 12.2
> THIRTEEN AREAS TO ASSESS IN EVALUATING TASKS CHILDREN MIGHT
> DO FOR A PARENT WITH A DISABILITY
>
> 1. The age and developmental level of the child being asked to perform the task
> 2. The nature of the task itself (how arduous, time consuming, unpleasant)
> 3. The symbolic meaning of the task (e.g., related to toileting, sexuality, performed for an opposite gender parent)
> 4. Whether performing the task causes any pain or discomfort to the parent with the disability
> 5. The frequency the task must be performed by the child
> 6. If the child is the sole person responsible for performing the task and/or has primary responsibility for ensuring it is done
> 7. The consequences of not performing the task (e.g., life threatening, dire consequences, pain or discomfort, reduced mobility)
> 8. The degree of support the child has in performing the task
> 9. The relationship of the child to the person for whom the task is performed
> 10. The roles of the other able-bodied members of the house (is only one child the one to do the tasks?)
> 11. The time of day or night the task must be completed
> 12. The total number of such tasks
> 13. Any positive benefits to the child for performing the task

people in their social network (Aunos, Goupil, & Feldman, 2003). Rather, loss of custody was related to lower income, less involvement of the mothers in the community, lower satisfaction with services received, and older children. This suggests that it is factors outside the mothers' intellectual disability itself that make the difference in retaining custody.

One of the few studies that examined positive aspects about parenting with a disability did find that there were several. The first such study (Buck & Hohmann, 1981) was on fathers with spinal cord injuries, compared with nondisabled fathers matched for SES. They found that the fathers with spinal cord injury expressed verbal and physical affection significantly more often than the fathers without disabilities. The children of fathers with spinal cord injury reported more positive attitudes toward their fathers than did the comparison children. Other studies have found that families with parents with disabilities have more fluid gender roles, enhanced problem-solving skills, and more positive attitudes toward disability (see Preston, 2012, for a review of parents with disabilities).

Readers are encouraged to be skeptical about findings in the literature and to approach their clients with disabilities who are parents as they might any parent. As with any parent, it is important to assess a history of childhood abuse or neglect, substance abuse, separations from parents, and other childhood critical incidents or traumas. It is helpful to ask about the history of the disability onset or changes in the disability in relation to childbearing and child rearing. All of these factors are likely to be more pronounced in their effects on parenting than the disability itself.

Discussion Questions

1. What is the recent paradigm shift in the research on children with disabilities and their families?
2. How do pre-disability marriages fare in comparison to post-injury marriages?
3. Find an article on a gay couple with a disability (not HIV or AIDS).
4. What were two important findings in Olkin, Abrams, Preston, and Kirshbaum (2006)?
5. A parent who is blind asks a son who is 8 to read the recipe on the back of a box. Use Box 12.2 to evaluate the task.

13 Disability-Affirmative Therapy Applied to the Case of "Sam"

THE PURPOSE OF this chapter is to walk through the sample case of "Sam" using the D-AT template. By addressing each of the nine areas of D-AT, we should be able to derive a case formulation that appropriately includes the disability, without over-inflating or underestimating its role in Sam's life and the problems he presents in therapy. I suggest that readers go back and review the case (Chapter 3). You might want to use the template (Table 13.1) to make your own notes before reading on in this chapter.

D-AT I: Current Disability Status and Sequelae

Sam's daily life is very much regulated by his disability. He has several ancillary conditions. One shoulder hurts, as does his back, probably from years of using (Canadian—forearm) crutches. The foot most affected by polio gets swollen, and Sam wears a compression sock to reduce swelling, and lies with it elevated twice a day. The space between two toes on that foot gets infected frequently, and nothing seems to completely clear up the spot. If the infection is left untreated, the infection becomes systemic, resulting in hospitalization to receive IV antibiotics. Sam cuts the toes off his compression socks to air out the toes of his foot. When his foot is infected or swollen he is unable to wear his leg brace, resulting in very limited ability

TABLE 13.1

THE D-AT TEMPLATE FOR NOTE TAKING

D-AT	Content	Notes
I	Current Disability Status	
II	Developmental History	
III	Models of Disability	
IV	Disability and Other Demographics	
V	Disability Culture and Community	
VI	Social Interactions	
VII	Effects of Microaggressions	
VIII	Affective regulation	
IX	Intimacy	
	Case Formulation	
	Treatment Goals	

to walk (with crutches). He uses an electric wheelchair or scooter outside the apartment and has a van with a lift—all of these are subject to frequent breakdowns and lengthy repair times. In the apartment there is a chair lift to the second story, but this, too, breaks about once a year.

Fatigue management is also a part of daily life. After weekends of activities with his husband, Sam generally does very little on Mondays so he can recoup his energy. He usually plans only one activity a day (e.g., a doctor appointment, physical therapy, swimming, therapy). Sometimes he does not participate in activities (e.g., events with his partner's family) because they are too fatiguing, or because they are in places difficult to access (e.g., friends' houses with stairs). He frequently comments in therapy on his "need to rest"—the rest may be partly physical/systemic, and partly efforts at emotion regulation.

The future degree of disability is uncertain. Sam is on Medicare, which is slow to approve purchases, making it slow to obtain necessary equipment (e.g., getting a wheelchair takes at least a year). Approval for repairs also is slow, and then repairs can only be done at certain places (where workers are grossly underpaid for the work and therefore take in too much work to handle it quickly). Pain and fatigue are likely to be ongoing, if not increasing, issues. Avoiding falls will be a critical issue, as will reduction in the number and severity of infections in his foot.

D-AT II: Developmental History

The Ur story for Sam is as follows: He is 2 years old, in the hospital with polio, his mother home with her two other children and 5 hours away. Sam tried to escape to get home, and ended up caught up in the bed sheets hanging from the crib, abandoned and alone. This became his core schema—I will be abandoned, I am ultimately alone, I will die alone. When he was in fact abandoned in a foreign country by his first love, this schema was reinforced.

Two other memories are key to Sam's current functioning. One involves the need to be as good as other children in all activities, even if those activities were affected by his polio. The second is that he should not cry or complain. From these experiences he learned that there was something wrong with having polio and that the disability should be masked to the greatest extent possible. Emotions about inabilities or pain or falling were to be kept hidden, never discussed.

D-AT III: Models of Disability

Sam was raised with the medical model (polio is a medical condition that should be remediated to the greatest extent possible, which means walking even if a wheelchair is a more efficient method of ambulation) and the moral model (disability should never be discussed and is inherently shameful; be like all the other boys). Being gay compounded the models, that is, his family was very negative about homosexuality (moral model) and initially wanted him to be "converted" to being straight (medical model).

Sam was exposed to the social model in college (both for disability and for being openly gay). He was a part of gay rights movements, and the analogy to disability rights was not lost on him. However, his head believes he should embrace the social model, but his heart and emotions are ensconced in the moral and medical models. Sam's resultant models of disability are shown in Figure 13.1, and his desired models of disability are in Figure 13.2. It is the discrepancy between the two versions that causes Sam significant discomfort.

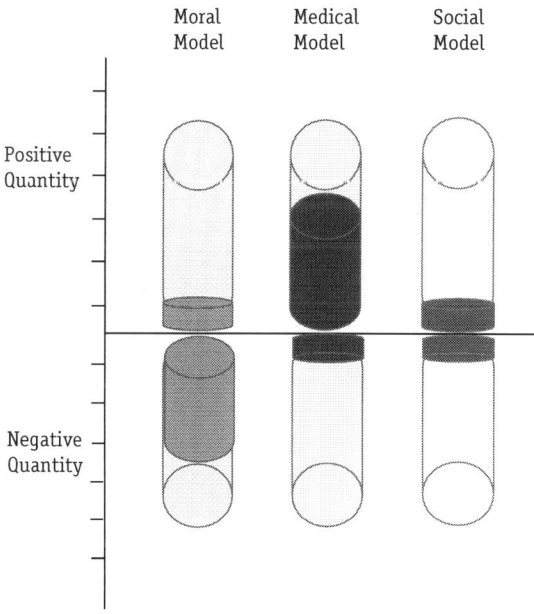

FIGURE 13.1 Sam's *actual* models of disability, showing high belief in the moral model, medium belief in the medical model, and low belief in the social model.

Disability-Affirmative Therapy

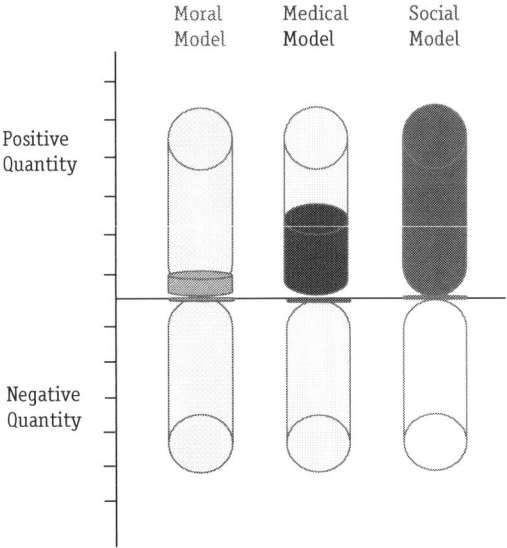

FIGURE 13.2 Sam's *desired* models of disability, showing very little belief in the moral model, low–medium belief in the medical model, and high belief in the social model.

D-AT IV: Disability and Other Demographic Variables

Sam is an educated White male, but is quite unaware of the privilege that confers on him. He holds a college degree and worked in a white collar job but was forced to retire earlier than anticipated because of his disability. Good benefits allowed him to do this. He was slow to appreciate his husband's entrepreneurship in doing any job for money (e.g., boarding dogs).

Being gay has made him aware of minority status, and he applied some of that awareness to his ideas about being disabled and part of a disability community, but not to the same degree as for being gay. His cultural roots are middle America farmland, which promulgates hard work, productivity, and emotional reserve. The former two made retirement even more difficult. The latter gave him few tools to express his feelings about retirement, disability, or emotions.

D-AT V: Disability Culture and Community

Sam is part of a small group of gay men with disabilities. It is the one place where he is both gay and disabled, but, interestingly, he wants to share with the group only positive news of himself and his life. (Complaining was disallowed for him as a child.) He has great awareness of accessibility issues in his current home city, and is both drawn to and repelled by disability events. He does not belong to any organized disability groups (e.g., Californians for Disability Rights), and he stopped going to the local polio support group where he did not feel at all supported ("these old suburban women telling me what to do"). He and his friend with polio do read and discuss books about disability, particularly about polio (such as the history of FDR from a disability perspective). He has one foot in disability culture, but is much more ensconced in gay culture (which is more open and easier to find in his city).

D-AT VI: Social Interactions

Most of Sam's social interactions are with his partner and other gay male couples. He does go monthly to a group for gay men with disabilities, and talks by phone with his gay male friend with polio. He was a member of a church that was not very physically accessible to him, and he had a falling out with the leaders of that church, ultimately ending his attendance. This was a major rupture for him, and it took some time before he found another church he wanted to join. He attends church on Sundays about half the time, but hasn't made a close connection there. He did befriend someone from the church who has a significant mental illness, and he is very ambivalent about this friendship. He sees it as helping someone with a disability, but the person sometimes becomes too needy and Sam has phases when he has to greatly withdraw. However, it is through this friendship that Sam has learned how to set better boundaries for himself. The highlight of Sam's day is when his husband comes home in the evening, but Eddie has a very busy life, and Sam struggles with feeling abandoned by him. When he feels down, he ruminates about being abandoned and alone, growing old and dying alone, and feeling undeserving of anything better.

D-AT VII: Effects of Microaggressions

There are numerous and daily occurrences of microaggressions related to Sam's disability (rarely about his being gay), and he struggles mightily with his emotional responses to these. Sam tries to get out of the apartment twice a day (which he learned in therapy to do in response to depression), but homeless people camp on the sidewalk outside his apartment, making the sidewalk impassable. Trucks double park and block the few curbcuts. There are heavy doors to manage to get into many stores. Even in his own apartment he experiences significant difficulties: the place is very cluttered from his husband who collects many things, forcing Sam to use crutches or a walker instead of a wheelchair in the house and increasing the risk of falls. His apartment is on the second floor, and the elevator is often out of service for many hours. The homeowners' association does not want to pay for repairs on nights and weekends because it costs more, and Sam has gotten into rages with the leadership of that association over this issue. Additionally, maintaining two wheelchairs, a scooter, a van lift, a stair lift, and a leg brace all require a good deal of time and emotional energy. When Sam is unhappy his attention to all of these microaggressions is greatly increased, and his tolerance of them greatly decreased.

D-AT VIII: Affective Regulation

Sam's initial presenting problem was depression and rage, and these remain issues for him. The amount of time he is clinically depressed has greatly decreased over time in therapy, and his episodes of expressed rage likewise have decreased. But the shame and guilt he experiences when he does express rage has not diminished, though it no longer lasts for 3 to 4 days as it did before (1 to 2 days is more typical now). And once he gets into a rage his capacity for empathy and understanding are nil, and his ability to think through consequences greatly impaired.

On the converse side, Sam tries hard to present only a positive image. He won't write his yearly Christmas letter until he has enough good things to say. He won't talk about his depression or anger in his gay men with disabilities group. He has seemingly introjected the idea of the brave and cheerful person with a disability whose real experiences of inaccessibility and discrimination are not to be aired. Thus, when he is in fact depressed or enraged, he simultaneously feels shameful. This stew of bravery, depression, rage, and shame is a potent mix for him, and one of the main things he struggles with daily.

D-AT IX: Intimacy

Sam is in a long-term stable relationship; he married his husband Eddie several years ago. Nonetheless, he is ever fearful that he will be abandoned, that his husband will leave him over something minor, and fearful of expressing his true self. Eddie, in turn, can be somewhat unsympathetic to Sam's daily frustrations with access, particularly in the home. However, he is very thoughtful and caring when Sam is hospitalized or laid up with an injury. Neither of them talk openly about their sexual relationship, which is fairly minimal, and Sam will not share his desires for particular activities. He does not readily open up to others and mostly feels that part of himself is always hidden, in whatever venue he is in. Despite this, he has some long-term friendships and real loyalty from a few people.

Summary from D-AT Template

Sam has significant polio-related issues, including pain, fatigue, infections, and limited mobility. His childhood taught him to put on a brave front and to mask his disability as much as possible. His core schema is that he will be abandoned and left to die alone. There is great discrepancy between the models of disability to which he actually subscribes and the models he aspires to. Despite his status as an educated White male who held a good job, as a gay man and a person with a disability he feels so disenfranchised that he cannot experience his privilege. He has one foot in disability culture and community but no place where the pressures of putting on a brave front are significantly alleviated, or where he can be just another disabled person such that the disability becomes irrelevant. His mobility impairments prevent him from visiting friends' houses and limit his social activities when he desires more frequent social interaction. He experiences pronounced rage and sadness when places are not accessible to him and when others have not anticipated his needs, but he also has great difficulty asking others to help him. As a person with depression, rage, anxiety, and shame, he struggles with being the kind of disabled person his mother expected him to be. Even in his most intimate relationship (with his husband) he holds much of himself back, in large part out of fear that the real self is not loveable and would be abandoned.

Case Formulation

Sam is a man who is only partly known to others, with segments of himself in different places. He can be openly gay, but not disabled. He can be disabled but not complaining. He can be intimate but only by hiding parts of himself. His core belief is that he is unlovable, that knowing all of who he is would prove this. Thus to avoid being abandoned, he must hide parts of himself from everyone. He courts abandonment through his rage but then is terrified of being abandoned. This paradox fuels his depression and anxiety. He perceives limited behavioral and emotional options, using dichotomous thinking of abuser or abused. When in a rage he is the abuser. When depressed he is abused, abandoned, and believes himself deserving of both.

Therapy is the one place where he has shared all aspects of his being, though he feels that the heterosexual female therapist can never truly understand him as a gay male. The key tasks for therapy are emotion regulation, work on his core schema of being unlovable and thus worthy of abandonment, increasing his ability to manage microaggressions and inaccessibility, and allowing greater degrees of intimacy in his closer relationships through more genuine expression of himself.

Comments

Of course, there are clients without disabilities with similar schemas. How does Sam's disability affect the formulation and the treatment? What the template in disability-affirmative therapy has provided is a way to conduct a cultural evaluation. Through this evaluation we have seen that disability has been a key element in his developmental history (actual abandonment, pressure to be "normal"). Disability greatly affects his current life (fatigue and pain) and his interactions with the world (inaccessibility, limited ability to visit friends, daily microaggressions). Cognitive discordance arises from the contrast between Sam's actual and desired models of disability, and from his actual mood (enraged and depressed) and the prohibition against anger, coupled with the prescription for cheerfulness imposed on people with disabilities. In short, disability has affected almost every part of Sam's past and current life. Therefore, the treatment will include disability issues to a significant degree.

For example, in working with Sam's schema of abandonment, his current life will have more examples that reinforce this schema because of his disability. When he has to sit out a party due to fatigue, or can't go to someone's (inaccessible) house, or watch his husband plays tennis, Sam will feel left out and abandoned yet again. The realities of having a disability will intersect with his schema over and over, making it harder to temper or eradicate it.

To give another example, regarding Sam's schema of being unlovable, the daily microaggressions are constant reminders of his second-class citizenship. These reminders bring feelings of rage, followed by shame. The constant repetition of this cycle (microaggression → rage → acting out → shame), which is reinforced by the way it fits into Sam's schema of being unlovable, will make it harder to weaken this schema. Treatment may include some stress inoculation, or higher tolerance for microaggressions, but I think the more important part of the treatment would be helping derive a decision-making process for choosing which microaggressions and inaccessibility issues to address and how to do so.

What we see from the case study of Sam is that although his schemas may be similar to those of many other clients without disabilities, the treatment of those schemas will be greatly influenced by the daily realities of living with a disability. Addressing Sam's presenting problems without including his disability issues is unlikely to be effective. The D-AT template has guided us to recognize that disability will be an essential and even major part of the case formulation and the treatment. This may not be the case for all clients with disabilities. But without a systematic evaluation of the role of disability, it can be difficult to know how much to include it in the formulation and hence into the treatment. D-AT is designed to provide clinicians with a methodology for that systematic evaluation.

Although the case presentation focused on the first 3 years of therapy, after 5 years Sam was significantly improved in mood, problem solving, emotion regulation, setting boundaries, and handling microaggressions, and he was able to cut back on therapy frequency. This suggests that incorporation of D-AT into case formulation and treatment can make therapy more disability-appropriate and culturally sensitive. Even in therapy shorter than the longer treatment for Sam, D-AT should help therapists target areas for goals and hone treatment to fit the client with a disability and his or her family.

Discussion Questions

1. Go through and fill out Table 13.1. Compare answers with another person.
2. How much is disability a part of Sam's presenting problems? His relationship with the therapist? His relationship with his partner? How did you decide your answers?
3. How might the therapy have been different with a non-disabled therapist? Be as specific as you can.

APPENDIX

Other Works by R. Olkin

Books

Olkin, R. (1999). *What psychotherapists should know about disability.* New York: Guilford Press.

Chapters in Books

Olkin, R. (2013). Clinical applications with persons with disabilities. In D. W. Sue, M. E. Gallardo, & H. A. Neville (Eds.), *Case studies in multicultural counseling and therapy* (Chapter 16). Hoboken, NJ: John Wiley & Sons.

Olkin, R. (2010). Limping towards Bethlehem: A personal history. In J. G. Ponterotto, J. M. Casas, L. A. Suzuki, & C. M. Alexander (Eds.), *Handbook of multicultural counseling* (3rd ed, pp. 79–85.). Thousand Oaks, CA: Sage Publications.

Olkin, R. (2006). Persons of color with disabilities. In M. Constantine (Ed.), *Clinical practice with people of color: A guide to becoming culturally competent* (pp. 162–182). New York: Teacher's College Press.

Olkin, R. (2006). Females with disabilities. In J. Worell & C. Goodheart (Eds.), *Handbook of girls' and women's psychological health* (pp. 144–157). New York: Oxford University Press.

Olkin, R. (2004). Disability and depression. In S. L. Welner & F. Haseltine (Eds.), *Welner's guide to the care of women with disabilities* (pp. 279–300). Philadelphia: Lippincott Williams & Wilkins.

Olkin, R. (1995). Matthew: Therapy with a teenager with a disability. In M. A. Blotzer & R. Ruth (Eds.), *Sometimes you just want to feel like a human being: Empowering psychotherapy with persons with disabilities* (pp. 37–51). Baltimore: Paul Brookes.

Journal Articles

Olkin, R. (2013). What should we teach when we teach about women with disabilities? *Women & Therapy, 37*(1-2), 94–108.

Taube, D., & Olkin, R. (2011). When is differential treatment discriminatory? Legal, ethical, and professional considerations for psychology trainees with disabilities. *Rehabilitation Psychology, 56*(4), 329–339.

Olkin, R. (2009). The three R's of supervising students with disabilities: Reading, writing, and reasonable accommodations. *Women and Therapy, 33*(1-2), 73–84.

Olkin, R. (2008). Social warrior or unwitting bigot? *Professional Psychology: Research and Practice, 39*(5), 488–497.

Breeden, C., Olkin, R., & Taube, D. J. (2008). Custody evaluations when one divorcing parent has a disability. *Rehabilitation Psychology, 53*(4), 445–455.

Olkin, R., Abrams, K., Preston, P., & Kirshbaum, M. (2006). Comparison of parents with and without disabilities raising teens: Information from the NHIS and two national surveys. *Rehabilitation Psychology, 51*(1), 43–49.

Olkin, R. (2005). Why I changed my mind about physician-assisted suicide: How Stanford University made a radical out of me. *Journal of Disability Policy Studies, 16*(1), 68–71.

Olkin, R. (2004). Making research accessible to participants with disabilities. *Journal of Multicultural Counseling & Development, 32*(extra), 332–343.

Olkin, R., & Pledger, C. (2003). Can disability studies and psychology join hands? *American Psychologist, 58*(4), 296–304.

Olkin, R. (2003). Women with physical disabilities who want to leave their partners: A feminist and disability-affirmative perspective. *Women and Therapy, 26*(3/4), 237–246.

Olkin, R. (2002). The rights of graduate psychology students with disabilities. *Journal of Social Work in Disability and Rehabilitation, 1*(1), 67–80.

Kirshbaum, M., & Olkin, R. (2002). Parents with physical, systemic or visual disabilities. *Sexuality and Disability, 20*(1), 65–80.

Olkin, R. (2002). Could you hold the door for me? Including disability in diversity. *Cultural Diversity & Ethnic Minority Psychology, 8*(2), 130–137.

Conley-Jung, C., & Olkin, R. (2001). Mothers with visual impairments or blindness raising young children. *Journal of Visual Impairment and Blindness, 91*(1), 14–29.

Olkin, R. (1999). The personal, professional and political when clients have disabilities. *Women and Therapy, 22*(2), 87–103.

References

Abels, A. V. (2008). Putting disability ethics into practice. *Professional Psychology: Research and Practice, 39*, 495–497.

Addiction Hope. (2016). Benzodiazepine abuse causes, statistics, addiction signs, symptoms, and side effects. Retrieved from https://www.addictionhope.com/benzodiazepine/

Aikens, J. E., Reinecke, M. A., Pliskin, N. H., Fischer, J. S., Wiebe, J. S., McCracken, L. M., & Taylor, J. L. (1999). Assessing depressive symptoms in multiple sclerosis: Is it necessary to omit items from the original Beck Depression Inventory? *Journal of Behavioral Medicine, 22*(2), 127–142.

Alegría, M., Cao, Z., McGuire, T. G., Ojeda, V. D., Sribney, B., Woo, M., & Takeuchi, D. (2006). Health insurance coverage for vulnerable populations: Contrasting Asian Americans and Latinos in the United States. *Inquiry, 43*(3), 231–254.

Alexopoulos, G. S., Jeste, D. V., Chung, H., Carpenter, D., Ross, R., & Docherty, J. P. (2005). The expert consensus guideline series. Treatment of dementia and its behavioral disturbances. Introduction: methods, commentary, and summary. *Postgraduate Medicine*, Spec. No., 6–22.

Ali, Z., Fazil, Q., Bywaters, P., Wallace, L., & Singh, G. (2001). Disability, ethnicity and childhood: A critical review of research. *Disability & Society, 16*(7), 949–967.

Alston, R. J., Bell, T. J., & Feist-Price, S. (1996). Racial identity and African Americans with disabilities: Theoretical and practical considerations. *Journal of Rehabilitation, 62*(2), 11.

Amado, A. N. E. (1993). *Friendships and community connections between people with and without developmental disabilities.* Baltimore, MD: Paul H. Brookes Publishing.

American Cancer Society. (2002). *Sexuality & cancer: For the man/woman who has cancer and his/her partner.* Atlanta, GA: Author.

American Psychiatric Association. (2013). *Diagnostic and statistical manual,* 5th ed. Washington, DC: Author.

American Psychological Association. (1999). Enhancing your interactions with people with disabilities. Retrieved from http://www.apa.org/pi/disability/enhancing.html.

American Psychological Association. (2012). Guidelines for assessment of and intervention with persons with disabilities. *The American Psychologist, 67*(1), 43.

Anastasiou, D., Kauffman, J. M, & Michail, D. (2016). Disability in multicultural theory: Conceptual and social justice issues. *Journal of Disability Policy Studies, 27*(1), 3–12.

Anderson, P., & Kitchin, R. (2000). Disability, space and sexuality: Access to family planning services. *Social Science & Medicine, 51*, 1162–1173.

Andrews, A. B., & Veronen, L. J. (1993). Sexual assault and people with disabilities. *Journal of Social Work and Human Sexuality, 8*(2), 137–159.

Andrews, E. E., & Lund, E. M. (2015). Disability in psychology training: Where are we? *Training & Education in Professional Psychology, 9*(3), 210–216.

Annon, J. (1976). *The behavioral treatment of sexual problems: Brief therapy*. New York: Harper & Row.

Antonak, R. F., & Livneh, H. (1995). Direct and indirect methods to measure attitudes toward persons with disabilities, with an exegesis of the error-choice test method. *Rehabilitation Psychology, 40*(1), 3.

Arruda, M. S., Petta, C. A., Abrao, M. S., & Benetti-Pinto, C. L. (2003). Time elapsed from onset of symptoms to diagnosis of endometriosis in a cohort study of Brazilian women. *Human Reproduction, 18*(4), 756–759.

Artman, L. K., & Daniels, J. A. (2010). Disability and psychotherapy practice: Cultural competence and practical tips. *Professional Psychology: Research and Practice, 41*(5), 442–448.

Asch, A. (1946). Forming impressions of personality. *Journal of Abnormal and Social Psychology, 41*, 258–290.

Asch, A. (1988). Disability: Its place in the curriculum. In P. A. Bronstein and K. Quina (Eds.), *Teaching a psychology of people* (pp. 156–167). Washington, DC: American Psychological Association.

Asch, A. (2002). Disability equality and prenatal testing: Contradictory or compatible. *Florida State University Law Review, 30*, 315–342.

Asch, A., & Fine, M. (1992). Beyond pedestals: Revisiting the lives of women with disabilities. In M. Fine, ed., *Disruptive voices: The possibilities of feminist research* (pp. 139–174). Ann Arbor: University of Michigan Press.

Asch, A., & Fine, M. (1997). Nurturance, sexuality and women with disabilities: The example of women and literature. In L. J. Davis (Ed.), *The disability studies reader* (pp. 241–259). New York: Routledge.

Asemota, A. O., George, B. P., Bowman, S. M., Haider, A. H., & Schneider, E. B. (2013). Causes and trends in traumatic brain injury for United States adolescents. *Journal of Neurotrauma, 30*(2), 67–75.

Ash, A., Bellew, J., Davies, M., Newman, T., & Richardson, L. (1997). Everybody in? The experience of disabled students in further education. *Disability & Society, 12*(4), 605–621.

Asper, K. (2010). Psychotherapy and congenital physical disability. In M. Stein (Ed.), *Jungian psychoanalysis: Working in the spirit of C. G. Jung* (pp. 296–306). Chicago: Open Court Publishing Co.

Atkins, B. J. (1988). An asset-oriented approach to cross cultural issues: Blacks in rehabilitation. *Journal of Applied Rehabilitation Counseling, 19*(4), 45–49.

Atkins, D., & Marston, C. (1999). Creating accessible queer community: Intersections and fractures with dis/ability praxis. *International Journal of Sexuality and Gender Studies, 4*(1), 3–21.

Atwal, A., Spiliotopoulou, G., Coleman, C., Harding, K., Quirke, C., Smith, N., . . . Wilson, L. (2014). Polio survivors' perceptions of the meaning of quality of life and strategies to promote participation in everyday activities. *Health Expectations, 18*(5), 715–726.

Aunos, M., Goupil, G., & Feldman, M. (2003). Mothers with intellectual disabilities who do or do not have custody of their children. *Journal on Developmental Disabilities, 10*(2), 65–79.

Avery, R. C., & Hogan, D. P. (2007). Family configurations of disability in the 2000 census. Presented at the annual meeting of the Population Association of America, 2006. As cited in Hogan, D. P., Shandra, C. L., & Msall, M. E. (2007). Family developmental risk factors among adolescents with disabilities and children of parents with disabilities. *Journal of Adolescence, 30*(6), 1001–1019.

Bakshi, R., Shaikh, Z. A., Miletich, R. S., Czarnecki, D., Dmochowski, J., Henschel, K., . . . Kinkel, P. R. (2000). Fatigue in multiple sclerosis and its relationship to depression and neurologic disability. *Multiple Sclerosis, 6*(3), 181–185.

Balcazar, F. E., Keys, C. B., Kaplan, D. L., & Suarez-Balcazar, Y. (1998). Participatory action research and people with disabilities: Principles and challenges. *Canadian Journal of Rehabilitation, 12*, 105–112.

Balcazar, F. E., Keys, C. B., & Suarez-Balcazar, Y. (2001). Empowering Latinos with disabilities to address issues of independent living and disability rights: A capacity-building approach. *Journal of Prevention & Intervention in the Community, 21*(2), 53–70.

Balcazar, F. E., Seekins, T., Fawcett, S. B., & Hopkins, B. L. (1990). Empowering people with physical disabilities through advocacy skills training. *American Journal of Community Psychology, 18*(2), 281–296.

Balcazar, F. E., Suarez-Balcazar, Y., & Taylor-Ritzler, T. (2009). Cultural competence: Development of a conceptual framework. *Disability and Rehabilitation, 31*(14), 1153–1160.

Ballan, M. (2008). Disability and sexuality within social work education in the USA and Canada: The social model of disability as a lens for practice. *Social Work Education, 27*(2), 194–202.

Balter, R. (2006). Psychotherapy with clients with physical disabilities. *NY State Psychologist, 5*(4), 29–33.

Barker, L. T., & Maralani, V. (1997). *Challenges and Strategies of Disabled Parents: Findings from a National Survey of Parents with Disabilities: Final Report.* Berkeley Planning Associates.

Barker, M., Power, C., & Roberts, I. (1996). Injuries and the risk of disability in teenagers and young adults. *Archives of Disease in Childhood, 75*(2), 156–158.

Barnartt, S. N. (1996). Disability culture or disability consciousness? *Journal of Disability Policy Studies, 7*(2), 1–19.

Barnes, C., & Mercer, G. (2001). Disability culture: Assimilation or inclusion? In G. L. Albrecht, K. D. Seelman, & M. Bury (Eds.), *Handbook of disability studies* (pp. 515–534). Thousand Oaks, CA: Sage.

Barnes, C., Mercer, G., & Shakespeare, T. (1999). *Exploring disability: A sociological introduction* (pp. 182–210). Cambridge, UK: Polity Press.

Bartram, P. (2013). Melancholia, mourning, love: Transforming the melancholic response to disability through psychotherapy. *British Journal of Psychotherapy, 29*(2), 168–181.

Basford, J. R., Rohe, D. E., Barnes, C. P., & DePompolo, R. W. (2002). Substance abuse attitudes and policies in US rehabilitation training programs: A comparison of 1985 and 2000. *Archives of Physical Medicine and Rehabilitation, 83*, 517–522.

Bates, P. S., Spencer, J. C., Young, M. E., & Rintala, D. H. (1993). Assistive technology and the newly disabled adult: Adaptation to wheelchair use. *American Journal of Occupational Therapy, 47*(11), 1014–1021.

Beail, N., & Warden, S. (1996). Evaluation of a psychodynamic psychotherapy service for adults with intellectual disabilities: Rationale, design and preliminary outcome data. *Journal of Applied Research in Intellectual Disabilities, 9*(3), 223–228.

Bech, P. (2012). *Rating scales for psychopathology, health status and quality of life: A compendium on documentation in accordance with the DSM-III-R and WHO systems.* New York: Springer Science and Business Media.

Beeseley, K., White, J. H., Alston, M. K., Sweetapple, A., & Pollack, M. (2011). Art after stroke: The qualitative experience of community dwelling stroke survivors in a group art programme. *Disability & Rehabilitation, 33*(23–24), 2346–2355.

Belgrave, F. Z. (1998). *Psychosocial aspects of chronic illness and disability among African Americans.* Santa Barbara, CA: Greenwood Publishing Group.

Belgrave, F. Z., & Jarama, S. L. (2000). Culture and disability in the rehabilitation experience: An African American example. In R. G. Frank & T. R. Elliott (Eds.), *Handbook of rehabilitation psychology* (pp. 585–600). Washington, DC: American Psychological Association.

Belgrave, F. Z., & Walker, S. (1991). Predictors of employment outcome of black persons with disabilities. *Rehabilitation Psychology, 36*(2), 111.

Bendelin, N., Hesser, H., Dalh, J., Carlbring, P., Nelson, K. Z., & Andersson, G. (2011). Experiences of guided Internet-based cognitive-behavioural treatment for depression: A qualitative study. *BMC Psychiatry, 11*, 107.

Benedict, R. H., Fishman, I., McClellan, M. M., Bakshi, R., & Weinstock-Guttman, B. (2003). Validity of the Beck Depression Inventory-fast screen in multiple sclerosis. *Multiple Sclerosis, 9*(4), 393–396.

Berger, S. (2012). Is my world getting smaller? The challenges of living with vision loss. *Journal of Visual Impairment & Blindness, 106*(1), 1–16.

Berman, H., Harris, D., Enright, R., Gilpin, M., & Cathers, T. (1999). Sexuality and the adolescent with a physical disability: Understandings and misunderstandings. *Issues in Comprehensive Nursing, 22*, 193–196.

Bernert, D. J. (2011). Sexuality and disability in the lives of women with intellectual disabilities. *Sexuality and Disability, 29*, 129–141.

Biklen, D. (1988). The myth of clinical judgment. *Journal of Social Issues, 44*, 127–140.

Black, R. S., & Pretes, L. (2007). Victims and victors: Representation of physical disability on the silver screen. *Research and Practice for Persons with Severe Disabilities, 32*(1), 66–83.

Blackford, K. A. (1993). Erasing mothers with disabilities through Canadian family-related policy. *Disability, Handicap & Society, 8*(3), 281–294.

Blackmore, D. E., Hart, S. L., Albiani, J. J., & Mohr, D. C. (2011). Improvements in partner support predict sexual satisfaction among individuals with multiple sclerosis. *Rehabilitation Psychology, 56*(2), 117–122.

Błeszyńska, K. (1995). Values attributed to marriage by persons with physical disabilities. *International Journal of Disability, Development and Education, 42*(3), 203–210.

Bloom, B., Cohen, R. A., & Freeman, G. (2009). Summary health statistics for US children: National Health Interview Survey, 2008. *Vital and Health Statistics. Series 10, Data from the National Health Survey, 244*, 1–81.

Blotzer, M. A., & Ruth, R. (Eds.). (1995). *Sometimes you just want to feel like a human being: Case studies of empowering psychotherapy with people with disabilities.* Baltimore, MD: Paul H. Brookes.

Blue-Banning, M., Summers, J. A., Frankland, H. C., Nelson, L. L., & Beegle, G. (2004). Dimensions of family and professional partnerships: Constructive guidelines for collaboration. *Exceptional Children, 70*(2), 167–184.

Bogart, K. R. (2015). Disability identity predicts lower anxiety and depression in multiple sclerosis. *Rehabilitation Psychology, 60*(1), 105–109.

Bogdan, R., & Taylor, S. (1989). Relationships with severely disabled people: The social construction of humanness. *Social Problems, 36,* 135–148.

Bombardier, C. H., & Turner, A. P. (2010). Alcohol and other drug use in traumatic disability. In R. G. Frank, M. Rosenthal, & B. Caplan (Eds.). *Handbook of rehabilitation psychology* (2nd ed., pp. 241–258). Washington, DC: American Psychological Association.

Booth, T., Booth, W., & McConnell, D. (2005). Care proceedings and parents with learning difficulties: Comparative prevalence and outcomes in an English and Australian court sample. *Child & Family Social Work, 10*(4), 353–360.

Boston Women's Health Collective (1996). *The new our bodies, ourselves.* New York: Touchstone.

Boyle, C. A., Boulet, S., Schieve, L. A., Cohen, R. A., Blumberg, S. J., Yeargin-Allsopp, M., Visser, S., & Kogan, M. D. (2011). Trends in the prevalence of developmental disabilities in US children, 1997–2008. *Pediatrics, 127*(6), 1034–1042.

Bradford, J., Ryan, C., & Rothblum, E. E. (1994). National lesbian health care survey: Implications for mental health care. *Journal of Consulting and Clinical Psychology, 62,* 228–242.

Braithwaite, J., & Mont, D. (2009). Disability and poverty: a survey of World Bank poverty assessments and implications. *ALTER-European Journal of Disability Research/Revue Européenne de Recherche sur le Handicap, 3*(3), 219–232.

Brault, M. W. (2012). Americans with disabilities: 2010. *Current Population Reports, 7,* 0–131.

Breeden, C., Olkin, R., & Taube, D. (2008). Child custody evaluations when one divorcing parent has a physical disability. *Rehabilitation Psychology, 53*(4), 445–455.

Breen, L. J., Wildy, H., Saggers, S., Millsteed, J., & Raghavendra, P. (2011). In search of wellness: Allied professionals' understandings of wellness in childhood disability services. *Disability & Rehabilitation, 33*(10), 862–871.

Brenes, G. A., Guralnik, J. M., Williamson, J. D., Fried, L. P., Simpson, C., Simonsick, E. M., & Penninx, B. W. (2005). The influence of anxiety on the progression of disability. *Journal of the American Geriatrics Society, 53*(1), 34–39.

Brown, S. (2002). What is disability culture? *Disability Studies Quarterly, 22*(2), 34–50.

Brownridge, D. A. (2006). Partner violence against women with disabilities: Prevalence, risk, and explanations. *Violence Against Women, 12*(9), 805–822.

Bruno, R. L., Cohen, J. M., & Frick, N. M. (1994). The neuroanatomy of post-polio fatigue. *Archives of Physical Medicine and Rehabilitation, 75,* 498–504.

Bryan W. V. (2007). *Multicultural aspects of disabilities: A guide to understanding and assisting minorities in the rehabilitation process* (2nd ed.). Springfield, IL: Charles C. Thomas.

Buck, F., & Hohmann, G. (1981). Personality, behavior, values, and family relations of children of fathers with spinal cord injury. *Archives of Physical Medicine and Rehabilitation, 62,* 432–438.

Bullock, K., Crawford, S. L., & Tennstedt, S. L. (2003). Employment and caregiving: Exploration of African American caregivers. *Social Work, 48*(2), 150–162.

Burgmann, T., Clara, I., Graff, L., Walker, J., Lix, L., Rawsthorne, P., ... Bernstein, C. N. (2006). The Manitoba Inflammatory Bowel Disease Cohort Study: Prolonged symptoms before diagnosis—how much is irritable bowel syndrome? *Clinical Gastroenterology and Hepatology, 4*(5), 614–620.

Burton, P., Lethbridge, L., & Phipps, S. (2008). Children with disabilities and chronic conditions and longer-term parental health. *Journal of Socio-Economics, 37*(3), 1168–1186.

Buzzelli, S., di Francesco, L., Giaquinto, S., & Nolfe, G. (1997). Psychological and medical aspects of sexuality following stroke. *Sexuality and Disability, 15*(4), 261–270.

Byrd, E. K., & Elliott, T. R. (1985). Feature films and disability: A descriptive study. *Rehabilitation Psychology, 30*(1), 47–51.

Camenga, D. R., Gaither, J. R., Leventhal, J., & Ryan, S. (2015). Increasing incidence of hospital admissions for opioid poisonings in adolescents and young adults: 2000–2009. *Drug & Alcohol Dependence, 146*, e237.

Carlson, D., & Ehrlich, N. (2006). Sources of payment for assistive technology: Findings from a national survey of persons with disabilities. *Assistive Technology, 18*(1), 77–86.

Carlson, G., Armitstead, C., Rodger, S., & Liddle, G. (2010). Parents' experiences of the provision of community-based family support and therapy services utilizing the strengths approach and natural learning environments. *Journal of Applied Research in Intellectual Disabilities, 23*, 560–572.

Carroll, J. L., & Loughlin, G. M. (1992). Diagnostic criteria for obstructive sleep apnea syndrome in children. *Pediatric Pulmonology, 14*(2), 71–74.

Caruso, S. M., Baum, R. B., Hopkins, D., Lauer, M., Russell, S., Meranto, E., & Stisser, K. (1997). The development of a regional association to address the sexuality needs of individuals with disabilities. *Sexuality and Disability, 15*(4), 285–291.

Castaneto, M. V., & Willemsen, E. W. (2006). Social perception of the personality of the disabled. *Social Behavior and Personality, 34*(10), 1217–1232.

Center for Behavioral Health Statistics and Quality. (2016). *Key substance use and mental health indicators in the United States: Results from the 2015 National Survey on Drug Use and Health* (HHS Publication No. SMA 16-4984, NSDUH Series H-51). Retrieved from http://www.samhsa.gov/data/

Centers for Disease Control and Prevention (2008). Racial/ethnic disparities in self-rated health status among adults with and without disabilities—United States, 2004–2006. *MMWR. Morbidity and Mortality Weekly Report, 57*(39), 1069.

Centers for Disease Control and Prevention (2015). *Insufficeint sleep is a public health problem*. Retrieved from http://www.cdc.gov/features/dssleep/

Chan, F., Lam, C. S., Wong, D., Leung, P., & Fang, X. S. (1988). Counseling Chinese Americans with disabilities. *Journal of Applied Rehabilitation Counseling, 19*, 21–25.

Chan, J., Edman, J. C., & Koltai, P. J. (2004). Obstructive sleep apnea in children. *American Family Physician, 69*(5), 1147–1160.

Chan, K. W. A., Felson, D. T., Yood, R. A., & Walker, A. M. (1994). The lag time between onset of symptoms and diagnosis of rheumatoid arthritis. *Arthritis & Rheumatism, 37*(6), 814–820.

Chance, R. S. (2002). To love and be loved: Sexuality and people with physical disabilities. *Journal of Psychology and Theology, 30*(3), 195–208.

Chang, L-H., & Wang, J. (2012). Institutional contexts contribute to the low priority given to developing self-care independence in a rehabilitation ward: A qualitative study. *Clinical Rehabilitation, 27*(6), 538–545.

Chapman, C., Laird, J., Ifill, N., & Kewal Ramani, A. (2011). Trends in high school dropout and completion rates in the United States: 1972–2009. Compendium report. NCES 2012-006. National Center for Education Statistics.

Chen, R. K., Brodwin, M. G., Cardoso, E., & Chan, F. (2002). Attitudes toward people with disabilities in the social context of dating and marriage: A comparison of American, Taiwanese, and Singaporean college students. *Journal of Rehabilitation, 68*(4), 5.

Chen, R. K., Jo, S. J., & Donnell, C. M. (2004). Enhancing the rehabilitation counseling process: Understanding the obstacles to Asian Americans' utilization of services. *Journal of Applied Rehabilitation Counseling, 35*(1), 29–35.

Cheng, C. (2001). Assessing coping flexibility in real-life and laboratory settings: A multimethod approach. *Journal of Personality and Social Psychology, 80*(5), 814.

Cheng, C., & Cheung, M. W. (2005). Cognitive processes underlying coping flexibility: Differentiation and integration. *Journal of Personality, 73*(4), 859–886.

Cheng, C., Lau, H. P. B., & Chan, M. P. S. (2014). Coping flexibility and psychological adjustment to stressful life changes: A meta-analytic review. *Psychological Bulletin, 140*(6), 1582.

Choi, K. H., & Wynne, M. E. (2000). Providing services to Asian Americans with developmental disabilities and their families: Mainstream service providers' perspective. *Community Mental Health Journal, 36*(6), 589–595.

Chou, C. C., Chan, F., Phillips, B., & Chan, J. Y. C. (2013). Introduction to positive psychology in rehabilitation. *Rehabilitation Research, Policy, and Education, 27*(3), 126–130.

Christle, C. A., Jolivette, K., & Nelson, C. M. (2007). School characteristics related to high school dropout rates. *Remedial and Special Education, 28*(6), 325–339.

Chwastiak, L., Ehde, D. M., Gibbons, L. E., Sullivan, M., Bowen, J. D., & Kraft, G. H. (2002). Depressive symptoms and severity of illness in multiple sclerosis: Epidemiologic study of a large community sample. *American Journal of Psychiatry, 159*(11), 1862–1868.

Closs, S. J., Barr, B., Briggs, M., Cash, K., & Seers, K. (2004). A comparison of five pain assessment scales for nursing home residents with varying degrees of cognitive impairment. *Journal of Pain and Symptoms Management, 27*(3), 196–205.

Cobb, H. C., & Warner, P. J. (1999). Counseling and psychotherapy with children and adolescents with disabilities. In H. T. Prout & D. T. Brown (Eds.), *Counseling and psychotherapy with children and adolescents: Theory and practice for school and clinical settings* (3rd ed., pp. 401–426). Hoboken, NJ: John Wiley & Sons.

Cohen, L. J. (1998). *Mothers' perceptions of the influence of their physical disabilities on the developmental tasks of children* (Unpublished doctoral dissertation). California School of Professional Psychology at Alliant International University, Alameda, CA.

Cohen, S., Kamarck, T., & Mermelstein, R. (1983). A global measure of perceived stress. *Journal of Health and Social Behavior, 24*, 385–396.

Conley-Jung, C., & Olkin, R. (2001). Mothers with visual impairments who are raising young children. *Journal of Visual Impairment and Blindness, 91*(1), 14–29.

Copel, L. C. (2006). Partner abuse in physically disabled women: A proposed model for understanding intimate partner violence. *Perspectives in Psychiatric Care, 42*(2), 114–129.

Cornish, J. A., Gorgens, K. A., Monson, S. P., Olkin, R., Palombi, B. J., & Abels, A. V. (2008). Perspectives on ethical practice with people who have disabilities. *Professional Psychology: Research and Practice, 39*, 488–497.

Coutinho, M. J., Oswald, D. P., & Best, A. M. (2002). The influence of sociodemographics and gender on the disproportionate identification of minority students as having learning disabilities. *Remedial and Special Education, 23*(1), 49–59.

Craig Hospital. (2015). *Sexual function for men after spinal cord injury*. Retrieved from https://craighospital.org/resources/sexual-function-for-men-after-a-spinal-cord-injury

Crewe, N. (1980). Quality of life: The ultimate goal in rehabilitation. *Minnesota Medicine, 63*, 586–589.

Crewe, N., & Krause, J. (1988). Marital relationships and spinal cord injury. *Archives of Physical Medicine and Rehabilitation, 69*, 435–438.

Crewe, N., & Krause, J. (1990). An eleven-year follow-up of adjustment to spinal cord injury. *Rehabilitation Psychology, 35*, 205–210.

Crewe, N., & Krause, J. (1992). Marital status and adjustment to spinal cord injury. *Journal of the American Paraplegia Society, 15*, 14–18.

Cronin, T., Levin, S., Branscombe, N. R., van Laar, C., & Tropp, L. (2012). Ethnic identification in response to perceived discrimination protects well-being and promotes activism: A longitudinal study of Latino college students. *Group Processes & Intergroup Relations, 15*(4), 393–407.

Crutchfield, M. (1997). Who's teaching our children with disabilities? *NICHCY News Digest, 27*.

Cumming, R. G., Salkeld, G., Thomas, M., & Szonyi, G. (2000). Prospective study of the impact of fear of falling on activities of daily living, SF-36 scores, and nursing home admission. *Journals of Gerontology Series A: Biological Sciences and Medical Sciences, 55*(5), M299–M305.

Curran, A. L., Sharples, P. M., White, C., & Knapp, M. (2001). Time costs of caring for children with severe disabilities compared with caring for children without disabilities. *Developmental Medicine & Child Neurology, 43*(08), 529–533.

Dajani, K. F. (2001). What's in a name? Terms used to refer to people with disabilities. *Disability Studies Quarterly, 21*(3), 196–209. Retrieved from http://www.dsq-sds.org.

Darke, P. A. (1999). *The cinematic construction of physical disability as identified through the application of the social model of disability to six indicative films made since 1970: A day in the death of Joe Egg (1970), The raging moon (1970), The elephant man (1980), Whose life is it anyway?(1981), Duet for one (1987) and My left foot (1989)* (Unpublished doctoral dissertation). University of Warwick.

da Silva Cardoso, E., Pruett, S. R., Chan, F., & Tansey, T. N. (2006). Substance abuse assessment and treatment: The current training and practice of APA Division 22 members. *Rehabilitation Psychology, 51*(2), 175–178.

David, E. J. R. (2009). Internalized oppression, psychopathology, and cognitive behavioral therapy among historically oppressed groups. *Journal of Psychological Practice, 15*(1), 71–103.

Davila, D. G., Hurt, R. D., Offord, K. P., Harris, C. D., & Shepard Jr, J. W. (1994). Acute effects of transdermal nicotine on sleep architecture, snoring, and sleep-disordered breathing in nonsmokers. *American Journal of Respiratory and Critical Care Medicine, 150*(2), 469–474.

Deal, M. (2003). Disabled people's attitudes toward other impairment groups: A hierarchy of impairments. *Disability & Society, 18*(7), 897–910.

DeBerard, M. S., Spielmans, G. I., & Julka, D. L. (2004). Predictors of academic achievement and retention among college freshmen: A longitudinal study. *College Student Journal, 38*(1), 66.

Dembo, T., Leviton, G. L., & Wright, B. A. (1956). Adjustment to misfortune—a problem of social-psychological rehabilitation. *Artificial Limbs, 3*(2), 4–62. Reprinted in Dembo, T., Leviton, G. L., & Wright, B. A. (1975). Adjustment to misfortune: A problem of social-psychological rehabilitation. *Rehabilitation Psychology, 22*, 1–100.

Demissie, K., Rhoads, G. G., Ananth, C. V., Alexander, G. R., Kramer, M. S., Kogan, M. D., & Joseph, K. S. (2001). Trends in preterm birth and neonatal mortality among blacks and whites in the United States from 1989 to 1997. *American Journal of Epidemiology, 154*(4), 307–315.

DeRubeis, R. J., Siegle, G. J., & Hollon, S. D. (2008). Opinion: Cognitive therapy versus medication for depression: Treatment outcomes and neural mechanisms. *Nature Reviews Neuroscience, 9*, 788–796.

Devlieger, P. J., Albrecht, G. L., & Hertz, M. (2007). The production of disability culture among young African–American men. *Social Science & Medicine, 64*(9), 1948–1959.

DiGiulio, G. (2003). Sexuality and people living with physical or developmental disabilities: A review of key issues. *Canadian Journal of Human Sexuality, 12*(1), 53–68.

DiMatteo, M. R., Lepper, H. S., & Croghan, T. W. (2000). Depression is a risk factor for noncompliance with medical treatment: Meta-analysis of the effects of anxiety and depression on patient adherence. *Archives of Internal Medicine, 160*(14), 2101–2107.

DiScala, C., Sege, R., Li, G., & Reece, R. M. (2000). Child abuse and unintentional injuries: A 10-year retrospective. *Archives of Pediatrics & Adolescent Medicine, 154*(1), 16–22.

Doig, E., Fleming, J., Cornwell, P., & Kuipers, P. (2011). Comparing the experience of outpatient therapy in home and day hospital settings after traumatic brain injury: Patient, significant other and therapist perspectives. *Disability & Rehabilitation, 33*(13-14), 1203–1214.

Dolk, H., Pattenden, S., & Johnson, A. (2001). Cerebral palsy, low birthweight and socio-economic deprivation: Inequalities in a major cause of childhood disability. *Paediatric and Perinatal Epidemiology, 15*(4), 359–363.

Doren, B., & Benz, M. (2001). Gender equity issues in the vocational and transition services and employment outcomes experienced by young women with disabilities. In H. Rousso & M. L. Wehmeyer (Eds.), *Double jeopardy: Addressing gender equity in special education* (pp. 289–312). Albany, NY: State University of New York Press.

Douglass, S., Palmer, K., & O'Connor, C. (2007). Experiences of running an anxiety management group for people with a learning disability using a cognitive behavioural intervention. *British Journal of Learning Disabilities, 35*, 245–252.

Dovidio, J. F., Pagotto, L., & Hebl, M. R. (2011). Implicit attitudes and discrimination against people with physical disabilities. In R. L. Wiener & S. L. Wilborn (Eds.), *Disability and age discrimination: Perspectives in law and psychology* (pp. 157–184). New York: Springer.

Duckro, P. N., Chibnall, J. T., & Tomazic, T. J. (1995). Anger, depression, and disability: a path analysis of relationships in a sample of chronic posttraumatic headache patients. *Headache: The Journal of Head and Face Pain, 35*(1), 7–9.

Due-Christensen, M., Zoffmann, V., Hommel, E., & Lau, M. (2011). Education and psychological aspects: Can sharing experiences in groups reduce the burden of living with diabetes, regardless of glycaemic control? *Diabetic Medicine, 29*, 251–256.

Duke, T. S. (2011). Lesbian, gay, bisexual, and transgender youth with disabilities: A meta-synthesis. *Journal of LGBT Youth, 8*(1), 1–52.

Dune, T. M. (2012). Sexuality and physical disability: Exploring the barriers and solutions in healthcare. *Sexuality and Disability, 30*, 247–255.

Dunn, C., Chambers, D., & Rabren, K. (2004). Variables affecting students' decisions to drop out of school. *Remedial and Special Education, 25*(5), 314–323.

Dunn, D. S. (2015). *The social psychology of disability*. New York: Oxford University Press.

Dunn, D. S., & Andrews, E. (2015). People-first and identity-first language: Developing psychologists' cultural competence using disability language. *American Psychologist, 70*(3), 255–264.

Dupré, M. (2012). Disability culture and cultural competency in social work. *Social Work Education, 31*(2), 168–183.

Dwight, M. M., Kowdley, K. V., Russo, J. E., Ciechanowski, P. S., Larson, A. M., & Katon, W. J. (2000). Depression, fatigue, and functional disability in patients with chronic hepatitis C. *Journal of Psychosomatic Research, 49*(5), 311–317.

East, L. J., & Orchard, T. R. (2014). 'Why can't I?': An exploration of sexuality and identity among Canadian youth living with physical disabilities. *Journal of Youth Studies, 17*(5), 559–576.

Eddey, G. E., & Robey, K. L. (2005). Considering the culture of disability in cultural competence education. *Academic Medicine, 80*(7), 706–712.

Ehde, D. M., & Jensen, M. P. (2004). Feasibility of a cognitive restructuring intervention for treatment of chronic pain in persons with disabilities. *Rehabilitation Psychology, 49*(3), 254–258.

Ehrensperger, M. M., Grether, A., Romer, G., Berres, M., Monsch, A. U., Kappos, L., & Steck, B. (2008). Neuropsychological dysfunction, depression, physical disability, and coping processes in families with a parent affected by multiple sclerosis. *Multiple Sclerosis Journal, 14*(8), 1106–1112.

Elliott, T. R., & Umlauf, R. L. (1991). Measurement of personality and psychopathology following acquired physical disability. In L. A. Cushman & M. Scherer (Eds.), *Psychological assessment in medical rehabilitation*. Hyattsville, MD: American Psychological Association.

Emmett, T. (2005). Disability and poverty. In *Augmentative and alternative communication interventions: Beyond poverty* (pp. 68–94). London: Whurr.

Erickson Cornish, J. A., Gorgens, K., Monson, S. P., Olkin, R., Palombi, B. J., & Abels, A. V. (2008). Perspectives on ethical practice with people who have disabilities. *Professional Psychology: Research and Practice, 39*(5), 488–497.

Esmail, S., Darry, K., Walter, A., & Knupp, H. (2010). Attitudes and perceptions towards disability and sexuality. *Disability and Rehabilitation, 32*(14), 1148–1155.

Estell, D. B., Jones, M. H., Pearl, R., & Van Acker, R. (2009). Best friendships of students with and without learning disabilities across late elementary school. *Exceptional Children, 76*(1), 110–124.

Ewing, J. A. (1984). Detecting alcoholism: the CAGE questionnaire. *Journal of the American Medical Association, 252*(14), 1905–1907.

Falicov, C. J. (1995). Training to think culturally: A multidimensional comparative framework. *Family Process, 34*, 373–388.

Falicov, C. J. (1998). *Latino families in therapy: A guide to multicultural practice*. New York: Guilford Press.

Fallon, A. E., & Rozin, P. (1985). Sex differences in perceptions of desirable body shape. *Journal of Abnormal Psychology, 94*(1), 102.

Falvo, D. R. (2014). *Medical and psychosocial aspects of chronic illness and disability* (5th ed.). Burlington, MA: Jones & Bartlett Learning.

Farber, R. S. (2000). Mothers with disabilities: In their own voice. *American Journal of Occupational Therapy, 54*(3), 260–268.

Fawcett, S. B., White, G. W., Balcazar, F. E., Suarez-Balcazar, Y., Mathews, R. M., Paine-Andrews, A., Seekins, T., & Smith, J. F. (1994). A contextual-behavioral model of empowerment: Case studies involving people with physical disabilities. *American Journal of Community Psychology, 22*(4), 471–496.

Ferguson, P., & Asch, A. (1989). Lessons from life: Personal and parental perspectives on school, childhood, and disability. In D. Biklen, P. Ferguson, & A. Ford (Eds.), *Schooling and disability: Eighty-eight yearbook of the National Society for the Study of Education, 11* (pp. 108–140). Chicago, IL: National Society for the Study of Education.

Finkelstein, V. (1987). Disabled people and our culture development. *London Disability Arts Forum, 8*, 1–4.

Fisher, B., & Galler, R. (1988). Friendship and fairness: How disability affects friendship between women. In M. Fine & A. Asch (Eds.), *Women with disabilities. Essays in psychology, culture, and politics* (pp. 172–194.) Philadelphia: Temple University Press.

Fiske, S. T. (2011). *Envy up, scorn down: How status divides us.* New York: Russell Sage Foundation.

Fiske, S. T., Cuddy, A J. C., Glick, P., & Xu, J. (2002). A model of (often mixed) stereotype content: Competence and warmth respectively follow from perceived status and competition. *Journal of Personality and Social Psychology, 82*, 878–902.

Fitzgerald, E. (2007). Disability and poverty. In C. Mel (Ed.), *Welfare policy and poverty* (p. 229). Dublin: Institute of Public Administration and Combat Poverty Agency.

Foley, N. E. (2006). Preparing for college: Improving the odds for students with learning disabilities. *College Student Journal, 40*(3), 641.

Fraley, S. S., Mona, L. R., & Theodore, P. S. (2007). The sexual lives of lesbian, gay, and bisexual people with disabilities: Psychological perspectives. *Sexuality Research & Social Policy, 4*(1), 15–26.

Frank, R. G., Elliott, T. R., Corcoran, J. R., & Wonderlich, S. A. (1987). Depression after SCI: Is it necessary? *Clinical Psychology Review, 7*, 611–630.

Frankish, P. (2009). History and formation of the Institute of Psychotherapy and Disability. *Advances in Mental Health and Learning Disabilities, 3*(4), 10–12.

Frankish, P. (2013). Thirty years of disability psychotherapy, a paradigm shift? *Advances in Mental Health and Intellectual Disabilities, 7*(5), 257–262.

Frederick, D. A., & Haselton, M. G. (2007). Why is muscularity sexy? Tests of the fitness indicator hypothesis. *Personality and Social Psychology Bulletin, 33*(8), 1167–1183.

Fredriksen-Goldsen, K. I., Kim, H. J., & Barkan, S. E. (2012). Disability among lesbian, gay, and bisexual adults: Disparities in prevalence and risk. *American Journal of Public Health, 102*(1), e16–e21.

Fresco, D. M., Williams, N. L., & Nugent, N. R. (2006). Flexibility and negative affect: Examining the associations of explanatory flexibility and coping flexibility to each other and to depression and anxiety. *Cognitive Therapy and Research, 30*(2), 201–210.

Frick, N. M. (1985). Post-polio sequelae and the psychology of second disability. *Orthopedics, 8*(7), 851–853.

Friedman, R., & James, J. W. (2008). The myth of the stages of dying, death and grief. *Skeptic (Altadena, CA), 14*(2), 37–42.

Friedman, S. M., Munoz, B., West, S. K., Rubin, G. S., & Fried, L. P. (2002). Falls and fear of falling: Which comes first? A longitudinal prediction model suggests strategies for primary and secondary prevention. *Journal of the American Geriatrics Society, 50*(8), 1329–1335.

Fronek, P., Kendall, M., Booth, S., Eugarde, E., & Geraghty, T. (2011). A longitudinal study of sexuality training for the interdisciplinary rehabilitation team. *Sexuality & Disability, 29*, 87–100.

Fuchs, D., Mock, D., Morgan, P. L., & Young, C. L. (2003). Responsiveness-to-intervention: Definitions, evidence, and implications for the learning disabilities construct. *Learning Disabilities Research & Practice, 18*(3), 157–171.

Fujiura, G. T., & Yamaki, K. (2000). Trends in demography of childhood poverty and disability. *Exceptional Children, 66*(2), 187–199.

Gagnon, N., Flint, A. J., Naglie, G., & Devins, G. M. (2005). Affective correlates of fear of falling in elderly persons. *American Journal of Geriatric Psychiatry, 13*(1), 7–14.

Galli, U., Ettlin, D. A., Palla, S., Ehlert, U., & Gaab, J. (2010). Do illness perceptions predict pain-related disability and mood in chronic orofacial pain patients? A 6-month follow-up study. *European Journal of Pain, 14*(5), 550–558.

Galvin, R. (2003). The paradox of disability culture: The need to combine versus the imperative to let go. *Disability & Society, 18*(5), 675–690.

Garcia, J. G., & Zea, M. C. E. (1997). *Psychological intervention and research in Latino populations.* Needham Heights, MA: Allyn & Bacon.

Gavidia-Payne, S., & Stoneman, Z. (2006). Marital adjustment in families of young children with disabilities: Associations with daily hassles and problem-focused coping. *American Journal on Mental Retardation, 111*(1), 1–14.

Geers, A. E. (2003). Predictors of reading skill development in children with early cochlear implantation. *Ear and Hearing, 24*(1), 59S-68S.

Geisthardt, C. L., Brotherson, M. J., & Cook, C. C. (2002). Friendships of children with disabilities in the home environment. *Education and Training in Mental Retardation and Developmental Disabilities, 37*(3), 235–252.

Gentry, M. M., Chinn, K. M., & Moulton, R. D. (2004). Effectiveness of multimedia reading materials when used with children who are deaf. *American Annals of the Deaf, 149*(5), 394–403.

Getzel, E. E., & Thoma, C. A. (2008). Experiences of college students with disabilities and the importance of self-determination in higher education settings. *Career Development for Exceptional Individuals, 31*(2), 77–84.

Gibson, B. E., Teachman, G., Wright, V., Fehlings, D., Young, N. L., & McKeever, P. (2011). Children's and parents' beliefs regarding the value of walking: Rehabilitation implications for children with cerebral palsy. *Child: Care, Health & Development, 38*, 61–69.

Gill, C. J. (1994). A bicultural framework for understanding disability. *Family Psychologist, 10*, 13–16.

Gill, C. J. (1995). A psychological view of disability culture. *Disability Studies Quarterly, 15*(4), 16–19.

Gill, C. J. (1996). Dating and relationship issues. *Sexuality and Disability, 14*(3), 183–190.

Gill, C. J. (1997). Four types of integration in disability identity development. *Journal of Vocational Rehabilitation, 9*(1), 39–46.

Gilson, S. F., & Depoy, E. (2000). Multiculturalism and disability: A critical perspective. *Disability & Society, 15*(2), 207–218.

Gilson, S. F., Tusler, A., & Gill, C. (1997). Ethnographic research in disability identity: Self-determination and community. *Journal of Vocational Rehabilitation, 9*(1), 7–17.

Goldberg, A. E., & Perry-Jenkins, M. (2007). The division of labor and perceptions of parental roles: Lesbian couples across the transition to parenthood. *Journal of Social and Personal Relationships, 24*(2), 297–318.

Goldstein, S. B., & Johnson, V. A. (1997). Stigma by association: Perceptions of the dating partners of college students with physical disabilities. *Basic and Applied Social Psychology, 19*(4), 495–504.

Gordon, P. A., Feldman, D., & Chiriboga, J. (2005). Helping children with disabilities develop and maintain friendships. *Teacher Education and Special Education: The Journal of the Teacher Education Division of the Council for Exceptional Children, 28*(1), 1–9.

Gordon, P. A., & Perrone, K. M. (2004). When spouses become caregivers: Counseling implications for younger couples. *Journal of Rehabilitation, 70*(2), 27.

Gordon, P. A., Tschopp, M. K., & Feldman, D. (2004). Addressing issues of sexuality with adolescents with disabilities. *Child and Adolescent Social Work Journal, 21*(5), 513–527.

Gordon, R. M., Zaccario, M., Sachs, D. M., Ufberg, H., & Carlson, J. A. (2009). Psychotherapy with children and adolescents with physical disabilities. *Journal of Infant, Child & Adolescent Psychotherapy, 8*(2), 113–123.

Graham-Smith, S., & Lafayette, S. (2004). Quality disability support for promoting belonging and academic success within the college community. *College Student Journal, 38*(1), 90.

Grech, S. (2011). Poverty and disability. *Disability & Society, 26*(7), 888–891.

Greene, B. (2003). Beyond heterosexism and across the cultural divide—Developing an inclusive lesbian, gay and bisexual psychology: A look to the future (pp. 357–400). In L. D. Garnets & D. C. Kimmel (Eds.), *Psychological perspectives on lesbian, gay, and bisexual experiences.* New York: Columbia University Press.

Greene, B. (2005). Psychology, diversity and social justice: Beyond heterosexism and across the cultural divide. *Counseling Psychology Quarterly, 18*(4), 295–306.

Greenwell, A., & Hough, S. (2008). Culture and disability in sexuality studies: A methodological and content review of literature. *Sexuality & Disability, 26,* 189–196.

Greenwood, K. A., Thurston, R., Rumble, M., Waters, S. J., & Keefe, F. J. (2003). Anger and persistent pain: Current status and future directions. *Pain, 103*(1-2), 1–5.

Greer, B., Roberts, R., & Jenkins, W. (1990). Substance use among clients with other primary disabilities: Curricular implications for rehabilitation education. *Rehabilitation Education, 4,* 33–44.

Grzesiak R. C., & Hicok, D. A. (1994). A brief history of psychotherapy and physical disability. *American Journal of Psychotherapy, 48*(2), 240–250.

Guldin, A. (2000). Self-claiming sexuality: Mobility impaired people and American culture. *Sexuality & Disability, 18*(4), 233–238.

Gulseren, S., Gulseren, L., Hekimsoy, Z., Cetinay, P., Ozen, C., & Tokatlioglu, B. (2006). Depression, anxiety, health-related quality of life, and disability in patients with overt and subclinical thyroid dysfunction. *Archives of Medical Research, 37*(1), 133–139.

Gumus, H., Akpinar, Z., & Yilmaz, H. (2014). Effects of multiple sclerosis on female sexuality: A controlled study. *Journal of Sexual Medicine, 11*(2), 481–486.

Guo, B., Bricout, J. C., & Huang, J. (2005). A common open space or a digital divide? A social model perspective on the online disability community in China. *Disability & Society, 20*(1), 49–66.

Guter, B., & Killacky, J. R. (Eds.) (2004). *Queer crips: Disabled gay men and their stories.* New York: Harrington Park Press.

Hadfield, R., Mardon, H., Barlow, D., & Kennedy, S. (1996). Delay in the diagnosis of endometriosis: a survey of women from the USA and the UK. *Human Reproduction, 11*(4), 878–880.

Hafstrom, J. L., & Schram, V. R. (1984). Chronic illness in couples: Selected characteristics, including wife's satisfaction with and perception of marital relationships. *Family Relations, 33,* 195–203.

Hahn, H. (1988). Can disability be beautiful? *Social Policy, 18*(3), 26–32.

Hahn, H. (1993). The political implications of disability definitions and data. *Journal of Disability Policy Studies, 4*(2), 41–52.

Hahn, H. (1996). Antidiscrimination laws and social research on disability: The minority group perspective. *Behavioral Sciences & the Law, 14*(1), 41–59.

Hahn, H. D., & Belt, T. L. (2004). Disability identity and attitudes toward cure in a sample of disabled activists. *Journal of Health and Social Behavior, 45,* 453–464.

Haiman, C. A., Stram, D. O., Wilkens, L. R., Pike, M. C., Kolonel, L. N., Henderson, B. E., & Le Marchand, L. (2006). Ethnic and racial differences in the smoking-related risk of lung cancer. *New England Journal of Medicine, 354*(4), 333–342.

Halfon, N., Houtrow, A., Larson, K., & Newacheck, P. W. (2012). The changing landscape of disability in childhood. *The Future of Children, 22*(1), 13–42.

Hampton, N. Z. (2000). Meeting the unique needs of Asian Americans and Pacific Islanders with disabilities: A challenge to rehabilitation counselors in the 21st century. *Journal of Applied Rehabilitation Counseling, 31*(1), 40.

Hampton, N. Z., Zhu, Y, & Ordway, A. (2011). Access to health services: Experiences of women with neurological disabilities. *Journal of Rehabilitation, 77*(2), 3–11.

Hanjorgiris, W. F., Rath, J. F., & O'Neill, J. H. (2004). Gay men living with chronic illness or disability: A sociocultural, minority group perspective on mental health. *Journal of Gay & Lesbian Social Services, 17*(2), 25–41.

Hanna, W. J., & Rogovsky, B. (1991). Women with disabilities: Two handicaps plus. *Disability, Handicap & Society, 6*(1), 49–63.

Harley, D. A., Hall, M., & Savage, T. A. (2000). Working with gay and lesbian consumers with disabilities: Helping practitioners. *Journal of Applied Rehabilitation Counseling, 31*(1), 4–11.

Harley, D. A., Nowak, T. M., Gassaway, L. J., & Savage, T. A. (2002). Lesbian, gay, bisexual, and transgender college students with disabilities: A look at multiple cultural minorities. *Psychology in the Schools, 39*(5), 525–538.

Harris, L. (2002). Disabled sex and the movies. *Disability Studies Quarterly, 22*(4), 144–162.

Harrison, N. (2000). Gay affirmative therapy: A critical analysis of the literature. *British Journal of Guidance and Counselling, 28*, 37–53.

Harrison, T., Stuifbergen, A., Adachi, E., & Becker, H. (2004). Marriage, impairment, and acceptance in persons with multiple sclerosis. *Western Journal of Nursing Research, 26*(3), 266–285.

Hasnain, R., & Balcazar, F. (2009). Predicting community-versus facility-based employment for transition-aged young adults with disabilities: The role of race, ethnicity, and support systems. *Journal of Vocational Rehabilitation, 31*(3), 175–188.

Hassouneh-Phillips, D., & McNeff, E. (2005). "I thought I was less worthy": Low sexual and body esteem and increased vulnerability to intimate partner abuse in women with physical disabilities. *Sexuality and Disability, 23*(4), 227–240.

Hastings, R. P., & Taunt, H. M. (2002). Positive perceptions in families of children with developmental disabilities. *American Journal on Mental Retardation, 107*(2), 116–127.

Hatzichristou, D., Rosen, R. C., Broderick, G., Clayton, A., Cuzin, B., Derogatis, L., et al. (2004). Clinical evaluation and management strategy for sexual dysfunction in men and women. *Journal of Sexuality and Medicine, 1*(1), 49–57.

Hauk, A. (2009). *No Teacher Left Behind: The Influence of Teachers with Disabilities in the K-8 Classrooms. A Review of the Literature* (Unpublished doctoral dissertation). University of Alaska Southeast.

Huang, J. (2011). Work disability, mortgage default, and life satisfaction in the economic downturn: Evidence from the Panel Study of Income Dynamics. *Journal of Disability Policy Studies*, 1044207311410428.

Hawker, G. A., Mian, S., Kendzerska, T., & French, M. (2011). Measures of adult pain: Visual Analog Scale for Pain (VAS Pain), Numeric Rating Scale for Pain (NRS Pain), McGill Pain Questionnaire (MPQ), Short-Form McGill Pain Questionnaire (SF-MPQ), Chronic Pain Grade Scale (CPGS), Short Form-36 Bodily Pain Scale (SF-36 BPS), and Measure of Intermittent and Constant Osteoarthritis Pain (ICOAP). *Arthritis Care & Research, 63*(S11), S240–S252.

Hayhow, B., Gaillard, F., Velakoulis, D., & Walterfang, M. (2014). Delayed diagnosis of multiple sclerosis in a patient with schizoaffective disorder: A case of 'diagnostic overshadowing'. *Australian and New Zealand Journal of Psychiatry*, 0004867414551067. http://anp.sagepub.com/content/early/2014/09/17/0004867414551067.

Hebbeler, K., & Spiker, D. (2016). Supporting young children with disabilities. *The Future of Children, 26*(2), 185–205.

Heinrich, R., & Tate, D. (1996). Latent variable structure of the Brief Symptom Inventory in a sample of persons with spinal cord injuries. *Rehabilitation Psychology, 41*, 131–148.

Hendershot, G. E., Larson, S., & Lakin, K. C. (2003). An overview of the National Health Interview Survey on disability. *Research in Social Sciences & Disability, 3*, 9–40.

Hergenrather, K., & Rhodes, S. (2007). Exploring undergraduate student attitudes toward persons with disabilities application of the disability social relationship scale. *Rehabilitation Counseling Bulletin, 50*(2), 66–75.

Hernandez, B., Keys, C., & Balcazar, F. (2000). Employer attitudes toward workers with disabilities and their ADA employment rights: A literature review. *Journal of Rehabilitation, 66*(4), 4.

Hibbard, R. A., & Desch, L. W. (2007). Maltreatment of children with disabilities. *Pediatrics, 119*(5), 1018–1025.

Higgins, A., Sharek, D., Nolan, M., Sheerin, B., Flanagan, P., Slaicuinaite, S., McDonnell, S., & Walsh, H. (2012). Mixed methods evaluation of an interdisciplinary sexuality education programmer for staff working with people who have an acquired physical disability. *Journal of Advanced Nursing, 68*(11), 2559–2569.

Higgins, D. (2010). Sexuality, human rights and safety for people with disabilities: The challenge of intersecting identities. *Sexual and Relationship Therapy, 23*(3), 245–257.

Hill, C. E., O'Grady, K. E., & Elkin, I. (1992). Applying the Collaborative Study Psychotherapy Rating Scale to rate therapist adherence in cognitive-behavior therapy, interpersonal therapy, and clinical management. *Journal of Consulting and Clinical Psychology, 60*(1), 73.

Hill, S., Dziedzic, K., & Ong, B. N. (2011). Patients' perceptions of the treatment and management of hand osteoarthritis: A focus group enquiry. *Disability & Rehabilitation, 33*(19-20), 1866–1872.

Hirsche, R. C., Williams, B., Jones, A., & Manns, P. (2011). Chronic disease self-management for individuals with stroke, multiple sclerosis and spinal cord injury. *Disability & Rehabilitation, 33*(13-14), 1136–1146.

Hjelle, K. M., & Vik, K. (2011). The ups and downs for social participation: Experiences of wheelchair users in Norway. *Disability & Rehabilitation, 33*(25-26), 2479–2489.

Hogan, D. P., Shandra, C. L., & Msall, M. E. (2007). Family developmental risk factors among adolescents with disabilities and children of parents with disabilities. *Journal of Adolescence, 30*(6), 1001–1019.

Hollar, D., & Moore, D. (2004). Relationship of substance use by students with disabilities to long-term educational, employment and social outcomes. *Substance Use & Misuse, 39*(6), 931–962.

Hollon, S. D., Stewart, M. O., & Strunk, D. (2006). Enduring effects for cognitive behavior therapy in the treatment of depression and anxiety. *Annual Review of Psychology, 57*, 285–315.

Hon, A. (2012). Facors influencing the adherence of antipsychotic medication (Aripiprazole) in first-episode psychosis: Findings from a grounded theory study. *Journal of Psychiatric and Mental Health Nursing, 19*, 354–261.

Hostyn, I., & Maes, B. (2009). Interaction between persons with profound intellectual and multiple disabilities and their partners: A literature review. *Journal of Intellectual and Developmental Disability, 34*(4), 296–312.

Houtrow, A. J., Larson, K., Olson, L. M., Newacheck, P. W., & Halfon, N. (2014). Changing trends in childhood disability, 2001–2011. *Pediatrics, 134*(3), 530–538.

Huang, J. (2012). Work disability, mortgage default, and life satisfaction in the economic downturn: Evidence from the Panel Study of Income Dynamics. *Journal of Disability Policy Studies, 22*(4), 237–246.

Huang, J., & Guo, B. (2005). Building social capital: A study of the online disability community. *Disability Studies Quarterly, 25*(2).

Hubbard, P. A., Broome, M. E., & Antia, L. A. (2005). Pain, coping, and disability in adolescents and young adults with cystic fibrosis: A Web-based study. *Pediatric Nursing, 31*(2), 82.

Hunt, B., Matthews, C., Milsom, A., & Lammel, J. A. (2006). Lesbians with physical disabilities: A qualitative study of their experiences with counseling. *Journal of Counseling and Development, 84*(2), 163.

Hunt, B., Milsom, A., & Matthews, C. R. (2009). Partner-related rehabilitation experiences of lesbians with physical disabilities: A qualitative study. *Rehabilitation Counseling Bulletin, 52*(3), 167–178.

Hwang, W. C. (2006). The psychotherapy adaptation and modification framework: Application to Asian Americans. *American Psychologist, 61*(7), 702.

Hyland, A., & McGrath, M. (2013). Sexuality and occupational therapy in Ireland—A case of ambivalence? *Disability & Rehabilitation, 35*(1), 73–80.

Iacono, T., Lewis, B., Tracy, J., Hicks, S., Morgan, P., Recoche, K., & McDonald, R. (2011). DVD-based stories of people with disabilities as resources for inter-professional education. *Disability & Rehabilitation, 33*(12), 1010–1021.

Ide, M. (2004). Sexuality in persons with limb amputation: A meaningful discussion of reintegration. *Disability and Rehabilitation, 26*(14/15), 939–943.

Idler, E. L., & Kasl, S. V. (1992). Religion, disability, depression, and the timing of death. *American Journal of Sociology, 97*(4), 1052–1079.

Idler, E. L., & Kasl, S. V. (1997). Religion among disabled and nondisabled persons II: Attendance at religious services as a predictor of the course of disability. *Journals of Gerontology Series B: Psychological Sciences and Social Sciences, 52*(6), S306–S316.

Iezzoni, L. I. (2011). Eliminating health and health care disparities among the growing population of people with disabilities. *Health Affairs, 30*(10), 1947–1954.

Ingstad, B., & Whyte, S. R. (Eds.) (1995). *Disability and culture.* Berkeley: University of California Press.

Jaehne, A., Loessl, B., Bárkai, Z., Riemann, D., & Hornyak, M. (2009). Effects of nicotine on sleep during consumption, withdrawal and replacement therapy. *Sleep Medicine Reviews, 13*(5), 363–377.

James, M., DeVivo, M. J., & Richards, J. S. (1993). Postinjury employment outcomes among African-American and white persons with spinal cord injury. *Rehabilitation Psychology, 38*(3), 151.

Jensen, M. P., Turner, J. A., Romano, J. M., & Karoly, P. (1991). Coping with chronic pain: A critical review of the literature. *Pain, 47*(3), 249–283.

Jetten, J., Branscombe, N. R., & Spears, R. (2006). Living on the edge: Dynamics of intragroup and intergroup rejection experiences. In R. Brown & D. Capozza (Eds.), *Social identities: Motivational, emotional and cultural influences* (pp. 92–107). Hove, England: Psychology Press, Taylor & Francis.

Johnson, R. E. (1989). Unlocking the curriculum: Principles for achieving access in deaf education. Working Paper 89-3.

Johnston, S. S., & Evans, J. (2005). Considering response efficiency as a strategy to prevent assistive technology abandonment. *Journal of Special Education Technology, 20*(3), 45–50.

Johnstone, B., Glass, B. A., & Oliver, R. E. (2007). Religion and disability: Clinical, research and training considerations for rehabilitation professionals. *Disability and Rehabilitation, 29*(15), 1153–1163.

Jolly-Ryan, J. (2005). Disabilities to exceptional abilities: Law students with disabilities, nontraditional Learners, and the law teacher as a learner. *Nevada Law Journal, 6*, 116.

Jones, J. M. (2013, Dec. 19). *In U.S., 40% get less than recommended amount of sleep.* Gallup. Retreived from www.gallup.com/poll/166553/less-recommended-amount-sleep.aspx

Jorgensen, S., Ferraro, V., Fichten, C., & Havel, A. (2009). Predicting college retention and dropout: Sex and disability. Retrieved from http://eric.ed.gov/?id=ED505873

Jutai, J., & Day, H. (2002). Psychosocial impact of assistive devices scale (PIADS). *Technology and Disability, 14*(3), 107–111.

Karlen, A. (2002). Positive sexual effects of chronic illness: Case studies of women with lupus (SLE). *Sexuality & Disability, 20*(3), 191–208.

Kaye, H. S., Yeager, P., & Reed, M. (2008). Disparities in usage of assistive technology among people with disabilities. *Assistive Technology, 20*(4), 194–203.

Kaye, J., & Raghavan, S. K. (2002). Spirituality in disability and illness. *Journal of Religion and Health, 41*(3), 231–242.

Kazukauskas, K. A., & Lam, C. S. (2009). Importance of addressing sexuality in certified rehabilitation counselor practice. *Rehabilitation Education, 23*(2), 127–140.

Keany, K. C., & Glueckauf, R. L. (1993). Disability and value change: An overview and reanalysis of acceptance of loss theory. *Rehabilitation Psychology, 38*(3), 199.

Keller, R., & Galgay, (2010). Microaggressive experiences of people with disabilities. In D. W. Sue (Ed.), *Microaggressions and marginality: Manifestations, dynamics and impact* (pp. 241–267). Hoboken, NJ: Wiley.

Keller, R., Galgay, C., Robinson, L., & Moscoso, G. (2009). *Microaggressions experienced by people with disabilities in U.S. society.* Paper presented at the annual meeting of the American Psychological Association, San Francisco, CA.

Kennedy, J. (2001). Unmet and undermet need for activities of daily living and instrumental activities of daily living assistance among adults with disabilities: Estimates from the 1994 and 1995 disability follow-back surveys. *Medical Care, 39*(12), 1305–1312.

Kennedy, P. (Ed.) (2012). *The Oxford handbook of rehabilitation psychology.* New York: Oxford University Press.

Kenneson, A., Vatave, A., & Finkel, R. (2010). Widening gap in age at muscular dystrophy–associated death between blacks and whites, 1986–2005. *Neurology, 75*(11), 982–989.

Kerns, R. D., Rosenberg, R., & Jacob, M. C. (1994). Anger expression and chronic pain. *Journal of Behavioral Medicine, 17*(1), 57–67.

Khan, F., Baguley, I. J., & Cameron, I. D. (2003). 4: Rehabilitation after traumatic brain injury. *Medical Journal of Australia, 178*(6), 290–297.

King, N., Lancaster, N., Wynne, G., Nettleton, N., & Davis, R. (1999). Cognitive-behavioural anger management training for adults with mild intellectual disability. *Scandinavian Journal of Behaviour Therapy, 28*(1), 19–22.

Kirshbaum, M. (2000). A disability culture perspective on early intervention with parents with physical or cognitive disabilities and their infants. *Infants & Young Children, 13*(2), 9–20.

Kirshbaum, M., & Olkin, R. (2002). Parents with physical, systemic, or visual disabilities. *Sexuality and Disability, 20*(1), 65–80.

Kluwin, T. N. (1993). Cumulative effects of mainstreaming on the achievement of deaf adolescents. *Exceptional Children, 60*(1), 73–81.

Knight, W., Knessel, R. D., & Markle, L. (2016). Persistence to graduation for students with disabilities: Implications for performance-based outcomes. *Journal of College Student Retention: Research, Theory & Practice*, 1521025116632524.

Knis-Matthew, L., Falzarano, M., Baum, D., Manganiello, J., Patel, S., & Winters, L. (2011). Parents' experiences with services and treatment for their children diagnosed with cerebral palsy. *Physical & Occupational Therapy In Pediatrics, 31*(3), 263–274.

Kocher, M. (1994). Mothers with disabilities. *Sexuality and Disability, 12*(2), 127–133.

Konigsberg, R. D. (2011). *The truth about grief: The myth of its five stages and the new science of loss*. New York: Simon and Schuster.

Kotagal, S., Gibbons, V. P., & Stith, J. A. (1994). Sleep abnormalities in patients with severe cerebral palsy. *Developmental Medicine & Child Neurology, 36*(4), 304–311.

Kraayenoord, C. V. (2011). Movies and disability: Positive impact or harm? *International Journal of Disability, Development and Education, 58*(2), 103–106.

Kramer, J. M., & Hammel, J. (2011). "I do lots of things": Children with cerebral palsy's competence for everyday activities. *International Journal of Disability, Development & Education, 58*(2), 121–136.

Kübler-Ross, E. (1975). On death and dying. *Bulletin of the American College of Surgeons, 60*(6), 12–15.

Kübler-Ross, E., & Kessler, D. (2014). *On grief and grieving: Finding the meaning of grief through the five stages of loss*. New York: Simon and Schuster.

Kumpfer, K. L., Alvarado, R., Smith, P., & Bellamy, N. (2002). Cultural sensitivity and adaptation in family-based prevention interventions. *Prevention Science, 3*(3), 241–246.

Kwok, C., & White, K. (2011). Cultural and linguistic isolation: The breast cancer experience of Chinese-Australian women—A qualitative study. *Contemporary Nurse, 39*(1), 85–94.

Lai, S., Duncan, P. W., Keighley, J., & Johnson, D. (2002). Depressive symptoms and independence in BADL and IADL. *Journal of Rehabilitation Research and Development, 39*(5), 589–596.

Laird, J., & Green, R. (Eds.) (1996). *Lesbian and gays in couples and families: A handbook for therapists*. San Francisco: Jossey-Bass.

Lakoff, G. (2014). *The all new don't think of an elephant!: Know your values and frame the debate*. White River Junction, VT: Chelsea Green Publishing.

Landreville, P., & Gervais, P. W. (1997). Psychotherapy for depression in older adults with disability: Where do we go from here? *Aging and Mental Health, 1*(3), 197–208.

Lang, H. G. (2002). Higher education for deaf students: Research priorities in the new millennium. *Journal of Deaf Studies and Deaf Education, 7*(4), 267–280.

Langer, K. G. (1994). Depression and denial in psychotherapy of persons with disabilities. *American Journal of Psychotherapy, 48*(2), 181–194.

Lantéri-Minet, M., Radat, F., Chautard, M. H., & Lucas, C. (2005). Anxiety and depression associated with migraine: Influence on migraine subjects' disability and quality of life, and acute migraine management. *Pain, 118*(3), 319–326.

Larsson, I., Miller, M., Liljedahl, K., & Gard, G. (2012). Physiotherapists' experiences of physiotherapy interventions in scientific physiotherapy publications focusing on interventions for children with cerebral palsy: A qualitative phenomenographic approach. *BMC Pediatrics, 12*, 1–12.

Lawlor, K., Mihaylov, S., Welsh, B., Jarvis, S., & Colver, A. (2006). A qualitative study of the physical, social and attitudinal environments influencing the participation of children with cerebral palsy in northeast England. *Pediatric Rehabilitation, 9*(3), 219–228.

Lazarus, R. S., & Folkman, S. (1984). *Stress, appraisal, and coping.* New York: Springer.

Legters, K. (2002). Fear of falling. *Physical therapy, 82*(3), 264–272.

Lenker, J. A., & Paquet, V. L. (2003). A review of conceptual models for assistive technology outcomes research and practice. *Assistive Technology, 15*(1), 1–15.

Lenze, E. J., Rogers, J. C., Martire, L. M., Mulsant, B. H., Rollman, B. L., Dew, M. A., Schulz, R., & Reynolds, C. F. (2001). The association of late-life depression and anxiety with physical disability: A review of the literature and prospectus for future research. *American Journal of Geriatric Psychiatry, 9*(2), 113–135.

Leone, P. E., Christle, C. A., Nelson, C. M., Skiba, R., Frey, A., & Jolivette, K. (2003). *School failure, race, and disability: Promoting positive outcomes, decreasing vulnerability for involvement with the juvenile delinquency system.* Washington, DC: National Center on Education, Disability, and Juvenile Justice.

Li, L., & Ford, J. A. (1998). Illicit drug use by women with disabilities. *American Journal of Drug and Alcohol Abuse, 24*(3), 405–418.

Li, L., Ford, J. A., & Moore, D. (2000). An exploratory study of violence, substance abuse, disability, and gender. *Social Behavior and Personality, 28*(1), 61–72.

Li, L., & Moore, D. (2001). Disability and illicit drug use: An application of labeling theory. *Deviant Behavior: An Interdisciplinary Journal, 22*, 1–21.

Lichtenberg, P. (1997). The DOUR project: A program of depression research in geriatric rehabilitation minority inpatients. *Rehabilitation Psychology, 42*, 103–114.

Liddle, J., Fleming, J., McKenna, K., Turpin, M., Whitelaw, P., & Allen, S. (2011). Driving and driving cessation after traumatic brain injury: Processes and key times of need. *Disability & Rehabilitation, 33*(25-26), 2574–2586.

Linton, S. (1998). *Claiming disability: Knowledge and identity.* New York: New York University Press.

Lippold, T., & Burns, J. (2009). Social support and intellectual disabilities: A comparison between social networks of adults with intellectual disability and those with physical disability. *Journal of Intellectual Disability Research, 53*(5), 463–473.

Livneh, H., & Antonak, R. F. (2005). Psychosocial adaptation to chronic illness and disability: A primer for counselors. *Journal of Counseling & Development, 83*(1), 12–20.

Livneh, H., & Martz, E. (2012). Adjustment to chronic illness and disabilities: Theoretical perspectives, empirical findings, and unresolved issues. In P. Kennedy (Ed.), *The Oxford handbook of rehabilitation psychology* (pp. 47–48). New York: Oxford University Press.

Llewellyn, G., McConnell, D., & Ferronato, L. (2003). Prevalence and outcomes for parents with disabilities and their children in an Australian court sample. *Child Abuse & Neglect, 27*(3), 235–251.

Lobentanz, I. S., Asenbaum, S., Vass, K., Sauter, C., Klösch, G., Kollegger, H., Kristoferitsch, W., & Zeitlhofer, J. (2004). Factors influencing quality of life in multiple sclerosis patients: Disability, depressive mood, fatigue and sleep quality. *Acta Neurologica Scandinavica, 110*(1), 6–13.

Lockwood, P., Jordan, C. H., & Kunda, Z. (2002). Motivation by positive or negative role models: Regulatory focus determines who will best inspire us. *Journal of Personality and Social Psychology, 83*(4), 854.

Löfgren-Mårtenson, L. (2013). "Hip to be crip?" About crip theory, sexuality and people with intellectual disabilities. *Sexuality and Disability, 31*(4), 413–424.

Longmore, P. K. (1995). The second phase: From disability rights to disability culture. *Disability Rag ReSource, Sept/Oct, 4*–11.

Longmore, P. K. (2003). *Why I burned my book and other essays on disability*. Philadelphia: Temple University Press.

Louw, A., Diener, I., Butler, D. S., & Puentedura, E. J. (2011). The effect of neuroscience education on pain, disability, anxiety, and stress in chronic musculoskeletal pain. *Archives of Physical Medicine and Rehabilitation, 92*(12), 2041–2056.

Lund, E. M., Andrews, E. E., & Holt, J. M. (2014). How we treat our own: The experiences and characteristics of psychology trainees with disabilities. *Rehabilitation Psychology, 59*(4), 367–375.

Lund, E. M., & Johnson, B. A. (2015). Asexuality and disability: Strange but compatible bedfellows. *Sexuality & Disability, 33*, 123–132.

Lund, M. L., & Nygård, L. (2003). Incorporating or resisting assistive devices: Different approaches to achieving a desired occupational self-image. *OTJR: Occupation, Participation and Health, 23*(2), 67–75.

Lynch, R. T., & Gussel, L. (1996). Disclosure and self-advocacy regarding disability-related needs: Strategies to maximize integration in postsecondary education. *Journal of Counseling and Development, 74*(4), 352.

Lynch, S. G., Kroencke, D. C., & Denney, D. R. (2001). The relationship between disability and depression in multiple sclerosis: the role of uncertainty, coping, and hope. *Multiple Sclerosis, 7*(6), 411–416.

Mackelprang, R. W., & Salsgiver, R. O. (2015). *Disability: A diversity model approach in human service practice* (3rd ed.). Chicago, IL: Lyceum Books.

MacLeod, F. K., LaChapelle, D. L., Hadjistavropoulos, T., & Pfeifer, J. E. (2001). The effect of disability claimants' coping styles on judgments of pain, disability, and compensation: A vignette study. *Rehabilitation Psychology, 46*(4), 417.

Mallory, G. B., Fiser, D. H., & Jackson, R. (1989). Sleep-associated breathing disorders in morbidly obese children and adolescents. *Journal of Pediatrics, 115*(6), 892–897.

Mann, D. M., Ponieman, D., Leventhal, H., & Halm, E. A. (2009). Predictors of adherence to diabetes medications: the role of disease and medication beliefs. *Journal of Behavioral Medicine, 32*(3), 278–284.

Mannerkorpi, K., & Gard, G. (2012). Hinders for continued work among persons with fibromyalgia. *BMC Muskuloskeletal Disorders, 13*, 96.

Marcus, C. L., Keens, T. G., Bautista, D. B., von Pechmann, W. S., & Ward, S. L. D. (1991). Obstructive sleep apnea in children with Down syndrome. *Pediatrics, 88*(1), 132–139.

Marini, I., & Stebnicki, M. A. (2012). *The psychological and social impact of illness and disability* (6th ed.). New York: Spring Publishing.

Marschark, M., Sapere, P., Convertino, C. M., Mayer, C., Wauters, L., & Sarchet, T. (2009). Are deaf students' reading challenges really about reading? *American Annals of the Deaf, 154*(4), 357–370.

Martensson, L. (2001). Rehabilitation of patients with chronic pain in primary health care. *Scandinavian Journal of Occupational Therapy, 8*, 108–108.

Martin, J. J. (2006). Psychosocial aspects of youth disability sport. *Adapted Physical Activity Quarterly, 23*(1), 65–77.

Martin, J. J., & Smith, K. (2002). Friendship quality in youth disability sport: Perceptions of a best friend. *Adapted Physical Activity Quarterly, 19*(4), 472–482.

Mason, J., & Scior, K. (2004). 'Diagnostic overshadowing' amongst clinicians working with people with intellectual disabilities in the UK. *Journal of Applied Research in Intellectual Disabilities, 17*(2), 85–90.

Masters, W. H., & Johnson, V. J. (1986). *Human sexual response*. New York: Bantam Books.

Mathers, C., Fat, D. M., & Boerma, J. T. (2008). *The global burden of disease: 2004 update*. Geneva: World Health Organization.

Mattingly, C., & Garro, L. C. (2000). *Narrative and the cultural construction of illness and healing*. Berkeley: University of California Press.

McCabe, M. P., Cummins, R. A., & Deeks, A. A. (2000). Sexuality and quality of life among people with physical disabilities. *Sexuality and Disability, 18*(2), 115–123.

McCracken, L. M., Vowles, K. E., & Eccleston, C. (2004). Acceptance of chronic pain: Component analysis and a revised assessment method. *Pain, 107*(1-2), 159–166.

McCreary, D. R., & Sasse, D. K. (2000). An exploration of the drive for muscularity in adolescent boys and girls. *Journal of American College Health, 48*(6), 297–304.

McCubbin, H. I., Thompson, E. A., Thompson, A. I., McCubbin, M. A., & Kaston, A. J. (1993). Culture, ethnicity, and the family: Critical factors in childhood chronic illnesses and disabilities. *Pediatrics, 91*(5), 1063–1070.

McDaniel, S. H., Doherty, W. J., & Hepworth, J. (2014). *Medical family therapy and integrated care* (2nd ed.). Washington, DC: American Psychological Association.

McDonald, K. E., Keys, C. B., & Balcazar, F. E. (2007). Disability, race/ethnicity and gender: Themes of cultural oppression, acts of individual resistance. *American Journal of Community Psychology, 39*(1-2), 145–161.

McGoldrick, M., Giordano, J., & Garcia-Preto, N. (Eds.). (2005). *Ethnicity and family therapy*. New York: Guilford Press.

McGuigan, C., & Hutchinson, M. (2006). Unrecognised symptoms of depression in a community–based population with multiple sclerosis. *Journal of Neurology, 253*(2), 219–223.

Mckenzie, J. A., & Swartz, L. (2011). The shaping of sexuality in children with disabilities: A Q methodological study. *Sexuality and Disability, 29*, 363–376.

McNeff, E. A. (1997). Issues for the partner of the person with a disability. In M. Sipski & C. J. Alexander (Eds.), *Sexual function in persons with disabilities and chronic illness*. Gaithersburg, MD: Aspen.

Melamed, S., Groswasser, Z., & Stern, M. J. (1992). Acceptance of disability, work involvement and subjective rehabilitation status of traumatic brain-injured (TBI) patients. *Brain Injury, 6*(3), 233–243.

Memel, D. S., Kirwan, J. R., Sharp, D. J., & Hehir, M. (2000). General practitioners miss disability and anxiety as well as depression in their patients with osteoarthritis. *British Journal of General Practice, 50*(457), 645–648.

Mercer, S., Dieppe, P., Chambers, R., & MacDonald, R. (2003). Equality for people with disabilities in medicine: Time for action and partnerships. *British Medical Journal, 327*(7420), 882.

Meredith, P., Strong, J., & Feeney, J. A. (2006). Adult attachment, anxiety, and pain self-efficacy as predictors of pain intensity and disability. *Pain, 123*(1), 146–154.

Mereish, E. H. (2012). The intersectional invisibility of race and disability status: An exploratory study of health and discrimination facing Asian Americans with disabilities. *Ethnicity and Inequalities in Health and Social Care, 5*(2), 52–60.

Milberger, S., Israel, N., LeRoy, B., Martin, A., Potter, L., & Patchak-Schuster, P. (2003). Violence against women with physical disabilities. *Violence and Victims, 18*(5), 581–591.

Miller, E., Chen, R., Glover-Graf, N. M., & Kranz, P. (2009). Willingness to engage in personal relationships with persons with disabilities examining category and severity of disability. *Rehabilitation Counseling Bulletin, 52*(4), 211–224.

Miller, P. S. (2008). Disability civil rights and a new paradigm for the twenty-first century: The expansion of civil rights beyond race, gender and age. *University of Pennsylvania Journal of Labor and Employment Law, 1*(2), 511–526.

Milligan, M. S., & Neufeldt, A. H. (2001). The myth of asexuality: A survey of social and empirical evidence. *Sexuality and Disability, 19*, 91–109.

Miltiades, H. B., & Pruchno, R. (2002). The effect of religious coping on caregiving appraisals of mothers of adults with developmental disabilities. *The Gerontologist, 42*(1), 82–91.

Mishel, M. (1981). The measurement of uncertainty in illness. *Nursing Research, 30*, 258–263.

Mohr, D. C., Boudewyn, A. C., Goodkin, D. E., Bostrom, A., & Epstein, L. (2001). Comparative outcomes for individual cognitive-behavior therapy, supportive-expressive group psychotherapy, and sertraline for the treatment of depression in multiple sclerosis. *Journal of Consulting and Clinical Psychology, 69*(6), 942.

Mohr, D. C., & Cox, D. (2001). Multiple sclerosis: Empirical literature for the clinical health psychologist. *Journal of Clinical Psychology, 57*(4), 479–499.

Mohr, D. C., & Goodkin, D. E. (1999). Treatment of depression in multiple sclerosis: Review and meta-analysis. *Clinical Psychology: Science & Practice, 6*(1), 1–9.

Mohr, D. C., Goodkin, D. E., Islar, J., Hauser, S. L., & Genain, C. P. (2001). Treatment of depression is associated with suppression of nonspecific and antigen-specific TH_1 responses in multiple sclerosis. *Archives of Neurology, 58*(7), 1081–1086.

Mohr, D. C., Goodkin, D. E., Likosky, W., Beutler, L., Gatto, N., & Langan, M. K. (1997). Identification of Beck Depression Inventory items related to multiple sclerosis. *Journal of Behavioral Medicine, 20*(4), 407–414.

Mohr, D. C., Likosky, W., Bertagnolli, A., Goodkin, D. E., Van Der Wende, J., Dwyer, P., & Dick, L. P. (2000). Telephone-administered cognitive–behavioral therapy for the treatment of depressive symptoms in multiple sclerosis. *Journal of Consulting and Clinical Psychology, 68*(2), 356–361.

Moix, J., Kovacs, F. M., Martín, A., Plana, M. N., & Royuela, A. (2011). Catastrophizing, state anxiety, anger, and depressive symptoms do not correlate with disability when variations of trait anxiety are taken into account. A study of chronic low back pain patients treated in Spanish pain units [NCT00360802]. *Pain Medicine, 12*(7), 1008–1017.

Montero-Marin, J., Carrasco, J. M., Roca, M., SerranoBlanco, A., Gili, M., & Mayoral, F., . . . Garcia-Campayo, J. (2013). Expectations, experiences and attitudes of patients and primary care health professionals regarding online psychotherapeutic interventions for depression: Protocol for a qualitative study. *BMC Psychiatry, 13*, 64.

Moore, C. L. (2002). Outcome variables that contribute to group differences between Caucasians, African Americans, and Asian Americans who are deaf. *Journal of Applied Rehabilitation Counseling, 33*(2), 8.

Moran, P. J., & Mohr, D. C. (2005). The validity of Beck Depression Inventory and Hamilton Rating Scale for Depression items in the assessment of depression among patients with multiple sclerosis. *Journal of Behavioral Medicine, 28*(1), 35–41.

Morris, J. (1991). *Pride against prejudice: Transforming attitudes toward disability.* London: The Women's Press. Reprinted 2014 by BPCC Hazell Books, Aylesbury, England.

Murphy, J., & Isaacs, B. (1982). The post-fall syndrome: A study of 36 patients. *Gerontology, 28*, 265–270.

Nabili, S. N. (2015). *Sleep apnea.* MedicineNet. Retreived from http://www.medicinenet.com/sleep_apnea/page4.htm

Nadal, K. L., Issa, M. A., Leon, J., Meterko, V., Wideman, M., & Wong, Y. (2011). Sexual orientation microaggressions: "Death by a thousand cuts" for lesbian, gay, and bisexual youth. *Journal of LGBT Youth, 8*(3), 234–259.

Nakosteen, R. A., Westerlund, O., & Zimmer, M. A. (2005). Health-related disabilities and matching of spouses: Analysis of Swedish population data. *Journal of Population Economics, 18*(3), 491–507.

Narayan, N. (2014). *Interplay between cultural beliefs and attitudes in raising a child with intellectual disability—An Asian Indian study* (Unpublished doctoral dissertation). California School of Professional Psychology at Alliant International University, San Francisco, CA.

Nario-Redmond, M. R., Noel, J. G., & Fern, E. (2013). Redefining disability, re-imagining the self: Disability identification predicts self-esteem and strategic responses to stigma. *Self and Identity, 12*, 468–488.

National Sleep Foundation. (2014). *2014 sleep in American poll: Sleep in the modern family.* Arlington, VA: Author.

National Sleep Foundation (2015). *Sleep in America poll finds pain a significant challenge when it comes to Americans' sleep.* Arlington, VA: Author.

Neese, R. E., & Finlayson, F. E. (1996). Management of depression in patients with coexisting medical illness. *American Family Physician, 53*, 2125–2133.

Nerini, A., Matera, C., Baroni, D., & Stefanile, C. (2015). Drive for muscularity and sexual orientation: Psychometric properties of the Italian version of the Drive for Muscularity Scale (DMS) in straight and gay men. *Psychology of Men & Masculinity, 1*(1), 1–10.

Newacheck, P. W., & Halfon, N. (1998). Prevalence and impact of disabling chronic conditions in childhood. *American Journal of Public Health, 88*(4), 610–617.

Newman, L., Wagner, M., Cameto, R., & Knokey, A. M. (2009). The post-high school outcomes of youth with disabilities up to 4 years after high school: A report from the National

Longitudinal Transition Study-2 (NLTS2). NCSER 2009-3017. Washington, DC: National Center for Special Education Research.

Newman, L., Wagner, M., Knokey, A. M., Marder, C., Nagle, K., Shaver, D., & Wei, X. (2011). The post-high school outcomes of young adults with disabilities up to 8 years after high school: A report from the National Longitudinal Transition Study-2 (NLTS2). NCSER 2011-3005. Washington, DC: National Center for Special Education Research.

Nilsson, C., Bartfai, A., & Lofgren, M. (2011). Holistic group rehabilitation—A short cut to adaptation to the new life after mild acquired brain injury. *Disability & Rehabilitation, 33*(12), 969–978.

Norden, M. F. (1994). *The cinema of isolation: A history of physical disability in the movies.* Rutgers, NJ: Rutgers University Press.

Nosek, M. A., Foley, C. C., Hughes, R. B., & Howland, C. A. (2001). Vulnerability for abuse among women with disabilities. *Sexuality and Disability, 19*(3), 177–189.

Nosek, M. A., Howland, C., Rintala, D. H., Young, M. E., & Chanpong, G. F. (2001). National study of women with physical disabilities: Final report. *Sexuality & Disability, 19*(1), 5–39.

Nosek, M. A., Howland, C. A., & Young, M. E. (2013). Abuse of women with disabilities: Policy implications. *Journal of Disability Policy Studies, 8*(1-2), 157–175.

Nosek, M. A., Robinson-Whelen, S., Hughes, R. B., Petersen, N. J., Taylor, H. B., Byrne, M. M., & Morgan, R. (2008). Overweight and obesity in women with physical disabilities: Associations with demographic and disability characteristics and secondary conditions. *Disability and Health Journal, 1*(2), 89–98.

Novack, T. A., Sherer, M., & Penna, S. (2010). In R. G. Frank, M. Rosenthal, & B. Caplan (Eds.). *Handbook of rehabilitation psychology* (2nd ed.; pp. 165–178). Washington, DC: American Psychological Association.

Oliver, M. L., & Shapiro, T. M. (2006). *Black wealth, white wealth: A new perspective on racial inequality.* Philadelphia: Taylor & Francis.

Olkin, R. (1999). *What psychotherapists should know about disability.* New York: Guilford Press.

Olkin, R. (2003). Women with physical disabilities who want to leave their partners: A feminist and disability-affirmative perspective. *Women and Therapy, 26*(3/4), 237–246.

Olkin, R. (2004). Disability and depression. In S. L. Welner & F. Haseltine (Eds.), *Welner's guide to the care of women with disabilities* (pp. 279–300). Philadelphia: Lippincott Williams & Wilkins.

Olkin, R. (2005). *Disability culture: A baker's dozen.* Newsletter of the Contra Costa County Psychological Association.

Olkin, R. (2008). Social warrior or unwitting bigot? *Professional Psychology: Research and Practice, 39*, 488–497.

Olkin, R., Abrams, K., Preston, P., & Kirshbaum, M. (2006). Comparison of parents with and without disabilities raising teens: Information from the NHIS and two national surveys. *Rehabilitation Psychology, 51*(1), 43–49.

Olkin, R., Hayward, H., Schaff, M., & VanHeel, G. (2016). *Women with disabilities: Experiences of multiple identities, microaggressions, and stigma.* Paper presented at the Western Psychological Association, Long Beach, CA.

Olkin, R., & Howson, L. J. (1994). Attitudes toward and images of physical disability. *Journal of Social Behavior and Personality, 9*(5), 81.

Olkin, R., Loewy, M., Safron, G., Hall, K., & Crockett, A. (2016). *Lived experiences of gay men with disabilities*. Paper presented at the Western Psychological Association, Long Beach, CA.

Olkin, R., & Pledger, C. (2003). Can disability studies and psychology join hands? *American Psychologist, 58*(4), 296–304.

Olkin, R., & Taliaferro, G. (2005). Evidence-based practices have ignored people with disabilities; Dialogue. In J. Norcross, L. Beutler, & R. Levant (Eds.), *Evidence-based practices in mental health* (pp. 353–359; 365–367). Washington, DC: American Psychological Association.

Ormel, J., Petukhova, M., Chatterji, S., Aguilar-Gaxiola, S., Alonso, J., Angermeyer, M. C., ... Kessler, R. C. (2008). Disability and treatment of specific mental and physical disorders across the world. *British Journal of Psychiatry, 192*(5), 368–375.

O'Toole, C. J. (2000). The view from below: Developing a knowledge base about an unknown population. *Sexuality and Disability, 18*(3), 207–224.

O'Toole, C. J., & Bregante, J. L. (1992). Lesbians with disabilities. *Sexuality and disability, 10*(3), 163–172.

O'Toole, C. J., & Bregante, J. L. (1993). Disabled lesbians: Multicultural realities. In M. Nagler (Ed.), *Perspectives and disabilities* (2nd ed.). Palo Alto, CA: Health Markets Research.

O'Toole, C. J., & Brown, A. A. (2002). No reflection in the mirror: Challenges for disabled lesbians accessing mental health services. *Journal of Lesbian Studies, 7*(1), 35–49.

Ouellette, A. R. (2012). Patients to peers: Barriers and opportunities for doctors with disabilities. *Nevada Law Journal, 13*, 645–667.

Owens, J. (2015). Exploring the critiques of the social model of disability: The transformative possibility of Arendt's notion of power. *Sociology of Health & Illness, 37*(3), 385–403.

Ozcan, S., Sahin, N. H., Bilgic, D., & Yilmaz, S. D. (2011). Is sexual dysfunction associated with diabetes control and related factors in women with diabetes? *Sexuality and Disability, 29*, 251–261.

Pachman, L. M., Hayford, J. R., Chung, A., Daugherty, C. A., Pallansch, M. A., Fink, C. W., Gewanter, H. L., ... Hochberg, M. C. (1998). Juvenile dermatomyositis at diagnosis: Clinical characteristics of 79 children. *Journal of Rheumatology, 25*(6), 1198–1204.

Pager, D., & Shepherd, H. (2008). The sociology of discrimination: Racial discrimination in employment, housing, credit, and consumer markets. *Annual Review of Sociology, 34*, 181.

Palmer, M. (2011). Disability and poverty: A conceptual review. *Journal of Disability Policy Studies, 21*(4), 210–218.

Palombi, B. J. (2008). Focus on disability: It's about time. *Professional Psychology: Research and Practice, 39*, 494–495.

Parchomiuk, M. (2012). Specialists and sexuality of individuals with disability. *Sexuality & Disability, 30*, 407–419.

Parish, S. L., & Cloud, J. M. (2006). Financial well-being of young children with disabilities and their families. *Social Work, 51*(3), 223–232.

Parish, S. L., Rose, R. A., Grinstein-Weiss, M., Richman, E. L., & Andrews, M. E. (2008). Material hardship in US families raising children with disabilities. *Exceptional Children, 75*(1), 71–92.

Park, J., Turnbull, A. P., & Turnbull, H. R. (2002). Impacts of poverty on quality of life in families of children with disabilities. *Exceptional Children, 68*(2), 151–170.

Park, S. (2012). Korean American parents' communication with European American therapist during behavioral intervention services. *Education, 132*(3), 560–567.

Parker, M. G., & Yau, M. K. (2012). Sexuality, identity and women with spinal cord injury. *Sexuality and Disability, 30*, 15–27.

Parritt, S., & O'Callaghan, J. (2000). Splitting the difference: An exploratory study of therapists' work with sexuality, relationships and disability. *Sexual and Relationship Therapy, 15*(2), 151–169.

Patel, R. M., Kandefer, S., Walsh, M. C., Bell, E. F., Carlo, W. A., Laptook, A. R., . . . & Hale, E. C. (2015). Causes and timing of death in extremely premature infants from 2000 through 2011. *New England Journal of Medicine, 372*(4), 331–340.

Pattison, S. (2005). Making a difference for young people with elarning disabilities: A model for inclusive counselling practice. *Counselling and Psychotherapy Research, 5*(2), 120–130.

Pattison, S. (2010). Reaching out: A proactive process to include young people with learning disabilities in counselling in secondary schools in the UK. *British Journal of Guidance & Counselling, 38*(3), 301–311.

Perron, B. E., Mowbray, O. P., Glass, J. E., Delva, J., Vaughn, M. G., & Howard, M. O. (2009). Differences in service utilization and barriers among Blacks, Hispanics, and whites with drug use disorders. *Substance Abuse Treatment, Prevention, and Policy, 4*(1), 1.

Pert, C., Jahoda, A., Stenfert Kroese, B., Trower, P., Dagnan, D., & Selkirk, M. (2013). Cognitive behavioural therapy from the perspective of clients with mild intellectual disabilities: A qualitative investigation of process issues. *Journal of Intellectual Disability Research, 57*(4), 359–369.

Peters, S. (2000). Is there a disability culture? A syncretisation of three possible world views. *Disability & Society, 15*(4), 583–601.

Peterson, Y. (1979). The impact of physical disability on marital adjustment: A literature review. *Family Coordinator, 28*, 47–51.

Petrie, K. J., Perry, K., Broadbent, E., & Weinman, J. (2012). A text message programme designed to modify patients' illness and treatment beliefs improves self-reported adherence to asthma preventer medication. *British Journal of Health Psychology, 17*(1), 74–84.

Pfister, G. J., Burkes, R. M., Guinn, B., Steele, J., Kelley, R. R., Wiemken, T. L., . . . & Cavallazzi, R. (2016). Opioid overdose leading to intensive care unit admission: Epidemiology and outcomes. *Journal of Critical Care, 35*, 29–32.

Phillips, A., & Rakusen, J. (1989). *New our bodies, ourselves: A health book for and by women*. New York: Penguin Books, Limited.

Phillips, B., & Zhao, H. (1993). Predictors of assistive technology abandonment. *Assistive Technology, 5*(1), 36–45.

Phillips, K. (2015, July 9). *Age and sleep apnea: Does age affect the prevalence of sleep apnea?* Alaska Sleep Clinic. Retreived from http://www.alaskasleep.com/blog/age-and-sleep-apnea-age-affect-prevalence-sleep-apnea

Pienta, A. M., Hayward, M. D., & Jenkins, K. R. (2000). Health consequences of marriage for the retirement years. *Journal of Family Issues, 21*(5), 559–586.

Pihlstrom, B., L., Michalowicz, B. S., & Johnson, N. W. (2005). Periodontal diseases. *Lancet, 366*, 1809–1820.

Pope, C. A., Bowman, C. A., & Barr, K. (2001). Conversations from the commissions: Negotiating the tensions in the preparation of teachers with disabilities. *English Education, 33*(3), 252–256.

Porat, O., Heruti, R., Navon-Porat, H., & Hardoff, D. (2012). Counseling young people with physical disabilities regarding relationships and sexuality issues: Utilization of a novel service. *Sexuality & Disability, 30*, 311–317.

Porterfield, S. L. (2002). Work choices of mothers in families with children with disabilities. *Journal of Marriage and Family, 64*(4), 972–981.

Post, M. W. M., Bloemen, J., & De Witte, L. P. (2005). Burden of support for partners of persons with spinal cord injuries. *Spinal Cord, 43*(5), 311–319.

Postar, A. (2011). Selective bibliography relating to law students and lawyers with disabilities. *American Univerity Journal of Gender Social Policy & the Law, 19*, 1237.

Poston, D., Turnbull, A. P., Park, J., Hasheem, M., Marquis, J., & Wang, M. (2003). Family quality of life: A qualitative inquiry. *Mental Retardation, 41*(5), 313–328.

Pote, H., Mazon, T., Clegg, J., & King, S. (2011). Vulnerability and protection talk: Systemic therapy process with people with intellectual disability. *Journal of Intellectual and Developmental Disability, 36*(2), 105–117.

Preston, P. (2012). Parents with disabilities. *International Encyclopedia of Rehabilitation*. Retrieved from http://cirrie.buffalo.edu/encyclopedia/en/article/36/.

Prigatano, G. P. (1992). Personality disturbances associated with traumatic brain injury. *Journal of Consulting and Clinical Psychology, 60*(3), 360.

Prilleltensky, O. (2004). My child is not my carer: Mothers with physical disabilities and the wellbeing of children. *Disability & Society, 19*(3), 209–223.

Quittner, A., Opipari, L., Regoli, M. J., Jacobsen, J., & Eigen, H. (1992). The impact of caregiving and role strain on family life: Comparisons between mothers of children with cystic fibrosis and matched controls. *Rehabilitation Psychology, 37*, 275–290.

Rackensperger, T., Krezman, C., McNaughton, D., Williams, M. B., & D'Silva, K. (2005). "When I first got it, I wanted to throw it off a cliff": The challenges and benefits of learning AAC technologies as described by adults who use AAC. *Augmentative and Alternative Communication, 21*(3), 165–186.

Rehab International. (n.d.). *Vicodin addiction statistics*. Retreived from http://rehab-international.org/vicodin-addiction/statistics

Reinders, H. S. (2008). Persons with disabilities as parents: What is the problem? *Journal of Applied Research in Intellectual Disabilities, 21*(4), 308–314.

Reiss, S., Levitan, G., & Szyszko, J. (1982). Emotional disturbance and mental retardation: Diagnostic overshadowing. *American Journal of Mental Deficiency, 86*, 567–574.

Resnicow, K., Baranowski, T., Ahluwalia, J. S., & Braithwaite, R. L. (1998). Cultural sensitivity in public health: Defined and demystified. *Ethnicity & Disease, 9*(1), 10–21.

Revenson, T. A., & Felton, B. J. (1989). Disability and coping as predictors of psychological adjustment to rheumatoid arthritis. *Journal of Consulting and Clinical Psychology, 57*(3), 344.

Reynolds, S. (2010). Disability culture in West Africa: Qualitative research indicating barriers and progress in the greater Accra region of Ghana. *Occupational Therapy International, 17*(4), 198–207.

Richardson, J. L., Langholz, B., Bernstein, L., Burciaga, C., Danley, K., & Ross, R. K. (1992). Stage and delay in breast cancer diagnosis by race, socioeconomic status, age and year. *British Journal of Cancer, 65*(6), 922.

Riddell, S., & Watson, N. (2014). *Disability, culture and identity*. New York: Routledge.

Ridgeway, P. (2011). Restorying psychiatric disability: Learning from first person recovery narratives. *Psychiatric Rehabilitation Journal, 24*(4), 335–343.

Riemer-Reiss, M. L., & Wacker, R. R. (2000). Factors associated with assistive technology discontinuance among individuals with disabilities. *Journal of Rehabilitation, 66*(3), 44.

Rimmer, J. H., & Wang, E. (2005). Obesity prevalence among a group of Chicago residents with disabilities. *Archives of Physical Medicine and Rehabilitation, 86*(7), 1461–1464.

Rintala, D. H., Howland, C. A., Nosek, M. A., Bennett, J. L., Young, M. E., Foley, C. C., Rossi, C. D., & Chanpong, G. (1997). Dating issues for women with physical disabilities. *Sexuality and Disability, 15*(4), 219–242.

Ripat, J., & Booth, A. (2005). Characteristics of assistive technology service delivery models: Stakeholder perspectives and preferences. *Disability and Rehabilitation, 27*(24), 1461–1470.

Risdal, D., & Singer, G. H. (2004). Marital adjustment in parents of children with disabilities: A historical review and meta-analysis. *Research and Practice for Persons with Severe Disabilities, 29*(2), 95–103.

Roberts, E. L., Ju, S., & Zhang, D. (2016). Review of practices that promote self-advocacy for students with disabilities. *Journal of Disability Policy Studies, 26*(4), 209–220.

Robertson, C. T., Egelhof, R., & Hoke, M. (2008). Get sick, get out: The medical causes of home mortgage foreclosures. *Health Matrix: Journal of Law-Medicine, 18*(65).

Robbins, M. J., Wester, S. R., & McKean, N. B. (2016). Masculinity across the life span: Implications for older gay men. In J. Y. Wong, S. R. Wester (Eds.), *APA handbook of men and masculinities* (389–409). Washington, DC: American Psychological Association.

Robinson, M. E., & O'Brien, E. M. (2010). Chronic pain. In R. G. Frank, M. Rosenthal, & B. Caplan (Eds.). *Handbook of rehabilitation psychology* (2nd ed., pp. 119–132). Washington, DC: American Psychological Association.

Rogers-Dulan, J., & Blacher, J. (1995). African American families, religion, and disability: A conceptual framework. *Mental Retardation, 33*(4), 226.

Rojahn, J., Komelasky, K. G., & Man, M. (2008). Implicit attitudes and explicit ratings of romantic attraction of college students toward opposite-sex peers with physical disabilities. *Journal of Developmental and Physical Disabilities, 20*(4), 389–397.

Rolland, J. (1994). *Families, illness and disability.* New York: Basic Books.

Rolland, J. S. (1999). Parental illness and disability: A family systems framework. *Journal of Family Therapy, 21*(3), 242–266.

Rolland, J. S. (2003). Mastering family challenges in illness and disability. In F. Walsh (Ed.), *Normal family processes: Growing diversity and complexity* (3rd ed.). New York: Guilford Press.

Rose, J. L., & Gerson, D. F. (2009). Assessing anger in people with intellectual disability. *Journal of Intellectual and Developmental Disability, 34*(2), 116–122.

Rosenbaum, P., Paneth, N., Leviton, A., Goldstein, M., & Bax, M. (2007). A report: The definition and classification of cerebral palsy April 2006. *Developmental Medicine and Child Neurology, 49*, 8–14.

Russo-Gleicher, R. J. (2008). MSW programs: Gatekeepers to the field of developmental disabilities. *Journal of Social Work Education, 44*(2), 129–155.

Saetermoe, C. L., Scattone, D., & Kim, K. H. (2001). Ethnicity and the stigma of disabilities. *Psychology and Health, 16*(6), 699–713.

Safran, S. P. (1998). Disability portrayal in film: Reflecting the past, directing the future. *Exceptional Children, 64*(2), 227–238.

Sandahl, C. (2003). Queering the crip or cripping the queer? Intersections of queer and crip identities in solo autobiographical performance. *GLQ: A Journal of Lesbian and Gay Studies, 9*(1), 25–56.

Sandowski, C. (1993). Responding to the sexual concerns of people with disabilities. *Journal of Social Work and Human Sexuality, 8,* 29–43.

Sareen, J., Jacobi, F., Cox, B. J., Belik, S. L., Clara, I., & Stein, M. B. (2006). Disability and poor quality of life associated with comorbid anxiety disorders and physical conditions. *Archives of Internal Medicine, 166*(19), 2109–2116.

Sayar, K., Gulec, H., & Topbas, M. (2004). Alexithymia and anger in patients with fibromyalgia. *Clinical Rheumatology, 23*(5), 441–448.

Scanlon, D., & Mellard, D. F. (2002). Academic and participation profiles of school-age dropouts with and without disabilities. *Exceptional Children, 68*(2), 239–258.

Schaffalitzky, E., Gallagher, P., MacLachlan, M., & Ryall, N. (2011. Understanding the benefits of prosthetics prescription: Exploring the experiences of practitioners and lower limb prosthetic users. *Disability & Rehabilitation, 33*(15-16), 1314–1323.

Scheer, J. (1994). Culture and disability: An anthropological point of view. In E. J. Trickett, R. J. Watts, & D. Birman (Eds.), *Human diversity: Perspectives on people in context* (pp. 244–260). San Francisco: Jossey-Bass.

Scherer, M. J. (1996a). *Living in the state of stuck: How technology impacts the lives of persons with disabilities.* Brookline, MA: Brookline Books.

Scherer, M. J. (1996b). Outcomes of assistive technology use on quality of life. *Disability and Rehabilitation, 18*(9), 439–448.

Scherer, M. J., Sax, C., Vanbiervliet, A., Cushman, L. A., & Scherer, J. V. (2005). Predictors of assistive technology use: The importance of personal and psychosocial factors. *Disability and Rehabilitation, 27*(21), 1321–1331.

Schirmer, B. R., & McGough, S. M. (2005). Teaching reading to children who are deaf: Do the conclusions of the National Reading Panel apply? *Review of Educational Research, 75*(1), 83–117.

Schmelkin, L. P. (1984). Hierarchy of preferences toward disabled groups: A reanalysis. *Perceptual and Motor Skills, 59*(1), 151–157.

Schmitt, M. T., & Branscombe, N. R. (2002). The internal and external causal loci of attributions to prejudice. *Personality and Social Psychology Bulletin, 28*(5), 620–628.

Schmitt, M. T., Branscombe, N. R., Postmes, T., & Garcia, A. (2014). The consequences of perceived discrimination for psychological well-being: A meta-analytic review. *Psychological Bulletin, 140*(4), 921–248.

Schreiber, J., Benger, J., Salls, J., Marchetti, G., & Reed, L. (2011). Parent perspectives on rehabilitation services for their children with disabilities: A mixed methods approach. *Physical & Occupational Therapy in Pediatrics, 31*(3), 225–238.

Schulz, C. H. (2008). Collaboration in the marriage relationship among persons with disabilities. *Disability Studies Quarterly, 28*(1).

Schumm, D., & Stoltzfus, M. (2011). *Disability in Judaism, Christianity, and Islam: Sacred texts, historical traditions, and social analysis.* New York: Springer.

Schunk, D. H. (1987). Peer models and children's behavioral change. *Review of Educational Research, 57*(2), 149–174.

Schur, L. (2002). The difference a job makes: The effects of employment among people with disabilities. *Journal of Economic Issues, 36*(2), 339–347.

Schur, L., Shields, T., & Schriner, K. (2003). Can I make a difference? Efficacy, employment, and disability. *Political Psychology, 24*(1), 119–149.

Schwartz, C. E., & Rogers, M. (1994). Designing a psychosocial intervention to teach coping flexibility. *Rehabilitation Psychology, 39*(1), 57–72.

Sexuality Information and Education Council of the U.S. (2002). Sexuality and disability: An SIECUS annotated bibliography. *Sexuality & Disability, 20*(3), 209–231.

Shakespeare, T. W. (2000). Disabled sexuality: Toward rights and recognition. *Sexuality and Disability, 18*(3), 159–166.

Shakespeare, T. W. (2004). Disablism ain't the same as racism. Retrieved from http://www.bbc.co.uk/ouch/opinion/disablism_aint_the_same_as_racism.shtml.

Shakespeare, T. W. (2006). *Disability rights and wrongs.* London: Routledge.

Shakespeare, T. W., & Watson, N. (2002). The social model of disability: An outdated ideology. *Research in Social Science and Disability, 2,* 9–28.

Sharabi, A. (2007). *Loneliness, mood, motivation and internet friendships, among adolescents with and without learning disabilities: with regard to the educational environment and the severity of the disability* (Unpublished doctoral dissertation). Tel Aviv University, Israel.

Shinohara, K., & Wobbrock, J. O. (2011, May). In the shadow of misperception: Assistive technology use and social interactions. In *Proceedings of the SIGCHI Conference on Human Factors in Computing Systems* (pp. 705–714). New York: ACM.

Shott, S. R., Amin, R., Chini, B., Heubi, C., Hotze, S., & Akers, R. (2006). Obstructive sleep apnea: Should all children with Down syndrome be tested? *Archives of Otolaryngology–Head & Neck Surgery, 132*(4), 432–436.

Shuttleworth, R., & Mona, L. (2002). Disability and sexuality: Toward a focus on sexual access. *Disability Studies Quarterly, 22*(4), 2–9.

Silverstone, P. H. (1990). Changes in depression scores following life-threatening illness. *Journal of Psychosomatic Research, 34,* 659–663.

Singh, D. (1993). Adaptive significance of female physical attractiveness: Role of waist-to-hip ratio. *Journal of Personality and Social Psychology, 65*(2), 293.

Sipski, M., & Alexander, C. J. (1997). *Sexual function in people with disability and chronic illness: A health professional's guide.* Silver Springs, MD: Aspen Publications.

Sirgy, J. (2012). *The psychology of quality of life: Hedonic well-being, life satisfaction, and eudaimonia* (Vol. 50). New York: Springer Science & Business Media.

Skinner, M. E. (1998). Promoting self-advocacy among college students with learning disabilities. *Intervention in School and Clinic, 33*(5), 278–283.

Sleeter, C. (2010). Why is there learning disabilities? A critical analysis of the birth of the field in its social context. *Disability Studies Quarterly, 30*(2).

Slevin, K. F., & Linneman, T. J. (2010). Old gay men's bodies and masculinities. *Men and Masculinities, 12*(4), 483–507.

Smart, K. M., Blake, C., Staines, A., & Doody, C. (2012). Self-reported pain severity, quality of life, disability, anxiety and depression in patients classified with 'nociceptive','peripheral neuropathic'and 'central sensitisation'pain. The discriminant validity of mechanisms-based classifications of low back (±leg) pain. *Manual Therapy, 17*(2), 119–125.

Smith, C., Hale, L., Olson, K., & Schneiders, A (2009). How does exercise influence fatigue in people with multiple sclerosis? *Disability & Rehabilitation, 31*(9), 685–692.

Smith, C., Hale, L., Olson, K., & Schneiders, A. (2013). Health care provider beliefs about exercise and faitugue in people with multiple sclerosis. *Journal of Rehabilitation Research and Development, 50*(5), 733–744.

Smith, C., Olson, K., Hale, L., Baxter, G. D., & Schneiders, A. (2011). How does fatigue influence community-based exercise participation in people with multiple sclerosis? *Disability and Rehabilitation, 33*(23-24), 2362–2371.

Smith, I. C. (2011). A qualitative investigation into the effects of brief training in solution-focused therapy in a social work team. *Psychology & Psychotherapy: Theory, Research & Practice, 84*, 335–348.

Smith, M. J., & Ryan, A. S. (1987). Chinese-American families of children with developmental disabilities: An exploratory study of reactions to service providers. *Mental Retardation, 25*(6), 345.

Smith, M. T., & Haythornthwaite, J. A. (2004). How do sleep disturbance and chronic pain inter-relate? Insights from the longitudinal and cognitive-behavioral clinical trials literature. *Sleep Medicine Reviews, 8*(2), 119–132.

Smith, R. A., & Hancock, L. E. (2012). *Asian-Americans with disabilities.* Columbia University, Columbia University Academic Commons. Retrieved from http://hdl.handle.net/10022/AC:P:14858.

Snyder, T. D., & Dillow, S. A. (2012). *Digest of education statistics 2011.* Washington, DC: National Center for Education Statistics.

So, C., & Pierluissi, E. (2011). Attitudes and expectations regarding exercise in the hospital of hospitalized older adults: A qualitative study. *Journal of the American Geriatrics Society, 60*(4), 713–718.

Sobsey, D. (2004). Marital stability and marital satisfaction in families of children with disabilities: Chicken or egg? *Developmental Disabilities Bulletin, 32*(1), 62–83.

Solomon, P., O'Brien, K., Wilkins, S., & Gervais, N. (2014). Aging with HIV and disability: The role of uncertainty. *AIDS Care, 26*(2), 240–245.

Soundy, A., Benson, J., Dawes, H., Smith, B., Collett, J., & Meaney, A. (2012). Understanding hope in patients with multiple sclerosis. *Physiotherapy, 98*(4), 344–350.

Specht, J. A., King, G. A., Willoughby, C., Brown, E. G., & Smith, L. (2005). Spirituality: A coping mechanism in the lives of adults with congenital disabilities. *Counseling & Values, 50*, 51–62.

Stapleton, D., Honeycutt, T., & Schechter, B. (2012). Out of sight, out of mind: Including group quarters residents with household residents can change what we know about working-age people with disabilities. *Demography, 49*(1), 267–289.

Stebbings, S., Herbison, P., Doyle, T. C., Treharne, G. J., & Highton, J. (2010). A comparison of fatigue correlates in rheumatoid arthritis and osteoarthritis: Disparity in associations with disability, anxiety and sleep disturbance. *Rheumatology, 49*(2), 361–367.

Steinkuller, P. G., Du, L., Gilbert, C., Foster, A., Collins, M. L., & Coats, D. K. (1999). Childhood blindness. *Journal of American Association for Pediatric Ophthalmology and Strabismus, 3*(1), 26–32.

Steinmetz, E. (2006). *Americans with disabilities, 2002.* Washington, DC: U.S. Department of Commerce, Economics and Statistics Administration, U.S. Census Bureau.

Stone, J. H. (2004). *Culture and disability: Providing culturally competent services.* Thousand Oaks, CA: Sage Publications.

Strike, D. L., Skovholt, T. M., & Hummel, T. J. (2004). Mental health professionals' disability competence: Measuring self awareness, perceived knowledge, and perceived skills. *Rehabilitation Psychology, 49*(4), 321–327.

Strupp, H. H., & Binder, J. L. (1984). *Psychotherapy in a new key: A guide to time-limited dynamic psychotherapy.* New York: Basic Books.

Substance Abuse and Mental Health Services Administration (SAMSHA). (2016). Retrieved from https://www.samhsa.gov/data/sites/default/files/NSDUH-FFR2-2015/NSDUH-FFR2-2015.htm

Substance Abuse and Mental Health Services Administration (SAMSHA). (2015). Retrieved from https://www.samhsa.gov/atod/marijuana

Sue, D. W. (2010). *Microaggressions in everyday life: Race, gender, and sexual orientation.* Hoboken, NJ: Wiley.

Sullivan, P. M., & Knutson, J. F. (2000). Maltreatment and disabilities: A population-based epidemiological study. *Child Abuse & Neglect, 24*(10), 1257–1273.

Swain, J., & French, S. (2000). Towards an affirmation model of disability. *Disability & Society, 15*(4), 569–582.

Swami, V., & Tovée, M. J. (2008). The muscular male: A comparison of physical attractiveness preferences of gay and heterosexual men. *International Journal of Men's Health, 7*(1), 59–71.

Sweeney, E. P. (2000). *Recent studies indicate that many parents who are current or former welfare recipients have disabilities or other medical conditions.* Washington, DC: Center on Budget and Policy Priorities.

Taleporos, G., & McCabe, M. P. (2003). Relationships, sexuality and adjustment among people with physical disability. *Sexual and Relationship Therapy, 18*(1), 25–43.

Taunt, H. M., & Hastings, R. P. (2002). Positive impact of children with developmental disabilities on their families: A preliminary study. *Education and Training in Mental Retardation and Developmental Disabilities, 37*(4), 410–420.

Taylor, J. L. (2002). A review of the assessment and treatment of anger and aggression in offenders with intellectual disability. *Journal of Intellectual Disability Research, 46*(s1), 57–73.

Tepper, M. S. (2000). Sexuality and disability: The missing discourse of pleasure. *Sexuality and Disability, 18*(4), 283–290.

Test, D. W., Fowler, C. H., Wood, W. M., Brewer, D. M., & Eddy, S. (2005). A conceptual framework of self-advocacy for students with disabilities. *Remedial and Special Education, 26*(1), 43–54.

Thorpe Jr, R. J., Szanton, S. L., Bell, C. N., & Whitfield, K. E. (2016). Education, income and disability in African Americans. *Ethnicity & Disease, 23*(1), 12–17.

Thurlow, M. L., Sinclair, M. F., & Johnson, D. R. (2002). Students with Disabilities Who Drop Out of School: Implications for Policy and Practice. Issue Brief: Examining Current Challenges in Secondary Education and Transition.

Tilley, C. M. (1996). Sexuality in women with physical disabilities: A social justice or health issue? *Sexuality and Disability, 14*, 139–151.

Timm, R. (2002). Disability-specific hassles: The effects of oppression on people with disabilities. *Dissertation Abstracts International,* ProQuest Microform UMI #3069626.

Toms Barker, L. T., & Maralani, V. (1997). *Challenges and strategies of disabled parents: Findings from a national survey of parents with disabilities.* Oakland, CA: Berkeley Planning Associates.

Tremain, S. (2000). Queering disabled sexuality studies. *Sexuality and Disability, 18*, 291–300.

Tschannen, T. A., Duckro, P. N., Margolis, R. B., & Tomazic, T. J. (1992). The relationship of anger, depression, and perceived disability among headache patients. *Headache: The Journal of Head and Face Pain, 32*(10), 501–503.

Turk, D. C., & Winter, F. (2006). *The pain survival guide: How to reclaim your life.* Washington, DC: American Psychological Association.

Turnbull, H. R., Beegle, G., & Stowe, M. J. (2001). The core concepts of disability policy affecting families who have children with disabilities. *Journal of Disability Policy Studies, 12*(3), 133–143.

Turnbull, A. P., Blue-Banning, M., & Pereira, L. (2000). Successful friendships of Hispanic children and youth with disabilities: An exploratory study. *Mental Retardation, 38*(2), 138–153.

Turner, R. J., & Beiser, M. (1990). Major depression and depressive symptomatology among the physically disabled: Assessing the role of chronic stress. *Journal of Nervous and Mental Disease, 178*(6), 343–350.

Turner, R. J., & McLean, P. D. (1989). Physical disability and distress. *Rehabilitation Psychology, 34*, 225–242.

Turner, R. J., & Noh, S. (1988). Physical disability and depression: A longitudinal analysis. *Journal of Health and Social Behavior, 29*, 23–37.

United Spinal Association and The University of Alabama Model SCI System. (2007). *Sexuality for women with spinal cord injury*. Retrieved from http://www.spinalcord.org/resource-center/askus/index.php?pg=kb.page&id=1579

Valle, J. W., Solis, S., Volpitta, D., & Connor, D. J. (2004). The disability closet: Teachers with learning disabilities evaluate the risks and benefits of "coming out." *Equity & Excellence in Education, 37*(1), 4–17.

Valvano, A. K., West, L. M., Wilson, C. K., Macapagal, K. R., Penwell-Waines, L. M., Waller, J. L., & Stepleman, L. M. (2014). Health professions students' perceptions of sexuality in patients with physical disability. *Sexuality & Disability, 32*, 413–427.

van Baar, M., Dekker, J., Lemmens, A., Oostendorp, R., & Bijlsma, J. (1998). Pain and disability in patients with osteoarthritis of hip or knee: The relationship with articular, kinesiological, and psychological characteristics. *Journal of Rheumatology, 25(1)*, 125–133.

Van der Riet, P., Dedkhard, S., & Srithong, K. (2011). Complementary therapies in rehabilitation: Stroke patients' narratives. Part 2. *Journal of Clinical Nursing, 21*, 668–676.

van Haastregt, J. C., Zijlstra, G. R., van Rossum, E., van Eijk, J. T. M., & Kempen, G. I. (2008). Feelings of anxiety and symptoms of depression in community-living older persons who avoid activity for fear of falling. *American Journal of Geriatric Psychiatry, 16*(3), 186–193.

Van Huet, H., Innes, E., & Whiteford, G. (2009). Living and doing with chronic pain: Narratives of pain program. *Disability & Rehabilitation, 31*(24), 2031–2040.

van Ingen, D. J., Moore, L. L., & Fuemmeler, J. A. (2008). Parental overinvolvement: A qualitative study. *Journal of Developmental & Physical Disabilities, 20*, 449–465.

Van Nieuwenhuizen, A., Henderson, C., Kassam, A., Graham, T., Murray, J., Howard, L. M., & Thornicroft, G. (2013). Emergency department staff views and experiences on diagnostic overshadowing related to people with mental illness. *Epidemiology and Psychiatric Sciences, 22*(03), 255–262.

Veenhoven, R. (2013). The four quality of life ordering concepts and measures of the good life. In A. Delle Fave, *The exploration of happiness: Present and future perspectives* (pp. 195–226). Amsterdam: Springer Netherlands.

Vellas, B. J., Wayne, S. J., Romero, L. J., Baumgartner, R. N., & Garry, P. J. (1997). Fear of falling and restriction of mobility in elderly fallers. *Age and Ageing, 26*(3), 189–193.

Verza, R., Carvalho, M. L., Battaglia, M. A., & Uccelli, M. M. (2006). An interdisciplinary approach to evaluating the need for assistive technology reduces equipment abandonment. *Multiple Sclerosis, 12*(1), 88–93.

Vitiello, M. V., Rybarczyk, B., Von Korff, M., & Stepanski, E. J. (2009). Cognitive behavioral therapy for insomnia improves sleep and decreases pain in older adults with co-morbid insomnia and osteoarthritis. *Journal of Clinical Sleep Medicine, 5*(4), 355–362.

Von Korff, M., Ormel, J., Keefe, F. J., & Dworkin, S. F. (1992). Grading the severity of chronic pain. *Pain, 50*(2), 133–149.

Wagner, M. M., & Blackorby, J. (1996). Transition from high school to work or college: How special education students fare. *Special Education for Students with Disabilities, 6*(1), 103–120.

Wagner, M., Newman, L., Cameto, R., Garza, N., & Levine, P. (2005). After high school: A first look at the postschool experiences of youth with disabilities. A report from the National Longitudinal Transition Study-2 (NLTS2). SRI Project #P11182.

Waite, L., & Gallagher, M. (2002). *The case for marriage: Why married people are happier, healthier and better off financially.* New York: Broadway Books.

Walker, L. E. (1977). Battered women and learned helplessness. *Victimology, 2*(3-4), 525–534.

Walker, S. (1995). An examination of variables related to the cost of purchased rehabilitation services relative to the needs of persons with disabilities from diverse ethnic backgrounds; Revised. Retrieved from http://eric.ed.gov/?id=ED397592

Wampold, B. E., & Imel, Z. E. (2015). *The great psychotherapy debate: The evidence for what makes psychotherapy work.* New York: Routledge.

Wang, K., & Dovidio, J. F. (2011). Disability and autonomy: Priming alternative identities. *Rehabilitation Psychology, 56*(2), 123–127.

Wang, R. H., Mihailidis, A., Dutta, T., & Fernie, G. (2011). Usability testing of multimodal feedback interface and simulated collision-avoidance power wheelchair for long-term-care home residents with cognitive impairments. *Journal of Rehabilitation Research & Development, 48*(7), 801–822.

Warfield, M. E. (2005). Family and work predictors of parenting role stress among two-earner families of children with disabilities. *Infant and Child Development, 14*(2), 155–176.

Watermeyer, B. (2012). Disability and countertransference in group psychotherapy. *International Journal of Group Psychotherapy, 62*(3), 393–418.

Waxman, B. (1994). It's time to politicize our sexual oppression. In B. Shaw (Ed.), *The ragged edge: The disability experience from the pages of the first fifteen years of the Disability Rag* (pp. 82–87). Louisville, KY: The Avocado Press.

Waxman, B., & Finger, A. (1989). The politics of sex and disability. *Disability Studies Quarterly, 9*(3), 1–5.

Webb, P. M., Purdie, D. M., Grover, S., Jordan, S., Dick, M. L., & Green, A. C. (2004). Symptoms and diagnosis of borderline, early and advanced epithelial ovarian cancer. *Gynecologic Oncology, 92*(1), 232–239.

WebMD. (n.d.). Obstructive sleep apnea explained. Retreived from http://www.webmd.com/sleep-disorders/guide/understanding-obstructive-sleep-apnea-syndrome

Weeks, J., Heaphy, B., & Donovan, C. (2001). *Same sex intimacies: Families of choice and other life experiments.* Hove, UK: Psychology Press.

Weiller, E., Bisserbe, J. C., Maier, W., & Lecrubier, Y. (1997). Prevalence and recognition of anxiety syndromes in five European primary care settings. A report from the WHO study on Psychological Problems in General Health Care. *British Journal of Psychiatry, 173*(Suppl 34), 18–23.

Weissman, M. M., & Myers, J. K. (1978). Affective disorders in a US urban community: The use of research diagnostic criteria in an epidemiological survey. *Archives of General Psychiatry, 35*, 1304–1311.

Welner, S. L. (1999). Contraceptive choices for women. *Sexuality and Disability, 17*, 209–214.

Wessels, R., Dijcks, B., Soede, M., Gelderblom, G. J., & De Witte, L. (2003). Non-use of provided assistive technology devices, a literature overview. *Technology and Disability, 15*(4), 231–238.

Westbrook, M. T., Legge, V., & Pennay, M. (1993). Attitudes towards disabilities in a multicultural society. *Social Science & Medicine, 36*(5), 615–623.

Western, B., & Pettit, B. (2005). Black-white wage inequality, employment rates, and incarceration. *American Journal of Sociology, 111*(2), 553–578.

Wiegerink, D., Roebroeck, M., Bender, J., Stam, H., & Cohen-Kettenis, P. (2011). Sexuality of young adults with cerebral palsy: Experienced limitations and needs. *Sexuality & Disability, 29*, 119–128.

Wiggins, L. D., Baio, J. O. N., & Rice, C. (2006). Examination of the time between first evaluation and first autism spectrum diagnosis in a population-based sample. *Journal of Developmental & Behavioral Pediatrics, 27*(2), S79–S87.

Wilson, S. (2003). *Disability, counseling and psychotherapy: Challenges and opportunities*. New York: Palgrave Macmillan.

Wineman, N. M. (1990). Adaptation to multiple sclerosis: The role of social support, functional disability, and perceived uncertainty. *Nursing Research, 39*(5), 294–299.

Witter, M. (2016). *Gay disabled men: A qualitative study* (Unpublished doctoral dissertation). California School of Professional Psychology at Alliant International University, San Francisco, CA.

Wiwanitkit, V. (2008). Sexuality and rehabilitation for individuals with cerebral palsy. *Sexuality & Disability, 26*, 175–177.

Wiwanitkit, V. (2009). Lower paraplegia in females: Sexuality aspect. *Sexuality and Disability, 27*, 61–63.

Wong, D. (2007). *Attitudes and beliefs of immigrant Chinese parents of children with disabilities: How they fit into theoretical models of disability* (Unpublished doctoral dissertation). California School of Professional Psychology at Alliant International University, San Francisco, CA.

Wong-Hernandez, L., & Wong, D. (2002). The effects of language and culture variables to the rehabilitation of bilingual and bicultural consumers: A review of literature study focusing on Hispanic Americans and Asian Americans. *Disability Studies Quarterly, 22*(2).

World Health Organization (2001). *International classification of functioning, disability, and health*. Geneva: Author.

Wright, B. A. (1960). Value changes in acceptance of disability. In *Physical disability—A psychological approach*. New York: Harper & Row.

Wright, B. A. (1972). Value-laden beliefs and principles for rehabilitation psychology. *Rehabilitation Psychology, 19*(1), 38–45.

Wright, B. A. (1983). *Physical disability: A psychosocial approach* (2nd ed.). New York: Harper & Row.

Wright, B. A. (1988). Attitudes and the fundamental negative bias: Conditions and corrections (pp. 3–21). In H. Yuker (Ed.), *Attitudes toward persons with disabilities*. New York: Springer.

Yoshida, K. K., Li, A., & Odette, F. (1999). Cross-cultural views of disability and sexuality: Experiences of a group of ethno-racial women with physical disabilities. *Sexuality and Disability, 17*(4), 321–327.

Young, M. E., Nosek, M. A., Howland, C., Chanpong, G., & Rintala, D. H. (1997). Prevalence of abuse of women with physical disabilities. *Archives of Physical Medicine and Rehabilitation, 78*(12), S34–S38.

Young, R., Gore, N., & McCarthy, M. (2012). Staff attitudes towards sexuality in relation to gender of people with intellectual disability: A qualitative study. *Journal of Intellectual & Developmental Disability, 37*(4), 343–347.

Younggren, J. N., Boisvert, J. A., & Boness, C. L. (2016). Examining emotional support animals and role conflicts in professional psychology. *Professional Psychology: Research and Practice, 47*(4), 255–260.

Yuker, H. E. (1983). The lack of a stable order of preference for disabilities: A response to Richardson and Ronald. *Rehabilitation Psychology, 28*(2), 93–103.

Yuker, H. E. (1988). Perceptions of severely and multiply disabled persons. *Journal of the Multihandicapped Person, 1*(1), 5–16.

Yuker, H. E. (1994). Variables that influence attitudes toward persons with disabilities: Conclusions from the data. Psychosocial Perspectives on Disability, a special issue of the *Journal of Social Behavior and Personality, 9*, 3–22.

Zaidi, A., & Burchardt, T. (2005). Comparing incomes when needs differ: Equivalization for the extra costs of disability in the UK. *Review of Income and Wealth, 51*(1), 89–114.

Zea, M. C., Belgrave, F. Z., García, J. G., & Quezada, T. (1997). Socioeconomic and cultural factors in rehabilitation of Latinos with disabilities. In J. G. Garcia & M. C. Zea (Eds.), *Psychological interventions and research with Latino populations* (pp. 217–234). Needham Heights, MA: Allyn & Bacon.

Zelman, D. C., Smith, M. Y., Hoffman, D., Edwards, L., Reed, P., Levine, E., Siefeldin, R., & Dukes, E. (2001). Acceptable, manageable, and tolerable days: Patient daily goals for medication management of persistent pain. *Journal of Pain and Symptom Management, 28*(5), 474–487.

Zhan, L. (1999). Xi young hong: Health practice in Chinese older women. In L. Zhan (Ed.), *Asian voices: Asian and Asian American health educators speak out* (pp. 26–40). Sudbury, MA: Jones and Bartlett Publishers.

Zhang, A. Y., Snowden, L. R., & Sue, S. (1998). Differences between Asian and white Americans' help seeking and utilization patterns in the Los Angeles area. *Journal of Community Psychology, 26*, 317–326.

Zigmond, N. (2003). Where should students with disabilities receive special education services? Is one place better than another? *Journal of Special Education, 37*(3), 193–199.

Zinn, M. B. (1994). Feminist rethinking from racial-ethnic families. In M. B. Zinn & B. T. Dill (Eds.), *Women of color in US society* (pp. 303–314). Philadelphia: Temple University Press.

Zola, I. K. (1993). Self, identity and the naming question: Reflections on the language of disability. *Social Science & Medicine, 36*(2), 167–173.

About the Author

Rhoda Olkin, Ph.D., graduated from Stanford (BA) and UC Santa Barbara (Ph.D.), and is a Distinguished Professor at the California School of Professional Psychology, at Alliant International University, San Francisco. She specializes in disability and has published extensively on the topic. She teaches graduate courses on working with clients with chronic illness and disability and provides therapy to individuals and families with disabilities. She is a polio survivor, a mom, and published author.

Index

Page numbers followed by *b, f* and *t* refer to boxes, figures and tables, respectively.

Abels, A. V., 26–27
Ableism, 7, 8
Abrams, K., 200
Abuse
   as cause of disability, 72
   childhood, and substance abuse, 58
   in developmental history, 74–75
   outpatient psychotherapy research on, 19–20
Acceptance
   as value of disability community, 118
Acceptance of disability, 10
Accessibility, 121
Accommodations
   under ADA, 78
   assistive technology and accessing, 65
   in educational history, 76–77
   individualization of, 89
Acquaintances, 149–50
ADA. *See* Americans with Disabilities Act
Adaptation to disability, 9–10
Adjustment to disability, 9–10
Admiration, for person with disability, 151
Adolescents with disabilities
   advocacy skills of, 77
   norms for, 123
   sexuality for, 175
   therapeutic relationship with, 25
   See also Teens
Adoption, of assistive technology, 64–65, 128–29
Advocacy skills
   in developmental history, 77
   and model of disability, 118–19
   for parents of children with disabilities, 168
   as value of disability community, 118
Affective Regulation (D-AT VIII), 156–64
   anger and rage, 160–61
   anxiety and trauma, 161–63
   cheerfulness, 158
   gratefulness, 159–60
   insightfulness, 159
   mourning and depression, 156–58
   for "Sam" case example, 193–94
   and scope of values, 158–59
Affect of others, managing, 137
Affirmative therapy, 9
Affordable Care Act (2010), 56, 167
African Americans, 106–8
Agency, 9

Age-related disabilities, 25
Aggrandizing, 136t
Aging
  and course of disability, 66
  limitations related to disability vs., 152
  partnership, disability, and, 173–74
Alcohol use, 56, 57, 59
Alexander, C. J., 182
Alexander, C. M., 199
ALLOW model, 180
ALS (amyotrophic lateral sclerosis), 66
"Amanda" case example, 110–11
American Psychological Association (APA), 29, 119, 153, 176, 179
Americans with Disabilities Act (ADA), 56, 78, 119
Amyotrophic lateral sclerosis (ALS), 66
Anger, 160–61
Ankylosing spondylitis, 66
Antonak, R. F., 11
"Antonio" case example, 109–10
Anxiety, 16, 54, 161–63
APA. *See* American Psychological Association
APA Publications Manual, 7
Arts, the, 120–21
Asexuality, 175
Asian Americans, 108, 109
Asking questions
  about current disability status and sequelae, 69
  about disability, 47, 48b
  about illnesses and medications, 56b
  in therapy, 153
Assistive technology (AT)
  and current disability status/sequelae, 63–66
  and developmental history, 75–76
  in disability culture and community, 128–29
  and fall prevention, 60–61
  funding for, 168–69
  lived experiences with, 19
  questions from strangers with disabilities about, 147–48
Attitudes, toward people with disabilities, 2
Attraction, romantic, 171
Attractiveness, sexual, 175
Avoidance, 135t

Balter, R., 25–26
Beck Depression Inventory (BDI), 112–13
Behavior
  fundamental attribution error for, 145, 160
  influence of family, culture, and disability on, 107–8

Beliefs
  dissonance in, 95–96
  about medications 55, 56b
  values-laden, 30, 31t–32t
"Ben" case example, 152–53
Benzodiazepines, 57
Biklen, D., 78
Biopsychosocial model of disability, 3, 92
Black, R. S., 85–86
Blame, 47, 137
Blind (term), 121
Blotzer, M. A., 199
Body image, 128, 129
Breeden, C., 200
Brown v. Board of Education of Topeka Kansas, 90
Built environment
  microaggressions in, 29, 134
  segregation in, 89–90
Burden of disability, 122, 165–66

CAGE questionnaire, 59
"Can disability studies and psychology join hands?" (Olkin and Pledger), 200
Caregiving, 107, 171, 185
Casas, J. M., 199
Case Studies in Multicultural Counseling and Therapy (Sue, Gallardo, and Neville), 199
Casual acquaintances, 149–50
CBT (cognitive behavioral therapy), 16, 28
Center for Women with Disabilities, 181
Central characteristic, 97
Cerebral palsy (CP), 72
Chair users, 121
Cheerfulness, 158
Children with disabilities
  demographics of, 71–72
  friendships of, 150
  impact of parents' reactions on, 104–5
  relationships between parents and, 165–69
  role models for, 124, 125
  therapeutic relationship with, 25
Children without disabilities
  custody of, 185, 186
  relationships between parents and, 182–87
  sleep hours for, 61
  social interactions with, 147
  tasks of, 185, 186b
Chronic pain, assessments of, 49
CinemAbility (film), 86
Civil Rights Movement, 85
Civil rights violations, 136t

Clinical language, 82*t*–83*t*
Clinical Practice with People of Color (Constantine), 199
Cloud, J. M., 167
Cognitive behavioral therapy (CBT), 16, 28
Cognitive rehearsal, 163
Collective history, 119–20
Coming Home (film), 87
Communication, 15, 105
Community. *See* Disability Culture and Community (D-AT V)
"Comparison of parents with and without disabilities raising teens" (Olkin, et al.), 200
Competence
  cultural, 27, 109, 130
  ethnic, 109
  in outpatient psychotherapy, 27
Concentration problems, 112
Conley-Jung, C., 200
Constantine, M., 199
Constructivist view of disability, 3
Conversion disadvantage, 90, 98–99
Copel, L. C., 20
Coping flexibility, 23, 30, 68–69
Coping style, 66–69
Corticosteroids, 50
"Could you hold the door for me?" (Olkin), 200
Couples therapy, sexual expression in, 179
Course of disability, 66–68
Courting issues, 171–72
CP (cerebral palsy), 72
CPAP machine, 128
Craig Hospital, 182
Crippled, 122
Cross-cultural therapy, 2, 25
Cultural competence, 27, 109, 130
Culturally-adapted interventions, 109
Cultural sensitivity, 109
Culture
  and client perspectives on psychotherapy, 17
  and course/outcome of disability, 67–68
  disability-affirmative therapy within context of, 4
  influence of, on behavior, 107–8
  and relationships of parents and children, 168
  and social interactions with medical professionals, 149
  and understanding of disability for client, 106–7
  See also Disability Culture and Community (D-AT V)

Current Disability Status and Sequelae (D-AT I), 46–70
  assistive technology, 63–66
  clinical applications, 69
  coping style, 66–69
  course and outcomes of disability, 66–68
  current symptoms, 47–60
  falls, 59–61
  medication, 50, 54, 56*b*
  pain, 48–50, 51*b*–54*b*
  for "Sam" case example, 188–90, 189*t*
  sleep quality, 61–63
  substance use and misuse, 56–59
Custody, child, 185, 186
"Custody evaluations when one divorcing parent has a disability" (Breeden, Olkin, and Taube), 200

Daredevil (film), 86
D-AT. *See* Disability-affirmative therapy
Dating issues, 171–72
D-AT template
  applicability of, 6
  for notetaking, 189*t*
  overview, 3–5
  for "Sam" case example, 188–97
  summary from, 195–96
  See also specific parts of template
David, E. J. R., 28
Day hospitals, 15–16
deaf (term), 121
Deaf children, mainstreaming of, 89
Deaf community, 117, 121
Death, disability as fate worse than, 86
Death-with-dignity laws, 127
Demographic variables. *See* Disability and Other Demographics (D-AT IV)
Denial
  and disability as loss, 157, 158
  of identity and privacy, 135*t*
Depersonalization, 135*t*, 136*t*
Depression
  as affective prescription, 157–58
  cognitive behavioral therapy for treatment of, 16
  and compliance with medical treatment, 162
  disability and, 111–13, 157
  and falls, 59, 60
  medications for treatment of, 54
  online treatments for, 22
Descriptive language, 82*t*
Desexualization, 136*t*
Developmental disabilities, 21, 167

Developmental History (D-AT II), 71–78
  abuse, 74–75
  advocacy skills, 77
  assistive technology, 75–76
  clinical implications, 77–78
  disability experiences, 71–72
  disability onset story, 72–74
  educational history, 76–77
  medical history, 75–76
  for "Sam" case example, 190
Diagnosis
  impact on children of parents' reaction to, 104–5
  lag between symptoms and, 148–49
"Diego" case example, 154–55
Diffability, 6
Diffability Hollywood (film), 86
Disability(-ies)
  acceptance of, 10
  adaptation and adjustment to, 9–10
  asking questions about, 47, 48*b*
  defined, 7, 46
  as defining characteristic, 3, 97
  hierarchy of acceptability for, 129
  influence of, on behavior, 107–8
  meaning of, 80*t*
  models of (*See* Models of Disability (D-AT III))
  response to, 10
  therapist's stance on, 3–4
  use of term, 122
Disability-affirmative therapy (D-AT)
  applicability of, 2–3, 6
  components of, 3
  cultural context for, 4
  and gay-affirmative therapy, 101
  need for, 1–2
  skill sets for, 2, 103
  value-laden beliefs and corollaries of, 30, 31*t*–32*t*
  See also D-AT template
Disability and Other Demographics (D-AT IV), 97–114
  education and socioeconomic status, 98–100
  ethnicity, 106–10
  mental disorders and psychiatric disabilities, 110–13
  for "Sam" case example, 192
  sexual orientation, 100–105
Disability civil rights movement, 119–20
Disability culture and community
  concept of, 115–16

exposure to, 130–31
  therapist's knowledge of, 2
Disability Culture and Community (D-AT V), 115–31
  the arts, 120–21
  assistive technology, 128–29
  common concerns, 126–27
  expertise, 127–28
  in-group identity, 116–17
  language, 121–22
  model of disability, 118–19
  norms, 122–24
  pride and values, 117–18
  in research, 129–30
  role models, 124–26
  for "Sam" case example, 192
  social and personal history, 119–20
Disability experiences, 71–72, 135*t*
Disability Hassles Scale, 139, 140*b*–143*b*
Disability identity stages, 116
Disability onset story, 72–74, 173
Disability-Specific Hassles Scales (DSHS), 28–29
Disabled, the, 122, 129
Disabled person (term), 6–7, 47
Disablism, 7–8
Disengagement coping strategies, 68
Dissonance, in belief systems, 95–96
Distributive justice, 90
Diversity
  disability in conceptualizations of, 26, 88–90
  of people with disabilities, 115
Doctors, social interactions with, 148–49
Doherty, W. J., 9
DSHS (Disability-Specific Hassles Scales), 28–29
DSM-5 (APA), 176, 179
Dunn, D. S., 10
Durable medical equipment, 128
Dying, response to, 156–57

Early-onset disabilities, people with
  anxiety experienced by, 162
  assistive technology use by, 128
  dating and sexual relationships for, 175
  medical histories of, 75
  use of assistive technology by, 64
Earning disadvantage, 90
Eating, in disability culture, 120–21
Economic disadvantages, 90, 167
Education, 99–100, 106

Educational history, 76–77
Education for All Handicapped Children Act, 76
Edward Scissorhands (film), 86
Effects of Microaggressions (D-AT VII), 132–44
 clinical applications, 139, 143
 Disability Hassles Scale, 140b–143b
 domains, 134, 135t–136t, 137–38
 perpetrators of, 132–34
 for "Sam" case example, 143–44, 193
 against women with disabilities, 138, 138f
"Ellen" case example, 100
Emergency rooms, overshadowing in, 112
Emotional-support animals, 134
Emotions, 132. *See also* Affective Regulation (D-AT VIII)
Empirical studies of outpatient psychotherapy, 24–25, 28
Employment, 19, 58, 99, 106, 175
Empowerment, 9
Engagement coping strategies, 68
Erickson Cornish, J. A., 26–27
Essentializing disability, 145–46
Ethical issues, 26, 27
Ethnic competence, 109
Ethnicity, 106–10, 168, 170
"Evie" case example, 67
Evil, disability portrayed as, 86
Exercise, MS-related fatigue and, 23–24
Expertise, 127–28
Exploitation, sexual, 175
Externalization of disability, 173
Extrapersonal functioning, 10
Extremely Loud and Incredibly Close (film), 87

Falls, 59–61
Falvo, D. R., 161
Family(-ies)
 assistive technology use and role in, 129
 culture and role of, 106–7
 resilience in, 166
Family members
 influence of, on behavior, 107–8
 microaggressions perpetrated by, 134
 See also entries beginning Children; *entries beginning* Parents
Fantasies, of teens with disabilities, 122, 169
Fast food restaurants, 121
Fatigue, 23–24, 112
Fear of falling, 59–60
Fiske, S. T., 58–59

Friendships, 150–53
Fundamental attribution error, 145, 160

Galgay, C., 29, 134, 135t–136t, 137
Gallagher, P., 19
Gallardo, M. E., 199
Gay-affirmative therapy, 101
Gay men with disabilities
 dating issues for, 172
 interplay of disability and sexual orientation for, 100, 104–5
 references on, 177b–179b
Gender role flexibility, 101, 173
Generalizations about people with disabilities, 129, 130
Gill, C. J., 116, 172
Glasgow Anxiety Scale, 16
Glee (television series), 125
Goodheart, C., 199
Gorgens, K., 26–27
Gratefulness, 159–60
Greene, B., 101
Group affiliation, 115–17
Group therapy, 27
Gupta, Devin, 93–94
Guter, B., 104

Handbook of Girls' and Women's Psychological Health (Worell and Goodheart), 199
Handbook of Multicultural Counseling (Ponterotto, et al.), 199
Handicap (term), 7, 46
Haseltine, F., 199
Hawking, Stephen, 66
Hayward, H., 138, 139
Health care professionals
 attitudes about disabilities and sexual orientation of patients, 102
 microaggressions perpetrated by, 137–38
 social interactions with, 148–49
 training for, 21–22
Health effects, of microaggressions, 138
Health services, 16
Helping professions, 107
Helplessness, 135t
Hepworth, J., 9
Heumann, Judy, 125
Hispanics, 107–9, 116, 171
HIV, outcome of, 66
Hjelle. K. M., 18
Home setting, rehabilitation treatment in, 15–16
Hospitalizations, 75

Hunt, B., 103–4
Hyde Park on Hudson (film), 181
Hydrocodone, 57

I am Sam (film), 87
IDEA (Individuals with Disabilities Education Act), 76–78
Identity
 denial of, 135*t*
 disability identity stages, 116
 in-group, 116–17
 sexual orientation and disability identity, 101, 102
 shared, 117
Identity-first language, 6–7, 47
Illnesses, questions about, 56*b*
Impairment (term), 7, 46
Inaccessibility lawsuits, 90
Inclusion, 118
Independence, 15, 19, 129, 169
Independent living movement, 119
Individualized education plans, 89
Individuals with Disabilities Education (IDEA) Act, 76–78
Infantilization, 135*t*
In-group identity, 116–17
Injustice, 161
Inside Moves (film), 88
Insightfulness, 159
Insurance coverage, 60–61, 98
Intellectual disabilities, people with
 cognitive behavioral therapy for, 16
 perspectives on psychotherapy of, 15
 provider perspectives on psychotherapy with, 21–22
 translation of, 68
Internalized ableism, 8
Interpersonal functioning, 10
Intersectionality
 in research on therapy with people with disabilities, 30
 of sexual orientation and disability, 100–105
 See also Disability and Other Demographics (D-AT IV)
Intimacy, 174, 194
Intimate Relationships (D-AT IX), 165–87
 with children, 182–87
 with parents, 165–69
 with partners, 170–82
 for "Sam" case example, 194
 and sexuality, 175, 177*b*–179*b*, 179–82
Intrapersonal functioning, 10

"Isabella" case example, 154
Isolation, 14, 169

"Jack" case example, 75
"Jenny" case example, 65–66, 118
"Joleen" case example, 108
"Jonathan" case example, 63

Keller, R., 29, 134, 135*t*–136*t*, 137
Keplinger, Dan, 125
Killacky. J. R., 104
King Gimp (film), 125, 168
Kirshbaum, M., 184–85, 200
Kübler-Ross, Elizabeth, 156–57

Language
 about course/outcomes of disability, 67–68
 in disability-affirmative therapy, 11
 in disability culture and community, 121–22
 and models of disability, 82*t*–83*t*
 people-first vs. identity-first, 6–7
Late-onset disabilities, people with
 assistive technology use by, 128
 misconceptions about, 102–3
Learning disabilities, 76–77, 150
Least restrictive environment, 89
Leisure activities, 17–18, 49–50
Lesbians with disabilities
 dating issues for, 172
 interplay of disability and sexual orientation for, 100, 102–4
 references on, 177*b*–179*b*
"Leticia" case example, 123–26
Lidocaine, 50
Lived experience, 17–20, 104–5
Livneh, H., 10, 11
Loss, disability as, 156–57
Low vision, 121
Lucky, person with disabilities as, 159

MacLachlan, M., 19
Mainstreaming, 124
"Making research accessible to participants with disabilities" (Olkin), 200
Manageable pain, 49
Marijuana, 57–58
Marriage(s)
 of parents of children with disabilities, 166
 post-injury and pre-injury, 172–73
 rates of, for people with vs. without disabilities, 170–71
Martz, E., 10

Mask (film), 87–88
Matlin, Marlee, 125
McDaniel, S. H., 9
Meaning of life, 87
Media, people with disabilities in, 85–88, 159
Medicaid, 56
Medi-Cal, 61
Medical family therapy, 55
Medical history, 75–76
Medical model of disability
    comparison of other models with, 79, 80*t*–81*t*, 84
    described, 84–85
    language associated with, 82*t*–83*t*
    media depictions of, 86–87
    and probability of self-disclosure, 93*t*
    in "Sam" case example, 190, 191–92*f*
Medical noncompliance, 122
Medical professionals. *See* Health care professionals
Medical stripping, 75
Medicare, 168–69
Medications, 50, 54, 56*b*, 57–58
Medscape, 55
Mental disorders, 110–13
Mental retardation, 122
Microaggressions
    as concern in disability community, 127
    defined, 9
    domains affected by, 134, 135*t*–136*t*, 137–38
    against lesbians or gay men with disabilities, 105
    perpetrators of, 132–34
    in quantitative research on psychotherapy, 27–30
    and social interactions, 146, 149–50
    against women with disabilities, 138, 138*f*
    See also Effects of Microaggressions (D-AT VII)
Million Dollar Baby (film), 86
Minimizing, 135*t*
Mishel, M., 66
Model of disability
    and culture, 107
    in disability culture and community, 118–19
    impact on interventions of, 21–22
Models of Disability (D-AT III), 79–96
    clinical implications, 91–93, 93*t*
    comparison of, 79, 80*t*–81*t*, 84–85
    critique of, 88–91, 92*f*
    for Devin Gupta, 93–94
    language associated with, 82*t*–83*t*

in media, 85–88
    for "Sam" case example, 95–96, 190, 191*t*
Monson, S. P., 26–27
Moral model of disability
    comparison of other models with, 79, 80*t*–81*t*, 84
    described, 84
    language associated with, 82*t*–83*t*
    media depictions of, 86
    and probability of self-disclosure, 93*t*
    in "Sam" case example, 191–92*f*
Moscoso, G., 29
"Mothers with visual impairments or blindness raising young children" (Conley-Jung and Olkin), 200
Mourning
    affective prescriptions related to, 156–58
    for parents of children with disabilities, 165
    quantitative research on, 25, 27
Multiple sclerosis (MS)
    course of disability for, 66
    and depression, 111, 157
    depression assessments by people with, 112–13
    exercise and fatigue related to, 23–24
Murderball (film), 87
Music Within (film), 88

National Health Survey Data, 116
Negating of disability, 151
Negative affect, 139
Negative language, 83*t*
Neville, H. A., 199
New Our Bodies Ourselves, The (Phillips and Rakusen), 182
'*Night Mother* (film), 86
Normal sexuality, model of, 176
Norms, 104, 122–24
Notting Hill (film), 86

Olkin, R., 26–27, 138, 139, 165, 184–85, 199, 200
Online treatments for depression, 22
Opioids, 50, 57
Outcomes of disability, 66–68
Out-of-home placements, for children, 185, 186
Outpatient psychotherapy with people with disabilities, 12–33
    client perspectives on, 14–17
    disability-affirmative therapy for, 6
    and lived experiences of people with disabilities, 17–20

Outpatient psychotherapy with people with disabilities (*Cont.*)
  program evaluations and protocols for, 22–23
  provider perspectives on, 20–22
  qualitative research studies on, 13–24
  quantitative research studies on, 24–30
  studies of MS-related fatigue and exercise, 23–24
  and values-laden beliefs, 30, 31*t*–32*t*
Overgeneralization, 183–84
Overinvolvement, by parents, 22
Overshadowing, 17, 97–98, 112

Pacific Islanders, 108, 109
Pain
  and anger, 161
  assessments of, 48–50, 52*b*–53*b*
  client perspectives on, 17
  describing experience of, 51*b*–54*b*
  and sleep, 62
Palombi, B. J., 26–27
Paralysis, sensation and, 181
Paranoia, 113
Parentification of children, 185
Parents of children with disabilities
  advocacy skills of, 77
  impact of reactions to diagnosis by, 104–5
  model of disability of, 94
  overinvolvement of, 22
  perspectives on psychotherapy from, 15, 17
  relationships between children and, 165–69
  views of children vs., 18–19
Parents with disabilities
  employment for, 99
  relationships between children and, 182–87
"Parents with physical, systemic or visual disabilities" (Kirshbaum and Olkin), 200
Parish, S. L., 167
Partners and partnerships, 170–82
  courting and dating issues for people with disabilities, 171–72
  effects of aging and disability on, 173–74
  marriages of people with disabilities, 170–73
  partnerships between people with disabilities, 174
  and sexuality for people with disabilities, 175, 177*b*–179*b*, 179–82
  and sexuality in quality of life, 180
  stigma and discrimination for partners, 173
Partner violence, against women with disabilities, 19–20

Patient (term), 121, 122
Patronization, 136*t*
Pattison, S., 20
Peer modeling, 125
People-first language, 6, 7, 46
Perceived control, 23–24
Perks, of disability, 159
Perlman, Itzhak, 120
Permission, Limited Information, Specific Suggestions, Intensive Therapy (PLISSIT) model, 180
Persistent depressive disorder, 111–12
"Personal, professional and political when clients have disabilities, The" (Olkin), 200
Personal history, 120
Personal space, violation of, 135*t*
Persons with disabilities (people with disabilities), 6–7, 46
"Persons with Disabilities as Parents" (Reinders), 184
Phantom-limb pain, 17
Phantom of the Opera, The (film), 86
Phillips, A., 182
Physical disabilities, 25–26
Pledger, C., 200
PLISSIT (Permission, Limited Information, Specific Suggestions, Intensive Therapy) model, 180
Polio, course of disability associated with, 66
Ponterotto, J. G., 199
Positive language, 83*t*
Post-injury marriages and partnerships, 172–73
Poverty, 98–99
Pregnancy, 183
Pre-injury marriages and partnerships, 172–73
Prejudice, 8, 184–85
Premature birth, 72
Prenatal testing, 127
Preston, P., 200
Pretes, L., 85–86
Pride, in disability, 117–18
Privacy, denial of, 135*t*
Program evaluations, 22–23
Protected class, 119
Protection, 14
Psychiatric disabilities, 110–13
Psychiatric disorders, 15, 158
Psychotherapy with clients with disabilities
  empirical literature on, 5–6
  language in, 11
  need for disability-affirmative therapy in, 1–2

See also Outpatient psychotherapy with people with disabilities

QOL (quality of life), 10–11, 180
Qualitative research studies on outpatient psychotherapy, 13–24
    client perspectives on, 14–17
    and lived experiences of people with disabilities, 17–20
    program evaluations and protocols for, 22–23
    provider perspectives on, 20–22
    studies of MS-related fatigue and exercise, 23–24
Quality of life (QOL), 10–11, 180
Quantitative research studies on outpatient psychotherapy, 12, 24–30
Queer Crips (Guter and Killacky), 104
Questions. *See* Asking questions

Radio (film), 87
Rage, 143, 160–61
Rain Man (film), 86
Rakusen, J., 182
"Rebecca" case example, 146
Recruitment, 105
Reeve, Christopher, 125
Rehabilitation Act (1975), 85
Rehabilitation psychology, 5–6, 30, 58, 84
Rehabilitation Psychology, 13
Reinders, H. S., 184
Religion, 106
"Renee" case example, 162–63
Repetition, of microaggressions, 133
"Requirement of mourning," 156–58
Resilience, in families, 166
Response to disability, 10
Riding the Bus with My Sister (film), 87
Rights, conflicts between individual's, 90
"Rights of graduate psychology students with disabilities, The" (Olkin), 200
"Robert" case example, 182
Roberts, Ed, 125
Robinson, L., 29
Role models
    for children with disabilities, 169
    in disability culture and community, 124–26
    for lesbians, 103
    for parents of children with disabilities, 167–68
    for people with disabilities, 103
Romantic attraction, 171
Rory O'Shea Was Here (film), 87
Rust and Bone (film), 181
Ruth, R., 199
Ryall, N., 19

"Sam" case example, 34–45, 188–97
    Affective Regulation (D-AT VIII), 160–61, 194–95
    case formulation, 42, 195
    context, 35
    Current Disability Status and Sequelae (D-AT I), 188–90, 189*t*
    current life circumstances, 36–37
    Developmental History (D-AT II), 190
    Disability and Other Demographics (D-AT IV), 192
    Disability Culture and Community (D-AT V), 192–93
    disability onset story in, 74
    Effects of Microaggressions (D-AT VII), 143–44, 193–94
    falls in, 59
    history, 37–38
    Intimate Relationships (D-AT IX), 194
    mental disorders in, 111–12
    mental status examination, 39–40
    Models of Disability (D-AT III), 91, 95–96, 191, 191–92*f*
    presenting problems, 35–36
    Social Interactions (D-AT VI), 149, 193–94
    summary from D-AT template for, 195–96
    therapeutic relationship, 40–41
    treatment, 42–44, 195–96
SAMHSA (Substance Abuse and Mental Health Services Administration), 57
"Sandra" case example, 61
"Sarah" case example, 160
Scent of a Woman (film), 86
Schaffalitzky, E., 19
School, staying in, 99–100
SCOPE, 8
Secondary gain, 135*t*
Second-class citizen, 136*t*
Segregation, 76, 89–90, 119–20
Self, assistive technology as part of, 129
Self-advocacy, 77
Self-destructive behaviors, 161
Self-disclosure of disability, 91–92, 93*t*
Sensation, paralysis and, 181
Sequelae. *See* Current Disability Status and Sequelae (D-AT I)
SES. *See* Socioeconomic status
Sessions, The (film), 181

SexAbility (film), 181
Sexual attractiveness, 175
Sexual dysfunction, 176, 179
Sexual experiences, 170
Sexual exploitation, 175
Sexual expression, 181
Sexual Function for Men after Spinal Cord Injury (Craig Hospital), 182
Sexual Function in People with Disability and Chronic Illness (Sipski and Alexander), 182
Sexuality
    misconceptions about, 102
    "normal" model of, 175, 179
    references on disabilities and sexual orientation, 177b–179b
    research on, 175, 179–82
Sexuality and Disability (journal), 182
Sexuality for Women with Spinal Cord Injury (United Spinal Association and UA Model SCI System), 182
Sexuality Information and Education Council of the U.S. (SIECUS), 180
Sexual orientation, 100–105
    and dating issues, 172
    intersectionality of disability and, 100–105
    references on disabilities and, 177b–179b
Shakespeare, T. W., 8, 9, 89, 176
Shared identity, 117
SIECUS (Sexuality Information and Education Council of the U.S.), 180
Simon Birch (film), 86
Sipski, M., 182
Sleep apnea, 62–63
Sleep quality, 61–63
Social activities, 17–18, 49–50
Social history, 119–20
Social inclusion, 181
Social Interactions (D-AT VI), 145–55
    with casual acquaintances, 149–50
    with friends, 150–53
    for "Isabella" and "Diego" case examples, 154–55
    for "Sam" case example, 192–93
    with strangers, 146–49
    with therapists, 153
    See also Intimate Relationships (D-AT IX)
Social interactions, coping style and, 68
Social media, 150
Social model of disability, 8–9
    comparison of other models with, 79, 80t–81t, 84
    critiques of, 88–90
    described, 85
    within disability community, 118
    language associated with, 82t–83t
    media depictions of, 87–88
    and probability of self-disclosure, 93t
    in "Sam" case example, 190, 191–92f
Social Security Disability Insurance, 169
"Social warrior or unwitting bigot?" (Olkin), 200
Social workers, 21
Socioeconomic status (SES), 98–99, 106, 168
Sociopolitical issues, 127
Some of my best friends response, 137
Sometimes You Just Want to Feel Like a Human Being (Blotzer and Ruth), 199
Soul-searching, 159
Soul-torturing, 159
Spastics, 122
Spinal cord injury, 57, 66
Spread effect, 27, 47, 97, 135t, 159
SSI (Supplemental Security Income), 56
Star Wars (film), 86
Status, disability. *See* Current Disability Status and Sequelae (D-AT I)
Stereotypes, 58–59, 85–86
Strangers
    with disabilities, 147–48
    without disabilities, 146–47
    microaggressions perpetrated by, 132–34
    reactions of, to assistive technology, 64
    social interactions with, 146–49
Substance Abuse and Mental Health Services Administration (SAMHSA), 57
Sue, D. W., 9, 132, 199
Supplemental Security Income (SSI), 56
Surgeries, 75
Survivor (term), 121
Suzuki, L. A., 199
Symptoms
    current, 47–60
    lag between diagnosis and, 148–49
    and social interactions with strangers with disabilities, 148

TANF (Temporary Assistance for Needy Families), 183
Taube, D. O., 200
TBIs (traumatic brain injuries), 72
Teens
    chores for, 185
    fantasies of teens with disabilities, 122, 169
    See also Adolescents with disabilities

Temporary Assistance for Needy Families (TANF), 183
TENS (transcutaneous electrical nerve stimulation) units, 50
"Teresa" case example, 73
Therapeutic relationship
  with children/adolescents with disabilities, 25
  in "Sam" case example, 40–41
  and social interactions with therapist, 153
Therapists
  able-bodied, 153, 169
  lived experiences of people with disabilities vs. views of, 18–19
  on outpatient psychotherapy with people with disabilities, 20–22
  research outside of sessions by, 103
  social interactions with, 153
"Three R's of supervising students with disabilities, The" (Olkin), 200
Timm, R., 28–29, 134, 135t–136t, 137–39
Tolerable pain, 49
Tolerance of disability, as basis for friendship, 151–52
Tragedy, disability as, 158
Training
  and clinical errors with people with disabilities, 26–27
  for people with disabilities, 99
  for psychotherapy with clients with disabilities, 1–2
  in sexuality and disability, 176
  for work with people with disabilities, 21–23
Transcutaneous electrical nerve stimulation (TENS) units, 50
Transgender people with disabilities, 178b–179b
Trauma, 161–63
Traumatic brain injuries (TBIs), 72
Treatment
  for anxiety, 162
  for depression, 16, 22, 54
  and disability-affirmative therapy, 4
  for mental disorders, 113
  model of disability and, 81t, 92, 93
  in "Sam" case example, 42–44, 195–96
Tripartite model of quality of life, 10

United Spinal Association, 182
University of Alabama Model SCI System, 182

Values
  in disability community, 118
  scope of, 158–59

Values-laden beliefs, 30, 31t–32t
Van Huet, H., 17
"Vernon" case example, 113
Vik, K., 18
Vulnerability, 14

Wade, Cheryl, 120
Walker, L. E., 20
"Walter" case example, 54–55
Warfield, M. E., 167
Waterdance, The (film), 87
Waxman, Barbara, 175
WebMD, 55
Well-being, 138
Welner, S. L., 199
Welner's Guide to the Care of Women with Disabilities (Welner and Haseltine), 199
What Psychotherapists Should Know About Disability (Olkin), 199
"What should we teach when we teach about women with disabilities?" (Olkin), 200
Wheelchair-bound (term), 122
Wheelchair Sex & Disability Love (film), 181
"When is differential treatment discriminatory?" (Olkin), 200
Where Hope Grows (film), 87
Whites, 106–8
WHO. *See* World Health Organization
"Why I changed my mind about physician-assisted suicide" (Olkin), 200
Women with disabilities
  abuse against, 74
  children of, 183
  dating issues for, 172
  employment for, 99
  friendships of, 150–51
  microaggressions against, 29–30, 137–38, 138f
  partner violence against, 19–20
  research on intimate relationships for, 170–71
  substance use by, 58
"Women with physical disabilities who want to leave their partners" (Olkin), 200
Worell, J., 199
World Health Organization (WHO), 3, 7, 10
Wright, B. A., 30, 31t–32t, 158, 159

Young adults, 150, 179
Yuker, H. E., 166

Zelman, D. C., 49
Zolpidem, 57

Made in United States
Orlando, FL
11 September 2024